DECIDING TO SOAR②

Unwrapping Your Purpose.

SHARRON JAMISON

THE BRAG MEDIA COMPANY
LAGOS. NEWYORK. LONDON.

DECIDING TO SOAR 2: UNWRAPPING YOUR PURPOSE

Copyright © 2020 by SharRon Jamison

Revised edition, September 2022

All rights reserved. No part of this book may be reproduced, stored in a retrieval system, or transmitted in any form or by any means, electronic, mechanical, photocopying, recording, scanning, or otherwise, without prior written permission, except in the case of brief quotation embodied in reviews or critical articles. The views expressed in this book are those of the author and are provided for motivational & informational purposes only. While every attempt has been made to provide information that is both accurate and effective, the author does not assume any responsibility for the use/misuse of the information.

Published by The BRAG Media Company.

This book may be ordered from booksellers and online retail stores or contact www.SharRonJamison.com

Printed in The United States of America

ISBN: 979-8-655-49886-0

DEDICATION

For every person who knows soaring is possible.

For every person who knows they are equipped to do something special in the world.

For every person who is courageous enough to claim their place in society.

For every person who knows they have a purpose.

For every person who knows they are divinely loved.

This book is for you!

CONTENTS

INTRODUCTION

The most important question that every person must ask themselves is, "Why was I born?" That question is illuminating because it provides the spiritual light that helps you see where you are going, and it is also liberating because it frees you up to do what really matters most. "Why was I born" is a powerful question because it is a clarifier, modifier, and amplifier. It is a demanding query that not only determines what you will do in life, but it is also a question that shapes how you will live. Discovering why you were born — your purpose — is the ultimate quest for meaning and mattering; it is your lifeline that informs your timeline.

Even though discovering your purpose is so essential for living a fulfilling life, I used to believe that discovering your purpose was something that only happened to spiritual gurus, genius-like scientists, or celebrated political figures, but not me. Growing up in a lower-middle-class African American family in the 1970s, I was convinced that I was disqualified from doing something meaningful in the world. Based on what I was taught and observed, I didn't have the goods – what it took – to be used by God. I knew I had talents, skills, and wisdom, but I had no lightning-bolt experiences or life-defining moments like those I read about in self-help books. I had hardships, frustrations, successes, and a few pivotal moments, but nothing I would define as earth-shattering or purpose-worthy. I actually thought my life events were too boring and too insignificant to prepare me for a divine calling because I assumed that purpose-defining and purpose-developing moments had to be burning-bush moments that took your breath away, or at least, near-death experiences that almost took your life away. Since I had neither, I resigned myself to being nothing and doing nothing because I was convinced that I was not included in God's cosmic plan.

But as I grew spiritually, I realized that having a purpose did not require a specific lighting-bolt moment. I realized that God uses **all** of our experiences to develop, sharpen, and tweak us for work, witness, and service. I realized that God is always sprinkling hardships with joys, peppering pain with pleasure, alternating the political with the practical, injecting the spiritual with the sensual, and testing us through the individual and the systemic to prepare us for what we have been called to do. We are constantly being groomed for greatness and shaped for significance.

After years of working with thousands of amazing truth-seekers, I realize that discovering your purpose is a continuous process. It is the relentless unlearning of beliefs, habits, narratives, and patterns that helps you see new possibilities and opportunities for your life. It is the close examination of everyday events and ordinary moments that helps you identify your talents and clarify your values in ways that galvanize you to act, risk, and pursue your dreams. It is the constant, courageous unpacking of childhood trauma, the untying of close familial bonds, the unraveling of embarrassing secrets, the unshackling from oppressive conditioning, and the untethering from societal traditions that reveal your life's mission. It is the unleashing of divine power undergirded by a spiritual practice that helps you develop the strength to stand up for what you believe in and have the audacity to declare what you want. Unveiling your divine calling, your purpose, is never a single event. It is often a series of challenges, political events, deaths, hurts, relationships, successes, failures, and a culmination of insights amassed over many years that help you clarify what you have been called to do.

As you are reading **Deciding to Soar 2**, I pray that each chapter demonstrates the power of the human spirit and helps you witness the transitions and shifts required to bravely uncover and radically pursue your life's work. I also hope you see your own experiences, especially those you feel are irrelevant, with fresh eyes so you can recognize essential clues that you have ignored, appreciate the struggles you have endured, and be more reflective about the victories you have enjoyed. By looking at your life through the lens of purpose, I am confident you will see how being bullied, minimized, or celebrated were parts of an overall strategy to help you access pieces of yourself that were asleep or develop aspects of your character that needed refinement for your unique call. I hope you see how various events ignited and activated you to become your purest and highest self to prepare you to deliver a supernatural message or lead a divine mission. Even if you feel that you are too old to contribute or to create something extraordinary in the world, I pray that you have an open mind to see what's possible for your life. Remember, purpose is not based on age; purpose is about impact, the willingness to be used, and the relentless commitment to be a vessel for God. Purpose is never solely based on ability; it is based on availability. It is not about educational degrees; it is about exemplary devotion. It is not about your job; it is about your joy. And purpose is not about popularity; it is about having a heart to serve people and follow Godly principles.

By reading **Deciding To Soar 2,** you have joined a movement that will support you as you courageously, confidently, and consistently travel on your own purpose-directed journey. Through a variety of resources and online support, I promise you that if you open your heart and mind to the purpose process, your purpose will grab you, pick you up, and empower you to accomplish everything that your Creator has preordained for your life.

So, please read the collection of essays, sermons, stories, elder wisdom, and reflections with an open mind and then pray. Hear the Spirit speak to you in a way that pricks your conscience, stirs up your gifts, and expands your mind so you can become more aware, more awake, and more alive to this glorious gift called purpose.

Here is the good news: the world is waiting for you. But most importantly, YOU are waiting for you. And when you embark on your path to your purpose, you will SOAR in ways that will challenge convention, support humanity, and bring you unspeakable joy.

I am excited about your journey, and I look forward to traveling with you.

Blessings to you as you SOAR Higher than you have ever soared before.

A WORD ABOUT THE STORIES IN THE BOOK

Some stories in *Deciding To Soar 2: Unwrapping Your Purpose* share the life experiences of people who agreed to let me use their names. For those who allowed me to share their experiences but not their names, I have changed details to protect their identity. For people who have similar stories, experiences, and situations, I created composites so that any resemblance to any actual person or persons with similar circumstances, names, and experiences is coincidental and unintentional.

THE UNFOLDING OF ME

Declare It: I Am More Than I Imagined.

When you finally realize how amazing you are, and accept that you have supernatural gifts, you will cease to see limits. You will stop looking around and start looking within to discover your purpose.

Come with me and let the unfolding begin.

1

YOU ARE AN ENDLESS TREASURE SO DON'T FORGET YOUR VALUE

It took years, really decades, before I realized I was a treasure. But I am a treasure, and so are you. We all are treasure troves full of riches – memories, miracles, and mysteries. We are full of passionate perspectives, valuable visions, dazzling dreams, and whimsical wealth. We are a unique collection of goodness, greatness, and grace. We are more precious than we can ever imagine.

But though we are full of priceless treasures, sometimes we don't value what we have and who we are. Sometimes we don't admire what we can do or appreciate what we can be. Sometimes we fail to honor ourselves, and we don't acknowledge our God-given identity. The unfortunate truth is that we rarely see ourselves through crystal-clear eyes.

So, how do we frequently see ourselves? Sometimes we see and evaluate ourselves through lenses that are obscured by shadows – shadows of stereotypes, shame, or subjugation – that cause us to dismiss ourselves. Sometimes we look through lenses smeared with the residue of failed relationships, failed business ventures, and failed parenting that makes us undervalue ourselves. Sometimes we can't see our own beauty because we look through the windows of wounds, the distortion of doubt, or the debris of dysfunction that convince us to disown ourselves. Sometimes we cannot see our brilliance because we look through lenses that have been cracked by confusion, mired by misery, and tarnished by toxic traditions that persuade us to disempower ourselves. Trust me, it's hard to see ourselves clearly and honor ourselves deeply when our sight is impaired by the crippling stories that we were taught about ourselves and about our communities.

But come with me. Look at your treasure. Look inside of your mind, heart, and soul and see your ability, strength, and wisdom. Move quickly to the right, and see your creativity, your intellect, and your ingenuity. Move your hand to the left and extract your buried dreams, your untapped potential, and your hidden capacity. Bend down and dig deep underneath the expectations of your family, the assumptions of your friends, and the programming of society and unearth your passion, joy, and truth. Reach deep down into your treasure chest and discover secrets about your power, your purpose, and your promise that God encoded in your DNA.

Don't stop there. Search the side pockets of your treasure chest that are abundant with talents that you have not touched, revelations that you have not heard, and visions that you have not seen. Notice the elaborate compartments that contain your unfulfilled hopes that are waiting to be cultivated, unmet needs that are waiting to be met, and unrealized goals that are waiting to be achieved.

Keep going! Notice the many dimensions of your personality, the many layers of your experiences, and the complex contradictions of your character. Do you see how multi-talented and multi-faceted you are? Do you see how magical and miraculous you are? Do you see how creative and courageous you are?

Keep going; there's more! Search the corners of the treasure; there are hidden passageways to your future. There are hallways to your healing, and pathways away from your pain. There are corridors to your freedom from anything and anyone that holds you back, holds you down, or pulls you away from what God has destined for your life. Look carefully. Explore with intention and great anticipation. There is beauty to behold and extreme joy to unfold.

Now, pause. Do you see the riches inside of you? Yes, you do. Do you see how valuable you really are? Yes, you do. Do you notice how unique, how elegant, and how exquisite you are? Yes, you do. Do you see how uniquely equipped and qualified you are to fulfill your divine assignment, life's calling, or life's work? Yes, you do. Do you realize that there will never be another YOU created in the world? Yes, you do.

Yes, you are an endless treasure! You were born rich. You arrived on the planet fully loaded with a one-of-a-kind combination of abilities, beauty, brilliance, and wisdom to do something that only you can do.

What's wonderful about your treasure is that you have a lifetime to discover all the intricate facets of your personality and the intricacies of your divine wiring. And it will take a lifetime because there's so much to learn about the wealth that God invested and deposited into you. There's so much to express, experience, and enjoy because you are absolutely remarkable! Exquisite! Phenomenal! Opulent! Impressive!

Just so you know: you will need to bring a brand new set of eyes, a new understanding, and a fresh perspective when you uncover and inspect your priceless jewels. Sometimes your childhood lenses are so blurred by labels, lies, and limitations that they prevent you from seeing yourself as comprehensively and accurately as God made you. Remember, in some ways, society has conditioned you to overlook, devalue, and deny how amazing you are. So without clear eyes and a renewed vision, you won't recognize and embrace your magnificence. And, trust me, you are incredibly extraordinary.

My friend, be patient and analyze what you find. Look beyond your current identity and past your current circumstances, so you can discover what your Creator carefully placed in your DNA. Delve deeply into your soul and hold on tight to what you learn because what you find contains the keys to your purpose. Yes, the keys to unlock your purpose are in the treasure that lives inside of you. So trust what you find. Collect it, cultivate it, be curious about it, and connect with it. Use what you discover to fulfill your dreams, to execute your God-given vision, and to offer something transformative to the world.

Always remember that the most breath-taking journey that you will ever take is the journey inside of your own soul. Yes, your soul! And as you journey, you will realize that everything you need to fulfill your purpose is already inside of you, waiting to be revealed, retrieved, and released to the world.

Declare Today: I am an endless treasure! I have everything I need! I will share what I have with the world.

It's time to Soar Higher!

2

IT DOES NOT MATTER IF OTHERS LIKE YOU IF YOU DON'T LIKE YOURSELF

You are a priceless treasure. You are brilliant, radiant, and gifted. But do you like you?

The question may seem too silly to ask, but it is a question you must always ask yourself. So, I will ask you again. Do you like yourself? *Really* like yourself? Are you fond of you? Can you answer this question honestly?

Even though most people think they like themselves, some honestly don't. And, if they do like themselves, they have a very peculiar way of showing it. For example, I often hear people talk about their flaws, failures, and fears but say very little about their strengths and successes. They highlight their mistakes and misfortunes, but share little about what they did right or what they did well.

Think about your own life. How many times have you heard people berate themselves? How often do you hear people complain about the color of their hair, the size of the hips, and the placement of their eyes? How many times have you heard people call themselves stupid, fat, ugly, lazy, or dumb? How many times have you overhead people ruminate about their shortcomings and exaggerate their weaknesses? How many times have you witnessed people speaking about themselves or speaking to themselves in disparaging and disrespectful ways? How many times?

Sometimes we speak to ourselves in ways that we would never allow another person to speak to us, at least without some retaliation. Yet, we say hurtful words to ourselves and about ourselves every single day without considering how those pejorative phrases negatively affect our bodies, minds, and spirits. Trust me, our toxic comments get lodged into our psyches and infect our souls. They wreak havoc in our lives, our relationships, and our careers. And the saddest part is – the mean-spirited comments we hurl at ourselves are seldom fair or true.

One of my clients, let's call her Kayla, lived for over forty years without really liking herself. By society's standards, Kayla was successful; she was educated, admired, and commanded a six-figure salary. But Kayla's success did not make her like herself or prevent her from engaging in self-destructive behavior. For example, Kayla was secretly addicted to prescription drugs and frequently overindulged in alcohol. She mismanaged her money and routinely made ill-advised business decisions, which jeopardized her employment, and her professional standing in her industry.

Kayla's personal life was also in shambles. For starters, she dated men who consistently cheated on her, and who verbally abused her. When she insisted that her lovers respect her and honor their agreement to date her exclusively, the men would leave the relationship. But, Kayla would buy them back. Yes, Kayla had literally maxed out her credit cards trying to hold on to men who did not appreciate her, love her, or honor her. And if you questioned her about being complicit in her own disrespect, she would defend the men who cheated on her and secretly maintain relationships with them.

Kayla's friendships with women were equally as challenging, and she constantly made poor friendship choices. For some reason, she always attracted and befriended friends who smiled in her face, but exploited her insecurities and gossiped behind her back. For example, three years ago, she joined a graduate chapter of a sorority, and soon after she joined she overheard a few of her sorority sisters making fun of her for being "around the way," which is an offensive way of saying that a person is unrefined, simple, and low class. Of course, Kayla was devastated, and because she had experienced so many "sister wounds," she was reluctant to develop the deep, intimate connections she needed and craved.

Kayla's job was just as demeaning. Her boss, who she trained, was an arrogant bully who could not be pleased. He constantly belittled her, yet she spent endless hours trying to earn his approval and appreciation. When it was promotion time, her boss, whom she had trained, overlooked her and hired his friend who had no prior experience. The obvious slight felt like a slap in the face, but she refused to leave the company even though the workplace environment was toxic to her soul. To add insult to injury, Kayla's family often called her a corporate "sellout." Yes, they made fun of her until, of course, they needed a loan, a job recommendation, or some other favor.

What an emotional load! Kayla was sinking and was headed for an emotional breakdown. The pressure she endured was almost unbearable, and the daily stress was taking a huge toll on her health and spirit.

So, why did Kayla tolerate so much abuse? Why did she treat herself so poorly and allow others to treat her so badly? Why did she ignore her own needs and abandon her own dreams? Why did she abuse her body and not protect her heart? Why did she feel that diluting her own strength and dimming her own light were requirements to be loved and embraced? Why was Kayla complicit in her own demise?

The answer is complex, yet simple: Kayla never fully learned to like or love herself. Since she didn't cherish herself, she relied on others to make her feel important. And we all know that depending on others to validate us is risky and sometimes reckless. It is extremely dangerous for our self-worth to live in the eyes, in the hands, in the beds, or in the mouths of others. Our self-worth is our own individual responsibility; we must always affirm our own self-worth within our hearts and by the actions of our own hands. When we give that responsibility to others, we abandon our own sovereignty. We compromise ourselves and confine ourselves to endless cycles of self-sabotage that have us seeking out crumbs of concern and temporary acceptance instead of demanding a feast of love and unconditional respect.

But here is the good news: Kayla changed. When she realized that she was a talented woman who had gifts, grace, and guts, her life expanded and improved. She stopped chasing love and hustling for external validation because she was no longer dependent on others to affirm her worthiness or authenticate her existence. She was no longer a victim of her societal conditioning, painful experiences, or childhood programming. Most of all, Kayla discovered the power of "positive self-talk" and began challenging all of the toxic stories, beliefs, and thoughts that had constantly fed the false narrative that she was not good enough and that she didn't matter.

How did she do it? First, Kayla took an inventory of her life and explored what she had been taught and told about herself. To her chagrin, she discovered that since her childhood, she had been consistently taught that she was ugly, dumb, and unwanted, which had made it nearly impossible for her to see her value and self-worth. And when she had attempted to affirm or assert herself to her abusers, they further ridiculed and rejected her, which squashed her budding self-esteem.

When Kayla realized that her negative inner dialogue, hunger for acceptance, and feelings of victimhood kept her trapped in cycles of dysfunction, she made monumental shifts in her belief systems. As my elders used to say, "she plucked the weeds and took the seeds" so that new disempowering beliefs could not take root and grow. And then, she planted, cultivated, and watered new seeds (thoughts) that promoted her agency, self-affirmation, and radical self-love.

Kayla also assessed her environments because when people don't like themselves, they unknowingly gravitate to places and situations that confirm and reinforce their *"un-likability."* I know that's a hard pill to swallow, but it's true. When I was a little girl, my elders used to say, *" if you don't heal, you will always get more of what you got."* Translation: if you don't like yourself, you will attract people who don't like you either. That's why it's essential to ask yourself if you like yourself, and if you are treating yourself with the respect and honor you deserve. Those questions are vital to the health of your psyche and soul. If not, you will constantly attract and surround yourself with people who will infect you with doubt, fear, and criticism, and any of those alone are stifling and corrosive to your identity, intuition, and image.

Next, Kayla hired a licensed therapist and a lifestyle coach to help her identify and shed old identities and limiting beliefs that kept her hustling for affection and approval. She also unraveled the toxic layers of her history, and learned how to reframe her life experiences through the lens of love. That was key. Because through the lens of love, Kayla finally realized that she didn't need to fix her family or be responsible for everyone's needs. She just needed to figure out what was true and necessary for who she was, what she needed, and what she was called to do. She just had to identify her values, make value-based choices, and live free from the needs and expectations of others. You can imagine how big of a relief that was for her.

Kayla invested in a nutritionist and a personal trainer to strengthen and sculpt her body. For her, looking good was not just about vanity; it was about feeling strong and bold enough to fulfill her vision. And feeling strong in one aspect of our lives always creates ripple effects that empower us in other areas, too.

Overall, Kayla rebuilt and upgraded her entire life. She updated her resume, activated her networks, and got a new job that valued and compensated her for her expertise. She found a church home that promoted love and didn't saddle her with shame and archaic rules. Most of all, Kayla allowed herself to experiment. She gave herself permission to try new activities, date different types of people, and attend unique events so she could discover what actually brought her joy and peace. The great news is that her exploratory journey provided fresh revelations that she used to re-think her career, re-prioritize her life, and re-position some folks, too!

Kayla's healing journey was expensive, but change will always cost you something; change is never free. What I have learned from coaching hundreds of women is that changing your life is always an investment. It is an investment of time and treasure, and it may even cost you a few friendships. But trust me, whatever the cost, healthy change is worth it because nothing is more expensive than regret, misery, or unhappiness. Nothing! Living with chronic sadness, misalignment, and fake belonging is extremely expensive to the soul, and can spiritually bankrupt you and everybody attached to you for generations to come.

Kayla learned and continues to discover how magnificent she is. She continues to grow and thrive in every aspect of her life. And with every internal shift, she releases another self-sabotaging pattern and replaces it with a life-affirming practice. With every new self-revelation, she calls forth additional gifts that were buried under years of dysfunction and self-loathing. With more self-awareness, she sheds more shame about what she did in her past when she didn't love herself. With every emotional release, she lets go of regret and replaces it with gratitude. Most importantly, with every new self-commitment, she inches closer to who God created her to be.

Just for the record: Kayla's process is not complete. Learning to like yourself is never a one-and-done process. Liking yourself is a lifelong journey full of great strides, messy slips, and a few backward stumbles. But as long as you are growing and are dedicated to unwrapping who you genuinely are, you will not only learn to like yourself, you will learn to appreciate and celebrate how resilient you really are. You will deeply cherish yourself and realize that the love you were yearning for already existed inside of you.

So, what does it mean for **YOU** to like yourself? What does it mean to like who you are and appreciate how you are uniquely wired? More importantly, why is liking yourself so important to pursuing your purpose?

For starters:

Liking yourself is fully accepting who you are — **all** of who you are. It is that unquestionable, unwavering, and non-negotiable belief that you are valuable. It is an inner belief that you were uniquely created and endowed with abilities, strengths, and talents that equip you to contribute to the world in a way that only you can contribute. It is an inner knowing that God created you, believed in you, trusted you, and lives inside of you. In other words, liking yourself means that you are convinced that you are priceless, and that you are intrinsically wealthy because you are a child of God.

Liking yourself is also a practice of taking care of yourself – your mind and spirit. It is a way of talking to yourself with compassion, love, and honesty when you make mistakes. It is the willingness to tell yourself the truth, even when the truth is inconvenient, embarrassing, or painful so you can learn valuable lessons and take inspired action. Liking yourself is knowing that you are so valuable that you have the right and the responsibility to establish healthy boundaries and standards of engagement to keep yourself emotionally, spiritually, and physically whole.

Liking yourself is possessing a strong commitment to your growth, development, and healing so you can function in the world with self-respect, self-confidence, and self-trust. It means being committed to being the best YOU at all times, irrespective of situations and circumstances because liking yourself is not conditional or situational. Liking yourself is consistent, undeniable, and immutable.

Liking yourself means knowing that you have a vision for your life; you have dreams, desires, and destiny. It means knowing that you have a voice (opinions, beliefs, and perspectives of your own) and that your voice has merit, meaning, and a message that need not be validated by others. Liking yourself is acknowledging that you have a vivid imagination, a keen intellect, and quick instincts to respond to life's challenges and uncertainties. It's an appreciation that you always have the insight and inner resources you need to fulfill your divine assignment and rise to every occasion.

Liking yourself means that you will do what it takes to become financially literate and independent, so you don't become imprisoned by debt or manipulated by money. It means investing in yourself so you can create your own income and resources without constant hustle or struggle. It does not mean that you worship money. However, liking yourself means that you realize that generating and having your own money provides the freedom you need to pursue your purpose without selling your soul, minimizing your talent, or compromising your character.

Liking yourself means taking care of your temple, your body. It means being a good steward of your organs, limbs, and faculties so you can fulfill your divine assignment. It means eating well and eating right. It means learning what helps your body function at its highest capacity. Let's face it. You will never get another body, so you must treat it well. You must exercise consistently, de-stress religiously, and rest daily to keep your body in tip-top shape. Remember: good health is both a tremendous gift and a divine responsibility.

Liking yourself means that you will take consistent breaks to revive your body and renew your mind. Now, that's hard for many of us because we were raised in a "do more" culture; we were taught that *busyness (doing a lot of things all of the time)* equals success. But liking yourself means that you won't push yourself beyond measure or to the brink of exhaustion. It means that you will love yourself enough to pause, pivot, and pray so you won't burn-out or become worn out by the cares of the world.

Liking yourself means that you will not engage in toxic relationships that disrespect or degrade you. I know that's a tough one. But how many times have you stayed around people who could not see your worth, your talent, or value? How many times have you dated people who made you feel undesirable, worthless, and unworthy? How many times has your family made you feel that you had to hustle to be heard, lie to be liked, or compromise to be accepted? How many times have you left an event or a job feeling insulted, ignored, and unappreciated? Liking yourself means that you won't tolerate mistreatment and mismanagement just to be in a clique or just to get paid. Liking yourself is an unwavering vow to surround yourself with people who value, welcome, and see you for the wonder that you are!

Liking yourself means revisiting your faith tradition and having the courage to abandon beliefs, doctrines, and practices that no longer connect you to God. It involves studying and thinking critically about sacred texts to learn the truth, so you don't blindly follow toxic traditions that you have outgrown. It means developing a spiritual practice to keep you aligned to your Creator so you can pursue your purpose with clarity and discernment.

Liking yourself means knowing that your body, your skin, your size, your gender, your color, your faith, your ability, your sexual orientation, and ethnicity are worthy of respect, dignity, and justice. It is an internal conviction that you are not more valuable than someone else, but you are also not less valuable than anyone else, either. It is self-validation at its best.

Liking yourself means that you will not diminish or mismanage your divine assignment. It means that you will not abandon your calling because of cowardice, laziness, lack of resources, or lack of discipline. It means that power and prestige will not seduce you and that you will not put yourself on sale for positions, popularity, or profit.

Liking yourself is all-encompassing; it affects every aspect of your being. It strengthens you in tough times; it upholds you in great times, and it stabilizes you in uncertain times. Liking yourself gives you spiritual power, and spiritual power gives you peace.

So, tonight, look in the mirror and ask yourself this critical question: do I like me? Tell yourself the truth. Listen to your spirit. Then make amends. Where you are strong, continue to strengthen and fortify. Where you are weak, heal, develop, and evolve. And slowly, with consistent work and ongoing healing, you will learn to like yourself and love yourself in a way that honors your soul.

Remember, you are a treasure; you are wealthy, valuable, and valued. God liked you and loved you so much that God created you and gave you a purpose, a divine assignment that was designed solely for you. God put something in your soul to help you contribute to the world and to bring you deep fulfillment. Now, it is up to you to learn to LIKE and affirm what God created so you can focus on your God-given assignment with faith, power, and love.

Declare Today: I like me, and I will treat me like I like me because I have a God-given purpose.

It's your time to Soar!

3

I WILL LOVE YOU
ONLY IF IT DOES
NOT REQUIRE
THAT I STOP
LOVING ME

I believe in compromises. Sometimes the only way to effectively deal with conflict is for both parties to make concessions so that everyone wins something. However, there are specific values that I will never compromise on, and one of those values is loving me.

You see, loving me is not optional; it's fundamental and foundational to my very survival. Without a modicum of self-love, I would become reliant and dependent on others to affirm my worth and value. I would become a hustler, a chameleon, and a beggar who scours the town looking for crumbs of affirmation in all the wrong places. If I don't love me first, I will undermine and disown my gifts, talents, abilities, and undervalue my unique contributions to the world.

Over the years, I have learned that loving myself means trusting that my Creator made me just the way I am because everything about me was based on a divine blueprint that was designed just for me. I have also learned that loving me means accepting and appreciating that my Creator gave me a purpose that fires up my life with joy and adventure. So, as I pursue my purpose, my God-given assignment, I erect and enforce healthy boundaries to create space for me to thrive, evolve, and transform without distractions, intrusions, and fear.

Loving me is essential but is not always easy because loving me angers some and intimidates others. But I have no choice. If I don't love me, I can't love you. If I can't extend grace, mercy, and compassion to me, I cannot extend them to you. If I can't tell myself the truth, I can't tell the truth to you. If I can't appreciate and celebrate me, I can never appreciate and celebrate you. If I can't give myself what I need, I will expect to get what I need from you. If I don't love me, my entire focus, and the substratum of my existence, would be about you! And expecting you to give me what I need, because I can't or won't give it to myself, is unfair to you; and it robs me of my own agency and self-respect.

I want to love you if I can. But first, I need to understand what love means to you. I need to understand what loving you requires. I need to know what love feels like, what love sounds like, what love tastes like, and what love looks like to you. I need to know what type of love makes your heart sing. By the way, do you really know how you like to be loved?

I need to understand what loving you may entail because no two people experience love the same way. Honestly, I may not have the capacity to share myself at the level that loving you may require. Loving you may be too emotionally taxing and spiritually draining for me. Loving you may require that I abandon aspects of my individuality and humanity, and that's too high of a price to pay for anything and anyone.

This is what I know for sure: loving me is necessary! Without my own self-love, I can't survive and thrive. Without my own self-love, I can't fulfill my purpose. Without my own self-love, I will feel unworthy, impotent, and inadequate. Without my own self-love, I will die a slow death of deferred dreams, empty hopes, and unrealized goals. Without my own self-love, I won't feel worthy of my purpose, my divine assignment, or my relationship with God. I will pay a high cost, maybe a fatal fee, for not loving me.

The bottom line is this: I can't love you until I love me! Even though I may not fully understand what loving me means right now, I am clear on one thing – me FIRST! I get the big piece of chicken. I will always get the best of my time. I will always be my main priority. I will always be my first investment. I will always take care of my body. I will always take care of my soul. I will always nourish my spirit. I will always feed my mind. I will always take care of me FIRST because loving you deeply and fully depends on my ability and my willingness to love me FIRST!

Remember, you can't give what you don't have. So, I will make sure that I have lots of love for me, and hopefully, I will have enough love to share with you. If not, I will understand that what I have to offer you is not what you want and need, and I will release you wishing you nothing but peace, love, and joy.

I love me! And because I love me, it… is… time… to…. SOAR!

4

THE MOST LIBERATING PLACE TO LIVE IS INSIDE YOUR OWN SKIN

I have lived in many places in my life. Due to my father's ministry, our family moved a lot, sometimes across the country. The constant relocations made me feel out of place and displaced. Constantly adjusting to new environments and new people filled me with anxiety. So much so that even today, I know I should move to a smaller house to maximize my resources. But I can't even stomach the idea of packing and purging; the thought of uprooting again makes me nauseous. I want to be in my own home. I want a safe, consistent place to rest my mind and restore my body. Have you ever felt that way?

Though having a physical home is extremely important to me,

life has taught me that a physical home, with all its comforts and conveniences, is not always the most liberating place to live. Often, it is our homes, behind the secured doors, where we feel the most trapped. It is in our rooms that are filled with our destructive secrets and dark shadows that steal our peace. It is at our kitchen tables where we yearn to be served love and acceptance but are only offered rejection and rebuke that disturb our souls. It is in our beds where we crave rest and restoration but are filled with fresh worries, old doubts, and childhood demons that deprive us of sleep. Sometimes our homes, though nicely decorated and well-appointed, restrict us and sometimes rob us of what we desire most—freedom and peace. So, where do you go to experience true liberation? In your own skin.

Living in your own skin is one of the most powerful, affirming, and liberating places to live. But after coaching hundreds of people, one thing that I know for sure is that learning to live in your own skin is not always easy. In fact, living in your own skin is quite challenging because we have been tricked into believing that living in our own skin is inferior at best and just plain irresponsible, at worst.

If you don't believe me, just take a look around. Everywhere you look, you are bombarded by images that try to fool you into believing that every place and any place is better than living in your own skin. Social media, digitally enhanced photographs, and carefully curated reels are marketed to you every day to convince you to reject who you authentically are. You and I, we, are continuously misled, manipulated, and misinformed about our contributions, value, and significance, so we will disown and doubt ourselves.

My friend, we are being hoodwinked. We are being tricked into comparing our actual lives with highlight reels. Trust me; those highly filtered images are not real. They are fantasies and fairytales to be enjoyed, not truth to be believed. We are just being deceived and seduced so we will crave, covet, and care about products and policies that make other people wealthy. That's right! Our insecurities and disappointments are just being exploited for financial gain, so we will prefer and chase the images of others and discard and despise our own. And when we abandon ourselves, we wander through life without a place to call our own; we become spiritual nomads or spiritually homeless without a firm foundation. Sadly, we don't live in our own skin.

So, how do you learn to live in your skin when you navigate in a culture that promotes and celebrates everything that you feel that you are NOT? What do you do when you become deluded and manipulated by ridiculous fabrications and never have an opportunity to hear the true facts? What do you do when you become so focused on the lives of others that you become disenchanted and enraged with your own existence? What do you do when you feel dis-eased because you feel defective, discarded, and denied? How do you get to that place called "happy, healthy and whole," a place that everybody seems to aspire to, but only a few actually arrive? How do you get back "home" to yourself so you live in your own skin?

What can you do? You go "home." You go home and learn who you are and who you are not. You study yourself; you interrogate yourself, and you challenge every narrative that you have been taught about yourself. You listen to your heart and unearth the parts of you that have been repressed by discontentment, lies, and misrepresentation. You go home and dis-identify with parts of your history that limit you so that you can be reunited with your true essence. You go home with the assurance that your Creator is also there. Yes, your Creator lives in your skin.

Granted, learning to live in your own skin will be a long, layered process. For me, it was a long journey, filled with pain, joy, failure, therapy, and lots of prayers. And honestly, I needed all of those modalities to overcome the ways I had been indoctrinated and domesticated to deny and disown everything that I was and hoped to be. From the color of my skin to the way I maneuvered in the world, I had been conned into renouncing every part of my being and even rejecting those who look and love like me.

But once I learned how to live in my own skin by accepting

myself, understanding myself, and honoring myself, I realized that I was whole. I realized that wholeness was my birthright, blueprint, and divine design. Most of all, I finally accepted that being anything other than what my Creator wanted me to be failed to honor my uniqueness, and it failed to honor my Creator, God. When I accepted that timeless truth, I went "home."

On my way "home," I reclaimed the beautiful skin that was customized for me and celebrated my beauty. I also recovered discarded pieces of me and owned the complicated truth of me. I cultivated the neglected parts of me and strengthen the weakened parts of me, so I could witness the true power of me. I got all of me and I went "home." "Home" in my own skin became my sacred place, my safe place, my healing place, and my SharRon place.

When we look at the people who have radically changed the world, we realize that the people who had the most significant impact "lived in their skin." They were not the most beautiful, the most brilliant, or the most talented people in the world. None were perfect. But they were people who embraced their differences, their quirkiness, their abilities, and their distinctness. They were people who had a sense of their divine purpose, a sense of knowing that they were on the right path, and a sense of being guided by their inner wisdom. They were at "home," or at least they worked at being "home" in their own skin, even if their skin was not celebrated by the masses.

What I now know for sure is that living in your own skin is the foundation for radical self-acceptance and inner peace. When you accept yourself, it releases you to be yourself, and you give others permission to be who they are, too. Just think about that…. LIBERTY! You are endowed by your Creator to have life, LIBERTY, and the pursuit of happiness. But, it is up to you to fiercely protect your LIBERTY so you are free from any influences that tempt you to betray who your Creator designed you to be!

My friend, go home. Go home to the YOU that existed before you were taught that you were unworthy, unqualified, and unlovable. Go home to the YOU that existed before your failures, trauma, and fear convinced you that you were limited and low-down. Go home to the YOU that was untainted by false narratives, unimaginable violence, and poisonous programming. Go home to the YOU that danced, dared, and dreamed freely, boldly, and joyously. Go home to the YOU that is hidden under layers of oppression and buried by historical burdens. Go home to the YOU that predates your physical birth when you knew and communed with God. Go home. Go home to your voice, your values, and your vision. Go home and stay home in your own skin.

Go home because home is your place of power. It's your source for freedom, it's your well of wisdom, it's your path to your creativity, it's the basis of your strength, it's your base for blossoming, and it's your connection to God. It's your grounding place. It's the substratum of everything you hold dear, YOU!

Tonight, look in the mirror, hug yourself and say, "Welcome, Home!" Then, continue to work to build your home and maintain your home so you always have a place to live, **in your own skin.**

Again, welcome home.

It's time to SOAR Higher!

5

FIND YOUR VOICE AND THEN SPEAK AS LOUD AS YOU CAN

When I was a little girl, maybe about nine years old, one of the church members told me to "find my own voice." Honestly, I didn't know that my voice was missing. After all, I could talk, sing, whisper, and yell. To me, my voice was not lost. It was right there inside of my mouth.

Since I didn't know that "finding your voice" was an idiom, I spent all day searching for my voice. I looked in the closet, in the basement, and in my bedroom. I looked in the kitchen, in the pantry, and in the toy box. I looked everywhere, and after searching all day, I told my Dad that I could not find my voice; it was missing, never to be seen again.

My Dad chuckled when I told him that my voice was missing. Patiently, he explained that "finding your voice" was just a figure of speech, and that my voice was not really lost. What? How was I supposed to know that?

Just thinking about that experience still makes me laugh today. I must have certainly looked crazy using my voice to explain that I could not find my voice! The irony, right?

Over the years, I learned that losing your voice meant not owning and not standing up for what you believe in – your truth. And after critical self-reflection, I realized, painfully, that I had indeed lost some of my voice. Somewhere along my journey in corporate America, I had begun to swallow my words, abandon my values, and suppress my opinions. Somewhere along my spiritual journey, I started downplaying my beliefs in exchange for respect and acceptance. Although I was naturally a protector and an activist who challenged bigoted tirades, over time, I had begun to overlook insults, excuse microaggressions, and accommodate demeaning behavior. When my views differed from my friends and colleagues, I started to lie or tell half-truths to win favors, appease the crowd, and maintain my social status. And when I felt threatened or targeted, I didn't speak up at all. I clammed up and shut down.

Painfully and regretfully, I had to accept the unfortunate truth. I had to acknowledge that I had allowed others to snuff and stunt the development and the honest expression of my authentic voice. And since I had lost my voice, I had also lost me.

But after decades of deep reflection and therapy, I reclaimed my voice and realized that my voice was more than my accent, my tone, and the pace of my speech. My authentic voice was my truth, a truth that emanated from a deep knowing in my soul. My authentic voice was a compelling force that spoke of expansion, demanded justice, and declared liberation. It was a courageous vessel of integrity and a catalyst for change. And most of all, I realized that my voice articulated my God-given purpose; it had power.

Yes, my voice had power because it brought healing salves to worried minds, wounded hearts, and weary souls. My voice had power because it could strengthen, empower, manifest, and pray to affect change. My voice had power because, despite what society said, my voice proclaimed who I was and declared all that I was destined to be. My voice had power because it was my brand, my signature, my image, and my influence. My voice was unique, and it was mine.

My friend, you also have an extraordinary voice. You may not have developed it, refined it, or acknowledged it yet, but you, too, have a voice that will speak words that only you can say. You, too, have a view that creates, connects, and comforts in a distinctive way. You, too, have an incredible, inimitable sound that summons greatness, shares insight, and serves a bigger purpose. You, too, have a voice that carries, moves, and inspires action. You, too, have a voice, and it is your responsibility to discover it, cultivate it, share it, and honor it. It is also your responsibility to ensure that your voice does not get tainted, twisted, or muted in a way that dishonors your divine call, your purpose.

However, I must warn you that your journey to discover your authentic voice will not be easy. There will be times when you think you are sharing original thoughts only to find out you are saying what someone else has already said or what someone else has programmed you to say. On your journey to find your authentic voice, you may even realize that you have internalized toxic narratives or oppressive assumptions and that you are merely parroting what's popular and what's expected.

But I promise you that with time, discipline, and deep introspection, your authentic voice will crystallize. As you delve deeper into your soul and deepen your relationship with God, your truth will gradually unfold, and you will feel spiritually aligned with your divine message and mission. With prayer, you will be activated and emboldened with a fierce determination to say what you have been born to say. You will be unflinching as you pursue and fulfill your God-ordained assignment, your purpose.

As you share and declare what God has told you to say, get ready. Some people may feel intimidated by your newfound or unconventional beliefs. Your original views may clash or compete with the status quo or push people beyond their comfort zones. Some of your closest supporters, as well as some of your fair-weather friends, may malign you or exclude you, and you may lose resources and relationships. Some people may even vehemently oppose you to such a degree that they may retaliate in ways that defy human decency. So, expect resistance, but never surrender your message or lower your voice.

Despite the risks and repercussions, and there will be many, I encourage you to FIND YOUR OWN VOICE! Refine your own beliefs. Articulate your own vision. Develop your own values. Think your own thoughts. Build your own life. Develop your own ideas. Draw your own conclusions. Reclaim your own "inner-standing." And then combine everything you learn and FIND your own unique voice.

When I think of people who found and used their unique voice, I immediately think of Dr. Martin Luther King, Jr. Dr. King's voice was distinctive in sound, spirit, and substance. It consoled hearts, it challenged injustice, and it called for change. It was passionate, prophetic, and authoritative. His voice reverberated with such clarity, conviction, and courage that it challenged the ethos of the world.

My friend, you may not be a Nobel Peace prize winner, a minister, or a political organizer, but you too have a unique voice. Your voice may be the way you design, the way you paint, or the way you sculpt. Your voice could be the way you sing, the way you write, or the way you motivate. Your voice could be the way you serve, the way you contribute, and the way you sacrifice. Your voice could be the way you advocate for others. Your voice can be expressed in a variety of ways because your voice is as varied as your divine assignment.

Remember that your voice is vital, and it communicates your purpose. It has been anointed to say something that ONLY you can say. So find your voice and speak as loudly as you can. Speak so loudly that you drown out doubt, fear, and shame. Speak so loudly that you inspire people to love, lead, and live in a way that honors others. Speak so loudly that you drown out the gremlins, critics, and haters around you and within you. Speak so loudly that you penetrate closed minds and pierce closed hearts. Speak so loudly that your YOUR voice is the voice that transforms the world.

Speak! Insert your voice where you have not been invited, included, or welcomed. Speak and speak loudly because people need to hear what you have to say. Remember, God is counting on you and You are counting on You!

Declare Today: God gave me something special to say to the world, and I am going to say it without apology and with great assurance.

It's time to Soar Higher!

THE POWER OF PURPOSE

You have something remarkable to offer the world.

God gave you a gift, and what you become is your gift to God!

Declare Today: I have a purpose. I have a divine job to do, and I have everything I need to do it.

6

REALITY WILL EVENTUALLY REVEAL WHAT THE SPIRIT ALWAYS KNEW

Have you ever really thought about how you grew up? Over the years, I have learned that sometimes it's useful to reflect on how you were raised. During our formative years, we were taught so many lessons about who we were and how we should act, that it is good to step back and evaluate the messages that shaped our lives. Knowing the source and origins of our core beliefs helps us understand why we say what we say and why we believe what we believe; it helps us conduct a belief audit. And when we understand what beliefs represent what we genuinely believe, we can determine what ideas need to be cultivated and which ideas need to be confronted so we can embrace and express our true essence.

Though it helps to reflect on our childhoods, walking down memory lane is easier for some than others. For example, if you grew up in a happy home and felt loved, seen, and valued, reminiscing about the good old days is easy. Let's face it; being brought up in a supportive environment full of doting relatives, fun traditions, and holiday gatherings makes it enjoyable to exchange stories and recall pleasant events. Just thinking about family vacations, piano recitals, and making cookies with grandma can put a smile on your face and joy in your heart.

But if you grew up in a haunted house without all of the childhood frills and thrills, revisiting your past may not be so easy. In fact, drudging up your past can be extremely painful. Reflecting on all the ways that your childhood was besieged by violence, disrupted by divorce, interrupted by illness, stolen by abuse, diminished by neglect, or marginalized by poverty can be re-traumatizing and reopen unhealed wounds. Let's be honest. Reminiscing about a childhood environment that was small on love but big on condemnation, discrimination and violation can still be detrimental to adult psyches and souls even today.

Although our childhoods were different in many ways, we all had something in common. As children, we knew something about ourselves. We could not explain it, and we didn't even know how we knew it. But we felt something because our souls knew something about us that our minds could not describe, and mouths could not articulate. Our young souls were wise and open; we could sense the presence of the Spirit. That's why we heard sounds that were inaudible to others, and we saw images that only we could see. We didn't know it then, but what we were seeing and sensing was the unveiling of our purpose. God, the Creator, was giving us a glimpse of our future and a preview of what we could become.

The unveiling of purpose can seem somewhat odd to those who don't believe that we all came to the world with divine assignments or sacred callings. It can even appear more confusing when we exhibit behaviors, interests, and tendencies that seem abnormal or even just plain weird. For example, when I was growing up, I used to walk around with an imaginary microphone preaching and teaching to dolls and make-believe congregants. I would stare in the mirror and preach while wildly waving my arms, making sure that I punctuated my impassioned phrases with extravagant gestures.

I know I was just a child, but I had something to say. I didn't understand everything I was saying, yet words and stories swirled in my head and jumped out of my mouth. It felt as if the words insisted on being spoken and heard; they demanded an audience.

To some of my relatives, I was a just crazy little girl yelling into a brush. To them, I was just imitating my Dad. Granted, my Dad was a preacher, and I admired him, but my preaching was more than mere imitation. It was more visceral and magical than childish mimicry. Preaching and teaching called out to me; both chose me, and my soul clung to them. I didn't need prompting either; my soul yearned to speak words that were beyond my experience and comprehension. I could not explain it, but somehow I knew that I was in my element because preaching was instinctive. It felt as natural as eagles must feel when they are flying in the sky.

I realize that me, a preacher's kid, being drawn to preaching could easily be rationalized. I was raised in the church; my relatives were active churchgoers and committed clergy. I get it. But what about children who had spiritual unctions, supernatural wisdom, and unexplained urges to do something or say something that was totally outside of their experience and environment? What about children who had visions and dreams of doing things that they never have seen or heard before, yet share detailed accounts of events and solutions that defy intellectual reasoning? What about children who were masters and prodigies at something even though they had little or no training? What about children who were born and raised in impoverished settings and toxic environments, who had little support yet changed cultural paradigms and started international movements with few resources or little expertise? How can you rationalize and explain such occurrences that altered the trajectory of the world?

You explain what's difficult to explain by understanding the power of purpose. Yes, purpose. You have a purpose. A seed was planted inside of you before you were born. Yes, you were created for a special assignment that only you can do. And God's providential orchestration does not require perfect circumstances to nurture and cultivate us for purpose either.

The truth is that you were "groomed in the womb" to shift the atmosphere and contribute something significant to the world. You were created with a divine blueprint and given a sacred roadmap to guide you to your highest good, which is God's good. You were born to be a solution to a problem, to be an antidote to end suffering, and to be a song that needed to be sung.

I know that the power of purpose might seem too far-fetched or not scientific enough for some. I understand the skepticism. It's hard to fathom that we were born with gifts and talents, and that we are on a God-ordained path. But even though our paths seem ordinary to us, our journeys are not ordinary to God. Our Creator always had an extraordinary plan for our lives. That's why Helen Keller, Oprah Winfrey, Nelson Mandela, Harriet Tubman, Abe Lincoln, and other world-changers were so effective. None of them were perfect. They endured hardships and setbacks, yet they persisted because they felt guided by the Force. They allowed their trials to unlock their potential and crystallize their commitment. They let the fires of life purify and refine them so they could illuminate the world. Like you, they allowed the Spirit to lead them through uncharted territory and over rough terrain to arrive at their purpose.

Purpose. You have one. Dysfunction can't disqualify it. Poverty can't prevent it. Your race, age, and gender can't deny it. Your mistakes and missteps can't eliminate it. People can't block it. Purpose. Even if nobody confirmed or affirmed your purpose as a child, you were born endowed with the grace, greatness, and giftedness to do something revelatory in the world. You were faithfully furnished and favored for your divine assignment, and nothing can stop you from achieving your purpose except YOU!

Purpose!

We can never underestimate who we are or what we have been called to do because our purpose is always unfolding; it is consistently revealed based on willingness to pursue it and our openness to remember it. And, if we open our hearts and spirits to the leading of God and embrace our purpose, we will live a life of amazement because God will surprise us over and over again. God will do the unbelievable and unimaginable if we walk courageously and faithfully toward what we are called to do.

Final Note: On your journey to purpose, you will make a few wrong turns, but don't worry. The detours will help you identify what is wrong for you and provide clues about what's right for you. Also, don't get sidetracked by your past because those pivotal moments provided the lessons, wisdom, and leverage you need to stand out and stand up for what you are called to do. Don't worry about your lack of resources or be concerned about your lack of training either. You know more than you think you know, and you have everything you need to accomplish your goal. Just stay committed and keep refining yourself because every new level will require a different version of you.

Here's the great news: clarity about your purpose will come through the faithful pursuit of it. And through constant pursuit, you will better understand why you were born and who you are. You will understand your desires, dreams, and most profound visions. You will realize why you were drawn and compelled to do something, say something, or see something. And through it all, your childhood experiences will make sense.

Purpose. You are a divine masterpiece. God had something special in mind when God created you. So be patient. Be prayerful. God will make your name great. And as you pursue your purpose, you will live in the perpetual awe of God as reality reveals what the spirit always knew.

Are you ready to pursue your purpose?

Declare Today: I was born for greatness, and greatness will be born from me.

It's time to Soar!

7

GOD TRUSTED YOU SO TRUST YOURSELF

The other day I was feeling pretty low. For those who remember the Color Purple, I probably sounded a lot like the character Sophia because I was feeling extremely despondent. I felt gripped by depression, and I was running as fast as I could to prevent being swallowed up by debilitating grief and intense sorrow. And trust me, I didn't feel like running, but I had no choice. I had to escape those unwanted emotions because I didn't want my productivity affected. I didn't have time to feel sad or lethargic. I had deadlines to meet, battles to win, goals to achieve, and a life to live.

But if you know anything about depression, you know that sometimes depression sneaks up on you and catches you off guard. Then it silently punches you as it gradually overtakes you. When it finally has you in a headlock, it saps your strength, stifles your creativity, and steals your focus. And after depression finally conquers you, it strips you of your hope, power, and self-worth. Trust me, depression is a fierce and unrelenting foe, and I was not interested in getting into the boxing ring with it. Because really? Who has time for all of that? Not me. I had books to write, meetings to attend, and classes to teach. I needed all of me; my life required my full attention and my full participation if I wanted to grow my business and take part in social change.

For days I tried my best to manage my extreme sadness with journal therapy. I wrote down my feelings and shared my thoughts without self-judgment. As we say in the coaching world, I leaned in, and "I stayed present" to my pain because I promised myself years ago that I would not resort to numbing. In the past, numbing with food and religion were my go-to, yet unsuccessful, coping strategies. But today, I was determined to live more courageously and honestly. I wanted to find a more loving way to deal with my intense emotional blues. No more putting temporary band-aids on oozing emotional wounds. Not today!

Despite weeks of feeling somewhat suicidal, I still could not pinpoint the cause of my intense sorrow. Yes, I had suffered some significant losses. A cherished relationship had ended, a business deal depleted my savings, my parents were experiencing health challenges, my son was dealing with job discrimination, and I was lamenting over some ill-advised life decisions. My sadness was explainable, but my pain was more profound than words. My head throbbed, my bones ached, and my spirit yearned. I felt buried by an avalanche of misfortune, and I felt trapped by the weight of my own despair.

When the depression lingered for months, I started to question my divine call. How could I have a purpose if I felt so discouraged? How could I have a divine assignment when I suffered from bouts of deep agony? How could I be a vessel if I sometimes felt like a victim? How could I have a platform when I sometimes struggled with my own inner demons? How could I be an advocate for others if I could not advocate myself? How could I talk about victory when I struggled in the valley?

How could I promote hope when I felt hopeless? How could I talk about elevation when I felt so empty? How can I encourage people to soar when I was sinking? How? Of course, I was a bit dramatic. I was an emotional mess, and my depression had intimidated me so much that I felt disqualified to do my life's work.

When I am extremely sad, I usually call my paid support, my therapist. On my three-decade mental health journey, I have learned that depression is an illness that requires questioning, truth-telling, and vision-casting because intense sadness is a sign that something is off, out of alignment, and gone awry. Most of all, depression is a clarion call to spend time with your Creator and seek clinical support because sometimes prayer needs a friend called Prozac.

During one of my weekly visits with my therapist, I shared how distraught and exhausted I was. As always, she was helpful, encouraging, and wise. But it was not until my father said something that I awakened from my emotional stupor. My father said, "God believed in you and trusted you to do something that only you can do, and you can do it." What? God still trusted me? Me? Even though I made poor decisions, even though I suffered from depression, and even though my childhood wounds kept showing up and showing out in my adult life? God still believed in and trusted me?

That night, I realized that my purpose was indeed encoded in my DNA in ways that circumstances could not touch or taint it. It was divinely protected and could not be taken away, even if anxiety and panic attacks interrupted my peace or siphoned my strength. It could not be revoked even if I felt unworthy and unsettled. It could not be rescinded even if I publicly stumbled or professionally tanked. My purpose was reserved for me. It was mine, all mine. Despite feeling emotionally flawed and fractured, I had a purpose because God trusted me. Yes, God trusted, and God anointed me. My imperfections did not surprise or sway God; God knew me before I knew myself.

Even though I still sometimes battle with depression, that

night, I finally accepted that nothing could disqualify me from pursuing and fulfilling what God had destined for me to do. Nothing. Not depression. Not anxiety. Not a disease. Nothing. If I kept moving in faith, God would order my steps and direct my path.

That night, my depression did not immediately go away, but my fear did, and I finally felt at peace. That night, though flawed, I knew that if I embraced my purpose completely, courageously, and conscientiously, that I would not be denied an opportunity to do something amazing, innovative, and beneficial in the world. That night I was convinced that I could and would contribute something significant to humanity, not despite my depression but because of my depression.

My friend, you have a purpose, too. You have something in your soul that makes you aware, awake, and alive in ways that defy reason. You have something deep in your soul that ignites your passion and excites your imagination. You have something that lives in you and gives you life. Yes, you have something that you were created and called to do, and nothing in the world can prevent you from doing it if you do not allow it. Not sickness, not tragedy, nor mistakes can sideline you if you stay committed to what God has called you to do.

Purpose. You have a purpose; you have a reason for living and giving. Despite your bad choices, despite your depression, and even after decades of riotous living, you are still worthy of your purpose.

My friend, God has not forgotten you. God still believes in you. God still trusts you. Now it is time for you to trust yourself to do what you were created to do.

So, wipe your tears. Forgive yourself. Heal your heart. Sharpen your mind. Cultivate your gift. Reclaim your power. Strengthen your body and passionately pursue what God has called you to do.

Declare Today: I am trusted and loved by God, and I will do great things.

Your purpose is waiting for you. It is time to Soar!

8

REMINDING ME OF MY PAST WON'T MAKE ME REPEAT IT

There will always be people in your life who love to remind you of your past. Even when you are making positive changes in your life, there will always be at least one person who will dredge up every mistake, misstep, and every messy thing that you have ever done to discredit you. And the motor-mouths will not even tell the WHOLE truth. They will exaggerate or add so much "flavor" that what they share will not even remotely resemble what actually occurred. You know that type. They tried to defame you, too.

Let's be clear... It is NOT that you and I, we, don't want to hear about our past, but we are tired of hearing about it. We know where we came from. We know what we did. We know where we fell, failed, and faltered. We know when we acted out, acted up, and sometimes acted a fool; we don't have amnesia. We just refuse to confine ourselves to yesterday because old conversations and stale thinking won't serve us today. We have moved on to greener pastures and to bigger possibilities.

Yes, we did a few mean-spirited, jacked up, and low-down things when we didn't love ourselves, know ourselves, or understand ourselves. We played ourselves cheap and sold ourselves short when we didn't know that we had a purpose. But we are different now. We are wiser now. We are stronger now. We are not who we used to be. We don't do what we used to do. We have transformed and elevated our lives. We have reinvented and reimagined ourselves. We have evolved, and we refuse to live in yesterday when tomorrow holds so much promise.

And just for the record, we hear what you are saying about us. We hear your petty comments like "she forgot where she came from." We hear the malicious murmuring about "he ain't all of that," and "she thinks she is all of that and a bag of chips." We hear all the nasty gossip that you are spewing in the atmosphere. We hear it, but we are not distracted by it.

So, keep talking about us if you want to; we won't participate in your slanderous public campaigns. We won't acknowledge your disparaging assumptions. We don't have time for empty conversations, no interest in changing your mind, and no desire to entertain insincere concerns. We are on a divine assignment. And we don't have time to be reminded of anything that infects us with shame, negativity, doubt, and insecurity. We don't have the energy to accommodate your hatred, jealousy, or manipulative schemes. We are on a mission to create and contribute something meaningful in the world. So, malign and criticize us if you want to. We refuse to be derailed or sidetracked by anything you do or say.

But, just for the record: we haven't forgotten where we came from. We are just more focused on where we are going and how to get there. We are looking in the mirror and finally seeing what God had in mind when we were created. We are looking in the mirror and noticing how our scars have prepared us for success. We see how our wounds have prepared us for greatness. We notice how our failures have filled us with wisdom. We see the frown lines on our foreheads that have filled our heads with intelligence and our hearts with resolve. We caress the skin that has survived the torrential storms and the freezing rain of abuse, rejection, and inequality. We see it all.

That's why we are excited about looking in the mirror daily and deeply to discover something new about our divine design. We are looking for talents that we have not used, gifts that we have not cultivated, and wisdom that we have not tapped. We are looking at ourselves through the lens of love, the filters of faith, and from the perspective of purpose. We are looking, and looking, and looking with sweet anticipation because we expect to see something new, spectacular, and unique in ourselves every single day. We are looking because God's greatness is unfolding in front of our very eyes.

No, we don't see ourselves as perfect people, but we do see ourselves as warriors and winners. We see ourselves as eagles who are ready to launch into a new stratosphere. And we are not worried about who is NOT going with us. We are focused on our fulfillment and not preoccupied with seeking your permission or validation.

We know we can walk with our heads held high, and we refuse to allow ourselves to retreat in fear and wallow in regret. We refuse to shrink or surrender to shame because we made some poor decisions. We refuse to grovel, beg, or hustle to be liked and loved. We know that we are capable and competent. We know that we are better and bolder. We know that we are bigger than any mistake, label, or social construct that attempts to discount us.

So, no... We have not forgotten where we came from. And reminding us about our blunders won't make us revert to what we used to do or who we used to be. We refuse to resurrect old, outdated versions of ourselves, and we are not interested in taking strolls down Memory Lane or Pot-hole Avenue. Our past is only a reference point that propels us further and faster into our purpose. And just so we don't get tempted to go back to an identity or situation that shrinks us, we keep looking in the mirror and saying loudly and confidently, *"It's time to Soar."*

Let's Dare to Soar Higher!

9

PURPOSE REQUIRES LIVING BELOW THE APPLAUSE AND ABOVE THE ATTACKS

People are fickle; they can be quite wishy-washy. Sometimes they love you; sometimes they don't. Sometimes they appreciate you; sometimes they don't. Sometimes they will support you; sometimes, they don't. Sometimes they defend you; sometimes they don't. People are quick to change their minds without notice or explanation. People are just unpredictable.

That's why at the end of the day, you can't be consumed or controlled by people's opinions. You can't let impressive accolades define you, and you can't let mean-spirited attacks derail you. You must stay balanced and sober in your own self-assessment. Why? You are not as bad as people say you are, and you are not as good as people say you are. You are just a person striving to be the best and the highest version of yourself, which is an ever-winding, bumpy road.

So, what do you do when people are applauding you or attacking you? You live below the applause and above the attacks. You stay composed and secure in knowing who you are and you "own" yourself. You own your self-esteem, self-confidence, and self-worth because it's your responsibility "to have your own back."

One of my clients (Sandy, not her real name) is a famous singer. Years ago, Sandy was at the top of the music charts. She had fame, money, and public acclaim. But then her music stop selling and producers stopped returning her calls. She was unceremoniously labeled a "has been" and was told that the masses no longer desired her sound or valued her creativity.

You can imagine how she must have felt. Sandy had dedicated years to her craft and devoted her time and energy to an industry that she loved and respected. Yet, she was suddenly ignored, and when she tried to revive her career, she was castigated. She was branded as pushy and hard to work with. And to add insult to more injury, she was rudely dismissed and discarded like an old, maggot-infested piece of meat despite her many contributions to the industry that she adored, supported, and helped to build.

What changed? Sandy's voice didn't change. Her talent didn't change. Her ability to invest in herself and her craft didn't change. What changed was the public's appetite for her music and her distinctive style of singing. But Sandy's intrinsic value didn't change. She was still gifted and glamorous, but she no longer believed in her ability or her worth because she had elevated the producers' opinions above her own.

Sandy is not alone. If we are honest, we all can point to at least one experience or event that made us question our competence, confidence, and our contributions. We don't want to dwell on it, but we all have been affected by "crowd chatter" and influenced by the peanut gallery and the non-descript "they." We may not want to admit it, but we all have internalized comments that crippled our creativity, snatched our hope, and suppressed our originality. We have all been there. And, unfortunately, many of us were never taught how to effectively deal with persistent peer pressure or how to value our own gifts. We were taught to let others assign value to our work and to our personhood. And as a result, we unknowingly gave people the power and the permission to put a price tag on our overall worth.

Thankfully, Sandy is reviving her singing career. She is creating music that she enjoys and is courageously owning and celebrating her unique singing style. She is now grounded in who she is, and is no longer chasing music producers, begging for gigs, or compromising her integrity to be accepted by the masses. She is doing what feels right for her because she now understands that true success comes from within; success is an inside job.

My friend, just like Sandy, as you pursue your purpose, remember that you are a treasure, too. Your value is not negotiable nor based on your performance. Your worth is not based on the endorsement and the approval of the crowd. Your value is inherent in who you because you are a divine being. You are God's child.

So, here's my advice. Enjoy the applause, but don't get so intoxicated by success that you crave endless praise. Also, expect some attacks, but don't become so intimidated and disillusioned by harsh critiques that you abort your mission. Most of all, keep your self-esteem, self-worth, and self-confidence in your own hands because the path to purpose is a bumpy ride. It's also an internal journey that includes big challenges, great opportunities, a few tears, but genuine fulfillment.

Now for a little shade: Remember that most people will judge you based on how they see themselves, not really how they see YOU! Most of their views about you are filtered through their own feelings of hypocrisy, inadequacy, fear, or guilt. So their applause and their attacks may not be about you, anyway. Did you get that?

Now, are you ready?
It's time to Soar!

10

A TRUE VISIONARY USES AN INTERNAL COMPASS, NOT A WELL TRAVELED MAP

Are you a visionary? Most successful people are because visionaries are people who follow the leading of the Spirit. They are true pioneers, innovators, and trailblazers. They don't rely on maps created by the masses, routes sanctioned by society, or courses created by culture. They listen to their own inner voices and bravely follow an internal compass that points the way.

Are you a visionary? Visionaries dare to be different, and they navigate in the world with confidence and intention. They may appear to be wandering in the wilderness, but they are not. They are listening carefully for guidance and inspiration because they expect to contribute to the world. No, they may not be able to give you exact details about their destination; they may not have dates, routes, or arrival times. But, they are NOT lost. They are following something that only they can see, sense, hear, smell, and touch.

Are you a visionary? Visionaries are attuned and in touch with the spiritual realm. They know that something higher or someone bigger is leading the way. And so, visionaries move with expectancy, courage, and gratitude, knowing that their ultimate destination will require a path that has never been traveled before. They confidently forge ahead, knowing that they have been equipped and endowed with the instincts, talents, and abilities needed for their customized, God-ordained journeys.

Are you a visionary? Visionaries are divinely directed by the Holy One. Despite the detours, the sometimes-rocky terrain, and the steep mountains they may scale along the way, visionaries are content. They believe deeply that the universe will unfold its grandeur as they proceed. And so they welcome the winding roads, the dark passageways, the deep ditches, the sharp cliffs, and the rough patches with hope, gratitude, and peace.

Are you a visionary? You may not know it, but you are a visionary too. You also have a unique journey to walk and experience in life. You, too, have something to do in the world that only you are qualified to do. You, too, will bring forth something that has never existed or been considered before. Yes, YOU, too, are a foreteller, seer, and a prophet replete with a mission, a message, and a purpose. You, too, are a visionary.

My friend, listen and heed the spirit. Your internal compass will serve as your GPS, God's Protection System, to guide you on your journey to destiny.

Are you ready to embrace your God-given purpose? I pray so because success, greatness, and fulfillment await.

It's time to Soar Higher!

BEING TRUE AND TRUSTING GOD

Own who you are.

When you see yourself through the lens of purpose, you will not bow to the crowd. You will not compete or compare. You will celebrate your true nature. You will honor your calling. You will refuse to accept limits. You will create your own narrative. You will shed the "shoulds." You will live your own life. You will stand out, stand up, and stand tall because you realize that greatness never compromises or surrenders to the crowd.

Declare Today: I will not cheat myself out of being Me!

11

IF YOU KEEP TRYING TO FIT IN, EVENTUALLY YOU WILL FADE OUT

Most of my life, I was called a misfit. Most of the groups that I so desperately wanted to join rejected me, excluded me, or ridiculed me. They said that I was weird, but what they didn't realize was that I was not weird; I was severely emotionally wounded. I was hurting. Life had beaten me up in ways that my young mind couldn't comprehend. But that's another story.

But as I healed and started to learn more about me, I continued to be a misfit. However, I realized that my definition of misfit was different from the definition of those who considered me to be an oddball. I was a "mis-fit" because I recognized that I was unwilling to fit into places or kiss-up to people who could not accept how God made me. I was a "mis-fit" because I realized that I was a circle, but people wanted me to be a square. I was a "mis-fit" because I demanded to live my own life without the permission or approval of others. I was a "mis-fit" because I refused to follow traditions that trapped me, norms that nullified me, or stereotypes that subjugated me. When I finally accepted that being normal required me to contort myself into unrecognizable caricatures that degraded me, I realized that I would never be "normal," whatever normal was. I accepted that I would never fit because I was too exceptional, too original, and too anointed to live as a fraction. I was a total human being who refused to be marginalized and minimized by society's rules. I was a one-of-a-kind woman who lived outside the confines of the crowd and beyond the constructs of a restrictive culture.

You are a wonderful "mis-fit" too. You were created and crafted to be rare and extraordinary. You were not made on an assembly line. You were not mass-produced. You were not a cookie-cutter clone; you are an original masterpiece customized to be YOU. God, the Creator, made you different to make a difference!

Let's be honest. Fitting in with the crowd could make your life easier, but you would never be happy, fulfill your purpose, or attract the people you need to support your destiny. However, standing out and stepping away from the "confinement of consensus" will help you see the world, be seen in the world, and help you serve the world in a bigger, bolder way. Stepping away from the group will give you the freedom you need to be a free-thinker, truth-teller, self-liberator, and a God-inspired activator.

Yes, you are different. You are a fantastic "mis-fit." Every detail, characteristic, and coincidence in your life has meaning. Every challenge, failure, and trial is part of your unfolding, strength-building, and development. Every heartbreak and love affair was instructive and purposeful. Every moment and mountain was formative. Every experience shaped you and molded you to be different, a "mis-fit," so that you could boldly express who you are. You were not born to float in the sea of sameness or live in a cage of conformity. You were born to be free and to fully express your Creator!

Never forget that when God, Destiny, calls you OUT, you will never again fit back into places that are not aligned with your divine CALL! So, when you are tempted to be like everybody else, resist the urge to fit in! Be courageous and be different. Be unconventional, be out of the box, and be unorthodox. Remember that you were born to add and accessorize the world with your greatness and to proudly demonstrate the diversity of a loving God.

I celebrate you! I honor you! Thank you for being you!

Let's Dare To Soar Higher!

12

YOU DON'T HAVE TO BE A REPLICA TO BE RELEVANT

We all want to be relevant, don't we? No one wakes up in the morning, aspiring to be invisible, inappropriate, or inconsequential. Feeling outdated, stagnated, and antiquated is nothing we desire or hope for, right? We all want to have an impact; we want to make a difference in the world and leave a legacy.

But to have impact and influence, we must be authentic; we must be ourselves because the world rewards originals, not duplicates. Even though imitators, clones, me-too-knock-offs, and second-rate copycats achieve some success, their success is never sustainable or memorable. The world craves and rewards fresh ideas, reframed thoughts, and innovative products to satisfy its insatiable and fickle appetite.

Real talk. When you see others experiencing the success that you desire for yourself, it is tempting to mimic them. The allure of fast fortune and instant fame can tempt us to compromise, conform, and cut a few corners. Don't you agree? This is a good place to say amen.

What we often forget is that we are only relevant if we don't disguise or dilute who we are. When we claim our true identities, share our narratives, and reflect our deepest convictions, then and only then, can we start revolutions and offer new revelations. Then, and only then, can we change lives, be a beacon of light, and dismantle systems that strangle justice. Then, and only then, can we shift the culture, restore faith, heal the land, and honor God.

I know it is easier to go along to get along; following the market, cavorting with the masses, and parroting socially approved messages are the paths of least resistance. And of course, it's easier to do what everybody else is doing or do what has already been done. But progress is only made when we move away from blind conformity and toward courageous originality. Progress is only made when we raise our voices and raise our hands to do what we were born to do, not what we were "allowed" to do or told to do. Social movements start when your conscience and your own moral compass compel you and propel you to do what the Divine Designer has called you to.

When I think about my life, I sometimes feel regret because I wasted so much time, energy, and money trying to be like everybody else, and you probably have, too. Even if we don't want to admit it, we all have experimented with being carbon copies of others, only to discover that imitation drains our joy and mutes our effectiveness. We all had to learn the hard way that what resuscitated our hearts and ignited our souls was accepting that we were purposeful prototypes of the Purpose-Giver, God. Am I right? You can say amen.

My friend, you were made to be relevant and there is nothing holy and humane about deleting parts of yourself. Destiny never requires that you divest of your God-given traits, erase your God-given personality, or abandon your God-given talents. Also, masquerading and mimicking others are not sacred acts. Both are rejections of your own personality and a rebuff of God's omniscient design.

You are relevant, which means that you might have to stand alone, stand up, and stand apart from the crowd. So, resist assimilation and impersonation. Reject conformity and compliance. Relinquish faking and masking. Refuse blending and borrowing. Renounce hiding and lying. Resist shrinking and settling. Reclaim YOU and listen to the urges and impulses of your soul so you can soar.

YOU are RELEVANT!

So, RISE!

Embrace your purpose!

Declare Today: I AM Relevant, and I WILL RISE AS ME!

Now, go forth and do what God has ordained you to do.

It's time to Soar!

13

YOU CAN'T FLY HIGH WITH SOMEBODY ELSE'S WINGS

I love the word *Soar.* Soar is not just about flying or rising high in the air; soaring is about maintaining height in the sky. It is about having the ability to ascend high, advance fast, and adjust quickly to opportunities and challenges. To me, soaring is power.

Often, I try to imagine what it feels like to soar. I close my eyes and try to envision myself effortlessly gliding in the sky. I try to take in the whole experience, and so I activate my senses to soak up the smells, hear the sounds, and taste the wind. I visualize how the air feels on my skin and how my limbs react to the speed. Then, I imagine what it feels like to be free, at ease, and at peace as I sail smoothly and naturally in the air. I imagine myself being engulfed by clouds, being tickled by the birds, and even peering into heaven. I know it sounds far-fetched, but I dream of soaring, not just flying. I dream of being up high – higher and farther than my eyes can see.

What about you? Do you ever dream of soaring? Right now, close your eyes. Imagine what it feels like to glide smoothly in the sky with purpose, precision, and proficiency. Can you feel it? Can you see it? Wow! It feels so right.

We all can SOAR. We all have wings that are composed of a unique combination of gifts, skills, and experiences that have prepared us to fly high in the sky. We all have wings that were specifically designed to help us SOAR in diverse environments, serve a variety of people, and to provide a distinctive purpose. We have wings that were tailored to overcome every obstacle that stands in our way. We have customized wings made to fit our own life specifications and journeys.

However, sometimes when we evaluate our own combination of talents, abilities, and experiences, we undervalue our wings, or we over-value the wings of our friends. Sometimes, we become so dissatisfied with our own beautiful wings that we degrade them, disown them, and disregard them. We act as if we have been cheated and ill-equipped with our own special set. So much so, that we don't exercise our wings, we don't cultivate our wings, and sometimes we curse our wings. And when we get really desperate, we try to steal the wings of others, not realizing that their wings will not fit us. Their wings were not made for us, and they cannot be remodeled and resized to accommodate who God created us to be or to do what God created us to do.

After we mismanage and mishandle our wings or steal ("borrow") our neighbors' wings, we become defeated and depressed. We complain, we compete, we compare, and we cry. And so, instead of launching into the sky of success, we sink and become anchored to the ground. We become so inflamed with jealousy and bitterness that we stop flying, or we abandon our wings altogether. We lose our way.

Sometimes it takes time for us to recognize how amazing, intricate, and powerful our own wings really are. But until we appreciate our own wings, which are treasured gifts from God, we stop flapping, flowing, and flying. We stop using what was explicitly designed for us, and we become imitators and spectators, not appreciating that we were created to be initiators and originators.

But after we suffer and struggle for a while, we accept our wings, and we realize how powerful and detailed they really are. We see their value, appreciate their abilities, and marvel at their beauty. We learn how far they can stretch and how fast they can surge. We learn what they can do, where they can go, and how far they can glide. We respect their uniqueness, and we thank the Divine Giver for the special gift.

You were created to SOAR with your own divinely customized WINGS. Your wings will always be loyal to you when you are loyal and loving to them. So, trust them, and they will help you launch into the sky, glide in the air, and SOAR to new heights!

Are you ready to fly?

Get ready, get set, go!

Your destiny is waiting for you!

It's time to Soar!

14

BE YOU EVEN IF IT MEANS YOU MUST BE ALONE

There will come a time in your life when you will refuse to be squeezed, shoved, silenced, and shrunk into being who you are NOT. You will refuse to accommodate, adjust, and alter your personality and your appearance to please others. You will no longer conceal your love life and your beliefs to make others feel comfortable. You will refuse to bow down, sit down or cow down to any policy, principle, or practice that fails to honor your divinity and your humanity. You will boldy stand UP!

You will realize that your personal integrity is worth more than money, fame, and popularity. You will realize that your personal integrity will not allow you to compromise your ethics, morals, and values to be accepted and included. You will realize that you won't be bought or bossed into believing or behaving in ways that violate your character. You accept that you may have to live and stand by yourself because you refuse to be a pawn, parrot, or punk to please people. You will be YOU! You will support you. You will love YOU even if it means being alone for a short while.

Yes, at first you may feel lonely. But if you think about it, you will not be lonely, alone maybe, but not lonely. Loneliness is what happens when you violate your moral compass and ignore your intuition. It's when you stop being your own best friend to suck up to others. It's when you fail to make courageous choices that align with who you are and who you desire to be. And that inner loneliness is what breeds desperation and depression, and unfortunately sometimes, suicide.

In contrast, being alone is a sign of inner strength and a time for great reflection. It is when you value yourself and your beliefs enough to step away from what does not support you. It's that inner peace that fills your soul because you know that you are willingly, boldly, and peacefully following your own convictions. It's those reassuring moments that provide peace because you know that you are doing precisely what God has placed in your heart to do. Now, that's power!

Be encouraged, my friend. Being alone right now means that you are on your way to something greater than aligns more perfectly with your purpose. It means that you are getting to know the new, improved you to prepare you for your next dimension of destiny. Being alone right now means that you are learning to discern and follow that still quiet voice that affirms you, directs you, and emboldens you. Being alone right now is a sacred time; it is a time of cultivation for your life-giving purpose.

Use this precious time alone wisely and thoughtfully. Journal daily. Meditate often. Just be still with the assurance that this alone time is holy, and will provide the power you need to embrace the next step of your journey.

Be YOU and SOAR because there are beautiful blessings in store.

Let's Dare To Soar Higher!

15

DON'T LET THE LACK OF THEIR ACCEPTANCE MAKE YOU LEAVE YOUR ASSIGNMENT

When we agreed to serve the world with our talents and gifts, nobody said it would be easy. Nobody said that we would have tons of friends, lots of support, or experience quick success (however you define success). Nobody said that the journey would be pain-free, stress-free, or just free. Nobody said that!

So, when you are attacked, understand that being unfairly criticized and publicly confronted is part of the process. When you feel minimized, understand that's part of the mission. When you feel punished, understand that's part of your path to purpose.

When people expose your dirty laundry, understand that exposure is a part of elevation.

Yes, the verbal jabs sting. And when you see pieces of your personal information on social media, you feel embarrassed. When people unfairly characterize you, and you see your name being dragged through the mud, you want to retaliate. I know. I have been there.

But, who told you that accepting your divine assignment would be comfortable, convenient, or conflict-free? Who said you would tiptoe through the tulips without some chaos? Who told you that people would not lie about your qualifications, your personal history, or your motives? Who told you that people would not turn against you? Who told you you would not have jealous saboteurs discrediting your reputation and undermining your influence? Who said that people would not harass and hinder you? Who promised you that your most trusted allies would always be faithful and protect your confidential information, your character, or your career? Who told you that?

Following your purpose is not the same thing as going to a party. It's not always simple, safe, or financially profitable. If following your purpose was easy, more people would follow their own purpose. Don't you agree?

So, how do you deal with constant criticism without growing resentful, cynical, and bitter? How do you proceed amid intense smear campaigns devised to defame you? How do you deal with envy that strains your relationships, sabotages productivity, and disrupts unity? How? You see opposition for what it is: a distraction!

Let's face it. Most of the people who viciously attack you are rarely doing something significant in their own lives. Since they lack the courage and discipline to pursue their own divine assignments, they use their valuable energy to disrupt you and to block your vision. That's why in a weird, pathetic way, it makes sense that your detractors are criticizing you. They need someone to blame for the lack of fulfillment and accomplishment in their own lives.

The moral of the story: Don't let other people distract you from your assignment. Stay focused. As my elders would say, "you can't pull your wagon and other wagons too." If people are sincerely committed to their own advancement, they will take some initiative themselves. If not, you must move forward alone, fortified by your belief in your purpose.

At first, being focused on your assignment may cost you a few friends. But trust me, you will be just fine. You have been endowed with the internal infrastructure needed to build and persevere. You have been graced to deal with hurts and hardships. You have the faith to stabilize you and steer you amid a storm. You can do it! You can do whatever needs to be done to fulfill God's purpose for your life.

Remember, you are a winner! You belong high in the sky. So, don't let the lack of acceptance convince you to abandon your assignment. Go forth, be fruitful, and flourish. It's activation and elevation time.

Declare Today: My assignment is non-negotiable, and I will not be deterred.

It's time to Soar!

16

DON'T PICK UP THINGS THAT DON'T BELONG TO YOU

When I was a little girl, my mother always told us, "Don't pick up things that do not belong to you." My mother gave us the same warning every time we went to the store. Not that my siblings or I ever forgot the rule, but my mother was not taking any chances. She was clear: stores were for seeing, not for touching. So, my siblings and I didn't touch anything; we kept our hands to ourselves. We didn't test Momma's patience because we knew Momma didn't play. She was clear: pick up something and die. Well, maybe not die, but you would feel like dying after one of her butt whoopings.

As I got older, I understood that being black and touching things in stores could be dangerous. If certain white people suspected that you were mishandling merchandise or stealing food, the entire family could get in trouble. Being young, curious, or innocent meant nothing. If you were black, to some people, you were a threat and a criminal. It didn't matter if you were three or thirty-three; it was assumed that you were a thief.

Even though my mother's warning was about shopping, life has taught me that her advice applies to all aspects of life. My mother's advice especially applies to picking up labels that society imposes on you. And let's be honest. Society imposes all types of labels on people, especially people considered as *"others."*

As a black woman, I am often labeled. For example, even though I am educated and accomplished, I am often labeled as incompetent, ignorant, angry, promiscuous, unethical, weak, emotional, loud, bossy, and other pejorative words that fail to represent my character. I have even heard labels attached to me that would have crushed my soul if I didn't know my history or know who I was. Suffice to say, labels were and continue to be affixed to me to discount and discredit me. It even hurts to acknowledge that fact; nevertheless, it's true.

Though extremely painful, my experience is not that unique. I know a few labels have been imposed on you, too. People who love to amass and abuse power always label "others" to marginalize them, dehumanize them, trivialize them, or villainize them. Labels have always been a form of control and disenfranchisement. Just look at history. When the colonizers labeled "coloreds and others" as less human, the colonizers easily justified their abuse, pillage, degradation, and savagery. Don't believe me? Pick up a history book – one that provides a little bit of truth, not the ones that omit the unsavory details.

Here's some friendly advice. As you are pursuing your purpose, don't pick up any labels that do not belong to you. And reject the labels you automatically impose on yourself because your purpose requires that you detach and dis-identify from any label that blurs your vision, restricts your movement, or saps your strength.

Why is rejecting labels so critical to your success and psyche? First, you don't fit into labels. No single label can describe all of who you are or all that you aspire to be. No single classification can celebrate all of your talents, gifts, and blessings that God has given you. No one label can comprehensively identify or define you; you are too majestic for that. You are too unique, too exclusive, too fantastic, too exceptional, too intricate, too complex, and sometimes too contradictory to be reduced to mere words. You are made in the image of God, which means that no human being can fully comprehend or convey your genius.

I have to admit that it took me almost thirty years to understand how societal labels were affecting my self-identity, my self-confidence, and my self-worth. Since I had grown up with a myriad of degrading labels pinned to me, I had unknowingly internalized many destructive ones that limited my life. The labels told me where I could go, what I could do, and what I should feel. The labels became the masters that minimized me, the rules that restricted, and the critical chaperons that coerced me. The labels were tyrants that terrorized me when I had elaborate dreams of success, mocked me when I had goals outside of my "culture," and scared me when I had accomplishments that were bigger than my experience. The labels ensured that I stayed in my place—the place where people who looked like me were socially *allowed* to dwell.

Thanks to decades of prayer and therapy, I learned that all societal labels imposed on me by human beings were beneath the divine label that God gave me. I now realize that people can never fully grasp all of me, and people cannot grasp all of you. That's the truth. The truth is tight, but it's right! You can say amen.

Here is the ultimate truth: it is YOUR responsibility to identify and define who you are and who you are not. When someone or a system places you in an unfavorable category, it is YOUR responsibility to remember that external labels do not determine YOUR reality or worth, only you do. It is also YOUR responsibility to never let a label demote you, demean you, deny you or dismantle you—NEVER! It is your responsibility to be so grounded in your purpose and personhood that people can't pimp, poison, or prevent you from doing what God has called you to do. It is up to you to let your understanding of who you are be a source of spiritual dynamite that detonates your gifts and launches your creativity into the atmosphere. Just YOU!

My friend, labels don't belong to you. Labels are societal stamps, stifling stickers, contaminated categories, deadly decals, and tainted tags. They are not divine dictates. They are human inventions, not God's instructions.

Remember what my mother said, *"Don't pick up things that don't belong to you,"* because, ultimately, only the labels that God gives you matter.

Declare Today: I release what God did not assign to me.

It's time to Soar!

17

THE STATUS QUO IS SOCIETY'S POSITION, BUT IT IS NOT YOUR DIVINE PLACE

When I entered corporate America, I was advised, but really warned, to stay in my place. My "trainer" admonished me to keep my head down and to do as I was told. Not only was I insulted that he talked to me like a child, but I was also furious that the other trainees did not get the same guidance. I was the only Black woman, and being warned to stay in my place and abide by the suffocating, degrading status quo was really a foreshadowing of what was to come. And being expected to willingly accommodate his request to be a second-class employee shattered my confidence. I was crushed and my spirit suffered a fatal, professional blow.

Over the years, abiding by the status quo became increasingly soul-depleting and heart-wrenching. I felt boxed in and blocked out. I felt trapped by an existing set of norms, beliefs, and policies that denied my humanity and devalued my talent. I felt oppressed by a heavy invisible system that would never let me grow, contribute, or shine. Reluctantly, I had to accept the unfortunate truth: the status quo was society's position, but it was not my place. The status quo could never see my talent, appreciate my worth, or let me navigate freely in the world.

Yes, the status quo may be the current state of the world. But, the current state of the world does not honor you. The current state expects you to conform and comply with policies, philosophies, and practices that society deems as acceptable, appropriate and allowed based on your societal designation. The status quo expects you to relinquish your ability to think for yourself and surrender your authority to decide for yourself. No, the status quo is not for you!

Yes, the status quo is the current state of things. But, the current state does not celebrate you. The current state does not honor your unique demonstration of beauty, your extraordinary brilliance, or God-given boldness. It attempts to shrink you down to average so you wallow in misery, mediocrity, and mess. It tries to marginalize you because even though YOUR difference is appealing, illuminating, and refreshing, it is outside of the standards of societal acceptability. No, the status quo is not for you.

Yes, the status quo is the current state of things. But, the current state does not accurately position you. You were created for greatness. God equipped you with genius, gifts, and guts to galvanize a movement, generate wealth, and to gather with the gifted to serve God's people. You were designed for success. You were positioned and set aside to contribute to the world in innovative ways, with life-giving words, and with soul-edifying wisdom. No, the status quo is not for you.

Yes, the status quo is the current state of things. But, the current state does not prepare you. It does little to help you discover who you are and develop who you were meant to me. It restricts your movement and reduces your thinking so you will follow the crowd and not your own conscience. It does not acknowledge that your ideas are novel or that your perspective is forward-thinking. It systematically tries to numb and neutralize you so you will acquiesce to the policing of the privileged. No, the status quo is not for you.

Yes, the status quo is the current state of things. But, the current state does not cultivate you. You were created to disrupt norms, develop minds, and discern the truth. You were designed to be a changemaker, a boundary-breaker, a trendsetter, and a truth-teller. You were made to shake some things up, shake some things off, and to shut some things down. You were divinely authorized to push the envelope, peel the onion, and press society's buttons to illuminate the darkness that has our nation sinking in spiritual disease, despair, and destruction. No, the status quo is not for you.

Yes, the status quo is the current state of things. But, the current state requires you to settle for what's beneath your potential and below God's promises. But you will not settle for crumbs or second-rate citizenship. You are a warrior. You were not made to concede; you will not accept defeat. You are strong, resilient, and relentless. Failure is only feedback to you. Losing is just a lesson for you. Rejection is only refinement to you. Being underestimated is just a strategy that allows you to build without distraction and win without detection.

My friend, the status quo is not for you because you have a purpose. Yes, you have a purpose. And because of your PURPOSE, the status quo can only be society's position, but it can never be YOUR place. Your place is bigger, brighter, and bolder. Your place is on the margins, on the fridges, and on the periphery of social conventions. Your place is beyond what's seen, what's available, and what's commonly known to others. So, step into that place. The place that God ordained just for you when you were only a thought in God's mind because YOU were made to SOAR!

Let's Dare To Soar Higher!

18

DOING YOU MAY OFFEND THEM

Pursuing YOUR purpose can sometimes spark some unexpected reactions from your friends and family. For example, instead of receiving words of encouragement and affirmation, you receive nasty personal attacks. It's the weirdest thing because you would think that those closest to you would applaud you for following your heart. You would hope that your inner circle would respect you for going after your vision, wouldn't you? You would expect that following your dreams would invoke admiration, right? Let's be honest. It's not every day that a person musters up the courage to do something new, to try something different, or to do something that makes their heart sing.

The other day one of my clients, Laura, decided to close her medical practice. She never wanted to be a physician. Truth be told, she hated it. She never enjoyed treating patients, she hated being around blood, and being in hospitals made her nauseous. For those reasons alone, I was happy that she was leaving the medical profession and not endangering the lives of unsuspecting patients. Well, maybe endangering is a bit of an exaggeration, but you get my point. Because really, who wants a frustrated physician operating on them? They may accidentally remove a kidney instead of a spleen.

But despite her apparent disdain for her profession, Laura's family was livid that she called it quits. Her "so-called" loved ones went off the deep end and expressed their disapproval in some rather hostile ways. They called her names, bombarded her with offensive notes, and sent some crazy, foul text messages condemning her decision. Some demanding family members even dared to show up at her house unannounced to protest her choice, a decision that had nothing to do with them.

What was shocking was that Laura's relatives felt that they actually had a voice and a vote in her personal affairs. Some of her family members even suggested that they should have been consulted before *she* decided to leave her profession, even if the change radically enhanced and enriched the quality of her life. A few relatives even told Laura that she was letting the entire family down. Really? The whole family would fall apart if she lived her own life and made decisions to honor her own mental health? Really? The well-being of the entire family rested solely on her continuing in a vocation that was giving her ulcers, migraines, and anxiety. Really? The reputation of the family will be damaged and doomed if she honored her truth and inner wisdom? Really?

I was shocked by the swiftness and meanness of the attacks. No crime had been committed. Laura's only offense was following her heart and embracing her truth. And honestly, her family should not have been shocked by her decision. They knew that she didn't enjoy medicine or being a doctor. Laura did not even want to go to medical school, and she tried to quit several times before she graduated. And after she graduated from medical school, she tried to quit again during her medical residency but felt forced to stay in a profession she knew she was ill-suited for.

Yes, Laura had the intelligence to practice medicine; she was a brilliant woman. But she never had the heart for medicine.

She had explained and shared her concerns repeatedly with her family but never felt confident enough to push back and go against the grain to live her own life, a fulfilling life.

During our sessions together, Laura shared how sad and scared she was about moving forward without her family's blessings. She didn't want to jeopardize her relationship with her loved ones because being disowned was a real possibility. At the same time, she was incredulous and outraged because none of her familial protestors, who were disparaging her, had made any significant investment in her career, a career that she hated.

None had paid for medical school. Nobody had contributed to her living expenses or volunteered to pay any of the $500K of educational debt that she felt crushed by. None of the protestors helped her study or even provided meals when she studied for her medical boards. None of her protesters helped her manage her practice, treat her patients, or stayed on the phone with insurance companies to get treatments approved. And most of all, nobody helped her when she was so depressed that she could barely crawl out of bed or drag herself to work. Nobody was there to relieve her or lighten her load. Yet, the same people who provided nothing but occasional verbal encouragement had the audacity to fiercely express their discontent with her decision.

Even though Laura's experience sounds a bit extreme, her experience is more common than you think. Unfortunately, many brave souls often receive criticism from loved ones when they make choices to honor themselves and to forge their own paths. When some courageous people make decisions that are not in alignment with their family's expectations, beliefs, needs, or timetables, some family members become unglued and emotionally abusive. Sometimes they retaliate in hurtful ways.

Laura and I spent months dissecting her deep-rooted beliefs and restructuring her life. During our time together, what was evident to me was that her family was not really upset at her. Laura's family was angry because she was doing something that they secretly, yet unconsciously, wanted for themselves. She was liberating herself from the traps of tradition and from the cage of conformity. She was challenging culture and defying societal norms. She was courageously rebelling against her family's narrative and establishing a new script for her happiness. She was demanding to be the main character, the (s)hero, the focus, and the chief priority in her own life. She was taking charge of her future in ways that caused disruption and discomfort to others.

My friend, as you revamp your life to be happier, healthier, and whole, some people will be furious with you too. But remember that their reactions have nothing to do with you. They are mainly upset because they feel stuck in a life or a system that is unexciting and unfulfilling, yet they lack the strength or willpower to change. And so, your loved ones unknowingly project their feelings of unhappiness onto you because they don't know how to confront the REAL internal issues that rob them of the agency and courage to direct their own lives.

I am happy to report that Laura is enjoying her new life. However, it has not been a "they lived happily ever after" story. There have been challenges, craziness, and casualties. She has lost some friends, tons of money, and some family members are still upset because, in their eyes, she has "thrown her life away."

Thankfully, Laura is finally happy. She sold her medical practice, moved to a new city, and started an online business helping other doctors leave their unfulfilling medical careers so they can live heart-centered lives, too. Despite the loss and struggle, Laura is finally at peace and has no regrets. She is actually proud of herself for creating a life she loves.

This is what I know for sure: doing you will offend "them," and you will encounter lots of "thems" on your purpose journey. So, take your time to get to know yourself and anchor yourself in that "knowing" so you can live your PURPOSE unapologetically and courageously.

Yes, Laura had an honorable profession, and to everybody else, she was successful and was living the American dream. But Laura wasn't living HER purpose. She was living a purpose imposed on her that was depleting her soul and draining her spirit. And we all know that consistent depletion will leave you limping, and not leaping, through life.

My father, Rev. Franklin Jamison, always says that "purpose will not add years to your life, but purpose will add life to your years." So, live with purpose and on purpose. And most of all, SOAR! SOAR HIGHER than you have ever SOARED before because the best is yet to come.

Let's Dare To Soar Higher!

19

REJECTION: IT'S NOT PERSONAL; IT'S PURPOSEFUL

I got deeply hurt today, so hurt that I felt sick. I couldn't put my finger on it, but the pain felt familiar. I don't want to sound too dramatic, but it felt like a stab in the heart, a punch in the stomach, and an uppercut to the eye. I felt like I had been jabbed in my most tender places, and the pain was excruciating.

After I shed a few tears and collected my thoughts, I realized that the emotion that was breaking my heart was the feeling of rejection. Yes, I had been rejected! I was officially notified that I was pushed out of a sister circle, but I didn't understand why. I hadn't disagreed with anyone. I hadn't shared any secrets. I hadn't crossed any emotional boundaries that I knew of. But for some reason, I was kicked to the proverbial curb with no explanation.

Being expelled from a group was not new to me because I never felt as if I really belonged anywhere. I spent a good portion of my life trying to find my team, my place, and my peeps because I was never really successful fitting into one clique or clan. Maybe it was hard for people to connect with me because I am a social nomad. I float and engage with many different types of groups because I always prefer conscious affinity over blind allegiance. And so, I guess to most people, my lack of commitment or loyalty to one demographic or faith tradition felt suspicious.

Needless to say, I was absolutely distraught and shocked when I learned that I had been ousted. I analyzed my untimely dismissal, my abrupt social expulsion, from a few perspectives, but none of the explanations made sense to me or made me feel better. I had to face the fact that I may never know why I received my walking papers. I also had to face another fact; rejection hurts, and it hurts a lot.

I don't want to sound morbid, but unfortunately, we all have and will experience rejection. We all will get dumped by someone we love. We may not get the job or position that we interviewed and prayed for. We may not get the part in the play that we practiced for. We may not get accepted to the school that we studied for. We may not get accepted by the crowd that we lied for, sold our souls for, or compromised our integrity for. We may not get as many "likes" on social media that we hoped for. We may not get the salary that we worked for. We may not even get our kindness returned as expected. During our lifetime, we will all get rejected. We will get excluded, banned, ignored, and abruptly dismissed from something and someone we desperately desire. And when it happens, we will be crushed!

Feeling crushed is extremely painful because rejection is a wound of the soul. You can't see it or touch it, but the pain is there, festering and causing havoc in our lives. And unfortunately, our invisible wounds rarely get adequately attended to, which makes them bleed the most and the longest. That's why many people behave so poorly today; their childhood soul wounds never healed, and they are reacting and reliving their long-standing trauma every day for the entire world to see.

Yes, my friend, rejection hurts. It makes you doubt yourself and question your self-worth. It makes you magnify your weaknesses, bemoan your inadequacies, rehash your mistakes, and fills you with fear. I don't know about you, but being rejected sent me straight down the *Beat-The-Hell-Out-Of-SharRon* lane and had me questioning my talents, insight, and judge of character. It had me crouching, crying, and, most of all, calling on Jesus.

Then, after I unmercifully beat myself up and emotionally tore myself to shreds for feeling sad about being excluded, I felt ashamed. I felt like an imposter because I was supposedly the "strong" one. I was the go-to chick. I was a Wonder Woman, right?

According to some of my former friends, being ostracized and shunned should not have bothered me. Instead of receiving support from them, I received questions like, "Where is your self-esteem? Where is your faith? Where is your strength? Why are you wimping out? And why are you letting people get to you?"

Being judged for feeling sad, being chastised for needing support, and having my Christian faith questioned by my so-called sister-girls felt like being pierced in an already oozing wound. Where was the empathy or compassion? Where were the close hugs of sisterhood and the words of encouragement? Why was I denied the same support and the same words of affirmation that I so generously gave to others in their time of need?

I didn't understand it then, but I later realized that their lack of support and empathy was not about me. Their inability to hold space for me was due to their own discomfort with my honest expression of pain. Since they appointed me as the "strong" one, seeing me cry made them feel weak. My blood-shot eyes, my quivering chin, and snot running down my nose reminded them of their own vulnerability. And being vulnerable is something that many "strong Black women" were taught to avoid at all costs.

My honest expressions of pain challenged the myth or the notion that Black women are stoic, immune to pain, and largely unaffected, which are lies forced on Black women by a society that fails to honor and protect us. And that's why the "strong Black women" myth is so harmful to us because it prevents Black women from getting the support, love, protection, and help we need to live and survive in the world. Even today, so many Black women are utterly overwhelmed and over-extended, trying to live up to a term and an expectation that denies us of our full humanity. We are literally forced and expected to be emotional mules and we are dying slow, emotionally excruciating deaths.

It took months to come to grips with being excommunicated. I discovered a lot about myself on my healing journey–some noble things and some unfavorable things. The greatest lesson that I learned was that rejection must be acknowledged and addressed to effectively heal the soul. The feelings of abandonment, being left out and banned, must be accepted and fully owned. If not, people will cover up their emotions with all types of antisocial behavior. They will lie, manipulate, numb, or retaliate. Some people will experience rejection so profoundly that they become aggressive, cynical, and, unfortunately, violent. Over the years, I have seen many people reel from rejection and nose-dive deep into depression and desperation because they attempted to hide their disappointment and agony. Despite my "*success*" and accomplishments, I have experienced some reeling too.

I can't tell you how to nurse your emotional wounds, but I can honestly admit that healing was difficult for me. My heart ached, my stomach boiled, and my head throbbed; I had a visceral reaction to being ousted. For months, my emotional reactions were all over the board. Sometimes I responded like a well-behaved, spiritually evolved adult, and sometimes, I just cussed people out. My thoughts and feelings ran the gamut and so did my behavior. And just for the super-saved, holier-than-thou people in the back, I am still saved and sanctified and my minister's card can't be revoked for being honest.

My friend, rejection, even though we don't volunteer for it, is a universal human emotion that you and I will experience many times in our lifetimes. But it's up to us to admit the sting of it so we can soothe our souls, get support and get on with our lives. It's up to us to affirm who we are, acknowledge our worth, and rebuild our self-esteem so we don't succumb to feelings that make us emotionally frail and spiritually weak. It's up to us to define rejection as a hurtful fact, but not a life-defining problem. (*Fact vs. problem. Know the difference and respond accordingly*).

Since rejection is inevitable, what can you do?

1) Remember that your value is not limited to someone else's vision. Some people won't, and some people can't see your value, and it is NOT theirs to see. You must see your own value. Just think about it. Many people didn't see how vital and valuable Jesus was, but their inability to see Jesus didn't diminish His value to the world. Honoring your value is your responsibility and can't be outsourced to others.

2) Remember that people are not always rejecting you. They may be responding to their assumptions about you and their beliefs about themselves. It may not be about you at all. Rejecting you may be the result of their inability and cowardice to ask you and themselves important questions. Never forget that cowards are not leaders; they are followers who are controlled by the crowd.

3) Remember that even though people didn't choose you, it does not mean that you are not chosen. God chose you; that's why you were born. The Best Chooser chose YOU to be on earth. Nobody else's opinion counts, so don't count it.

4) Remember, without healing, your injury could become your identity. When our egos get bruised, if not remedied, we tend to act out and act up in harmful ways to protect ourselves. We withdraw, worry, people-please, become abrasive, attack, or manipulate. We "*armor*" up so much that we become rigid, inflexible, and so brittle that we can't enjoy emotions like joy, peace, and contentment. So, address the bruise. Don't let being rejected today affect your opportunities and relationships tomorrow.

5) Remember that being rejected can be a gift. Every closed door in my life led me to a better, brighter place. Sometimes

being kicked out helps to stir up your dormant gifts. In some ways, rejection is God's redirection and protection.

My friend, you have a purpose, and eventually, you will be rejected. You will not always understand why people don't like you or don't choose you. And, even if you understood, it won't change a thing. So, remember that rejection is not personal; it's purposeful. And, being rejected may give you the greatest motivation and the best separation you need to do what you have been called to do.

Believe and Declare Today: I am a gift and the world is waiting for me.

Get ready. It's your time to Soar!

20

IF YOU LET YOUR TRUTH BE TOUCHED OR TAMED BY "THEM" AND "THEY," YOU WILL NEVER DO "THIS" OR "THAT"

"Girl, you are wrong about that. Let me tell you what you should do. You need to shut your mouth, keep your head down, and do your work. You got a good job."

My friend thought she was giving me sage advice. She thought compromising my humanity and self-respect were small prices to pay for a good corporate job that provided health benefits, a credit card, and a company car. But no! I was moving forward.

I didn't need her support or approval to file a sexual harassment claim. I was going to tell; my body nor my dignity was for sale.

What my friend didn't understand was that I was tired. I was tired of swallowing insults and dodging unwanted advances. I was weary of being brushed up against and constantly "undressed." I was offended that my personal space was constantly ignored and violated. I was sick of men being so close to me that I could smell their hot breath on my neck and feel the heat of their palms on my arm. I was tired of feeling dirty, nasty, and ashamed. I was tired and because I was tired, I had to tell. I had to tell because I had been touched. Violated. Dehumanized. Objectified. Humiliated. I had to tell because my body was mine, and I refused to let it be sullied by old, crusty, privileged men who treated me and eyed me like I was a slave on an auction block. I was going to tell.

Though I would have loved her support, I wasn't surprised that my friend didn't stand up for me or stand by me. I wasn't even upset that she didn't agree with my decision either. Her opinion meant nothing to me; it was my body, not hers. I was the one suffering from nightmares and stress-induced migraines. I was the one losing patches of hair and losing weight. I was the one suffering from stress-induced irritable bowel syndrome. I was the one bleeding and vomiting, not her.

I knew my friend was scared; her terror was palpable, but so was my truth. I knew I didn't deserve to be treated like a piece of meat. I knew it was not fair that I had to duck unwanted advances for a paycheck. I was not someone's whore; I was a college-educated Black woman in a white corporate setting who was already dodging emotional bullets and enduring soul-crushing comments because I had brown skin and textured hair. I was already doing quadruple duty. I worked a job, was expected to be the "black people" expert, walked on eggshells around racist colleagues, and tried to remain visible, yet invisible, all at the same time. I was working overtime just to be in the room and to have a rickety seat at the table. I damn sure was not going to be harassed by men, especially men who were older than my father. That was just disgusting. Not just no, but hell no! I was going to tell the truth and report their disgusting behavior with or without her support. I was going to tell.

I am not sure how or where I mustered the strength and courage to report their offensive behavior, but I knew one thing: I would survive. Somehow, I knew that I could trust my discernment and trust myself to weather a tumultuous storm. I had an inner wisdom and a silent knowing that brought me peace. I was going to tell, and regardless of the outcome, I knew that all would be well in my soul.

Bravely, I told. I shared details and dates about their vulgar advances. I answered questions that were explicit, and some that were voyeuristic. Some inquiries were not even germane to the case, but I answered them anyway because didn't believe I had a choice. And of course, the white man assigned to advocate for me never objected to their degrading questions or inferences. Even though I wasn't an attorney, I knew that he was deliberately letting me be attacked because he did nothing to stop the insulting questions that were clearly out of line and irrelevant to the sexual harassment complaint.

Though disgusted and belittled, I persevered. It took sheer will because the proceedings were intimidating, humiliating, and infuriating. I felt extremely violated because the entire process was absolutely repulsive and just downright hostile. At times, the cross-examinations were even comical because the old, crusty men tried to convince the power brokers that I actually pursued them. Yuck! Thankfully, the old, disgusting men had a history of womanizing and misogyny. Because if not, I may not have been believed, which would have victimized me again.

After I won my case, my friend admitted that she was wrong for not advocating for me. Again, I was not upset with her. However, I believe her apology was an attempt to deal with her own guilt. But let's be honest. She had reason to be frightened about publicly supporting me. As a Black woman in a toxic corporate environment, she didn't have allies or supporters either. She was constantly bullied, dismissed, and victimized too.

Diversity, equity, and inclusion policies were rarely enforced; the company's commitment to diversity was just mere corporate window dressing. So, it was understandable that she felt threatened by me speaking out. It was the 1980s and companies retaliated against women who spoke out against their corporate, yet abusive, leaders. Women, especially women of color, who reported offenses suffered extreme backlash so often that sexual harassment was commonly known as a CLIM, a career-limiting move. Now, how crazy is that? Women who reported sexual misconduct committed CLIMs while men who were sexually inappropriate and downright abusive received promotions? What?

My friend's fear was warranted because the odds were against me. Even though the truth was on my side, the company's leadership initially was not. It's unfortunate, but in a capitalist culture with no ethical oversight, the truth rarely matters. What's also true is that victimized and disenfranchised people can rarely support each other in meaningful ways. When you feel powerless, you can't protect yourself, let alone, others.

Why do I share this story? Because on the road to purpose, you will encounter many challenges and there will be many people who will presume to know what is best for you. They will give you advice, share their opinions, and infect you with their doubts. They will provide statistics, share research, and offer poisonous "prayers." Yet, their insights can't and don't compare to what you already know inside of your soul. Remember, you were born and equipped with wisdom. You know all types of information that are beyond your education, ability, and experience, and it is up to you to trust what you instinctively know, so you can respond to challenges and adversity with courage and clarity.

My friend, you were created for a purpose. And God, the Divine Knower, placed information inside of your soul because God knew that you would need divine wisdom and supernatural insight to navigate the vicissitudes of life. And most of all, God knew that you would need peace, a peace that only emanates from inner wisdom, which is your truth.

So, trust your truth because your truth cannot be tainted or tamed by the outside world. The truth knows, it sees, it understands, and it reveals. The truth dismantles, it connects, it builds, and it bolsters. The truth envisions, it excites, and it penetrates. Your inner truth is a well of wisdom that never runs dry; it's a deep, fresh, and supernatural reservoir that sustains and fortifies you. Truth.

Your inner truth is a gift and a guide to help you pursue your destiny. So, trust your truth. Listen to it. Protect it. Because when you trust it you can stand boldly against "them" or "they," and courageously conquer "this" and "that" with tenacity, grace, and love.

I know that I am right. It's my testimony. And it's probably your testimony, too.

It's time to Soar!

21

SOMETIMES LOSS IS THE COST OF LIBERATION

The other day I was looking through my wedding album. I am not sure what prompted me to do so, but there I was thumbing through the red binder, realizing that I never got around to placing some of the pictures behind the clear sticky paper that holds photographs in place. But then I tripped. Doggone it. Photos flew all over the room, and you can imagine how crazy I looked crawling around the floor retrieving pictures, trying my best not to ruin images that were already rapidly fading.

As I looked at some of the images that landed on the floor, I paused in disbelief. How could thirty years have passed by so quickly? Where did the time go? Time just seems to fly by so fast these days.

As I grow older and hopefully wiser, I notice that I see details in pictures that I missed decades earlier. So as I slowly turned the pages in my wedding album, and picked up the fading photos from the floor, I tried to remember what I was feeling on my wedding day. I tried to transport myself back to that special day to see if I could experience it through the eyes of wisdom. I wanted to see now what I could not see back then because some critical life lessons are only revealed when you are ready. And today, I felt ready. I was prepared to learn what my soul already knew.

I picked up the pictures and looked at them thoughtfully. There I was all dolled up in my cheap JC Penney wedding dress, and my thrift shop wedding veil. What I noticed first was the look in my eyes. It was obvious that I was terrified, dazed, or confused. I was forcing a smile on the outside, but I was not present. My eyes looked hollow, almost glass-like. But maybe what I saw in my eyes was fear or terror because a part of me was waiting for the earth to open up and swallow me whole. For weeks I had been warned that I was going to hell. Yes, hell! Yes, I was going to knock the bottom out of hell because I was marrying outside of my faith. You see, I was a Christian and was marrying a Muslim, and my Christian family fiercely opposed the marriage. So opposed that my father, who was a pastor, encouraged people not to attend my wedding. You can imagine how painful it was not having my parents' blessing and believing that I was going to hell all at the same time. That was a lot to juggle emotionally.

The morning of my wedding was filled with hair, makeup, the usual, I guess. Nothing spectacular. To me, getting ready for my wedding felt funeral-like, and my friend, Andrea, tried her best to add love, joy, and laughter to a supposedly festive occasion. But my sadness was palpable, and all day I wanted to weep, a deep soul-clearing cry, but I didn't. I couldn't. I was supposed to be happy; weddings are joyous events, right? But on my special day, all I wanted was my mommy and daddy. I wanted to feel special. I wanted to feel loved. I wanted to feel bride-like, whatever that felt like.

After we arrived at the bootleg wedding chapel, we lined up for the processional. My ex-husband and I almost burst out laughing as soon as we saw our officiant. The officiant recently had toe surgery and was upfront wearing too-short pants, thick white tube socks, and black orthopedic shoes with his bandaged toes sticking out. He looked ridiculous.

Thank God for the levity because as soon as the processional music started, I started to shake. First, it was nervous quivering, then the shaking escalated to wobbly legs, involuntary arm movements, and a trembling jaw. My mouth was dry, my stomach felt nauseous, and my eyes filled with tears. What was I doing? Was getting married the right thing to do?

I timidly shivered down the aisle in my cheap wedding dress, secretly hoping that my parents would come to the wedding; I was praying to be surprised. But as I stepped closer to the front of the chapel, the sadder I became. No parents. My soul tried to soothe my heart, but I was deeply disappointed, almost distraught. I had to face the truth; I was alone.

There were no bridesmaids or groomsmen. My little sister, Tiphanie, who was the only person I believed loved me, was secretly scheduled to attend. Unfortunately, my parents got wind of my plot to sneak her out of the house to attend my wedding, so she was not there. Thankfully, my best friend James came and escorted me down the aisle. He stood in place for my father and doubled as a groomsman. Andrea, who felt sorry for me, obligated, or both, was the maid of honor and a witness. A few church members who loved me showed up too. Michelle, Shawna, and Christy were right there to support me, and a few co-workers were there to encourage me as well. There were less than twelve of us in the chapel, and that's counting my ex-husband and me.

The wedding ceremony was quick. I remember little about the service or the reception. Everything was a blur, but I do remember that the wedding reception was a bit unsophisticated and amateurish. We were making Kool-aid and arranging food in front of the guests, which is a catering faux pas. It was hilarious. We had good intentions, but we didn't know what we were doing. Somehow, we were able to feed our handful of guests some sandwiches, fruit, and old wilted salad. I am glad we realized that catering was not our life's work.

What makes me proud of my low budget, low attended, and my much-maligned wedding was that I was twenty-three years old, and I was courageous enough to live my own life. I was able to stand up for myself and follow my own heart even amid extreme family and religious objections. I was able to articulate my own understanding of God and reframe my faith in a way that resonated with my soul. I was able to plan a wedding with no professional knowledge, no internet guidance, and no family support. I am most proud that I freed myself from the claws of conformity, and I liberated myself to love who I wanted to love and to love on my own terms.

My decision to marry a person of a different faith was costly because there is always a price to pay for following your conscience. Trust me, freedom is not free, and I paid dearly. There were social repercussions and much relational damage; I lost a lot.

Today, my parents regret not supporting me, and I regret holding a two-decade grudge against them too. Unfortunately, my grudge lasted longer than the marriage. Thankfully, my parents and I continue to heal our relationship and we are finding our way back to each other. I am grateful for that.

What does my ill-fated marriage have to do with purpose? Great question. I am glad that you asked.

My failed marriage was the perfect training ground for my purpose journey because divine assignments will always require you to stand your ground, activate your intuition, and solely depend on God. And you will need to depend on God because most people will not understand what you are doing or what you have been called to do. News flash: your divine purpose rarely comes with a map or an amen section; sometimes you may have to fend for yourself and be by yourself.

My friend, here is the unadulterated truth: your life's work will require you to deeply connect with your inner wisdom and your gut. If not, you will be manipulated by popularity, controlled by old narratives, and immobilized by fear. Without your inner discernment, you will not have the resolve to soar higher than social stigmas, cultural stereotypes, or the stifling status quo. And most of all, you won't possess the spiritual independence to do what God destined for your life.

Yes, I initially lost a lot—my family, my friends, and my support. But I experienced the power of liberation. I learned that I could withstand pressure, loneliness, and insults, and still survive. I learned that I didn't have to compromise my perspective to please people. I realized that self-acceptance was more transformative than crowd approval. I learned that I could count on myself to recover from terrible mistakes and rebound from public failures. I learned that I could recreate my own relationship with my Creator without adhering to religious dogmas and denominationalism.

Lessons! I learned many lessons. Yes, I lost a few things, but I learned lessons that developed my character, confirmed my fortitude, and strengthen my faith in God.

Marrying my ex-husband was a gutsy move. The relational damage was painful, and the losses were plentiful. But never forget that losing something valuable might be just what you need to liberate yourself from people, places, and beliefs, so you can SOAR!

Declare Today: I am not losing; I am being liberated to activate my divine purpose!

It's time to Soar!

THE PROCESS: BECOMING MORE OF YOU

An effective process prepares you for your divine purpose.

It's not always the arrival; it's who you become during the journey.

Declare Today: My steps are ordered by God

22

PEOPLE ARE SO QUICK TO BE BIG THAT THEY FAIL TO LEARN VALUABLE LESSONS WHEN THEY ARE SMALL

Have you ever met people who were so quick to make it big that they failed to learn valuable lessons when they were small? Have you? I don't mean to sound cynical, but I have met many people who tried to skip critical steps on their way to success. If you don't believe me, just look around. Trust me, "*skippers*" are easy to identify.

First, just look at your job. "Skippers" are usually the tyrants who boss people around to camouflage their incompetence and disguise their dysfunction. They didn't learn the job, and they don't have the expertise. So instead of admitting what they don't know, they become drill masters and micromanagers who hover over you instead of helping you. Nobody thrives under that type of scrutiny, and eventually, the most talented people leave.

"Skippers" are frequently egomaniacs who attempt to maximize their importance, dominate conversations, and control people. They always want to tell you something or tell you off because they feel insecure and inadequate about their ability to contribute and perform. They think they are hiding their feelings of inferiority under the guise of command, but their atrophied confidence is always on full display.

"Skippers" are sometimes shapeshifters who have multiple personalities and contort themselves to appease people in authority. They are suck-ups or brown-nosers. You can't trust them because they are so hungry for a promotion that they will step on your neck to move up. It's unfortunate and unscrupulous, but they have no choice. They have to resort to clandestine behavior because they are not really competent, confident, or committed. They moved up without mastery and now must rely on force, favors, and flattery to keep their positions.

"Skippers" are often liars who hide their mistakes, embellish the truth, or create their own reality. They have no choice because there are no statistics or track record to support their ascension. They sidestepped the developmental process and now they have a position but no proficiency. That's why they create and provide suspicious metrics and dicey data. Do you know anybody like that?

"Skippers" are serpentine thieves who are always "working" the room to steal your work, plagiarize your ideas, sully your reputation, and derail your dreams. Don't be shocked. They didn't attend the classes, attend the seminars, or pay their dues. They didn't get the training they needed to offer creative ideas, innovative solutions, or novel strategies. So, of course, they must take credit for your plans, results, and intellectual property. Don't forget that they are just professional thugs looking for prey to exploit, money to embezzle, and ideas to hijack.

"Skippers" are sometimes opportunists who feign support to get your personal information so they can sabotage you and overtake you when you are vulnerable. They act like they care and are empathetic to your plight, but they are not. Their only concern is their own aggrandizement and advancement. So, be careful. When you are emotional, watch what you say, how you say it, and when you say it. As I said in *Deciding To Soar 1*, people who are by your side are not always on your side. Word to wise: Don't get chummy with cut-throats.

"Skippers" are con-artists who masquerade as allies and assets, but are just adversaries, assassins, and agitators. You think that they "got" you, but they don't. They are trying to "get" what you "got." That's why you must be diligent and discerning. While skippers are playing checkers, you must play chess to guard against their manipulation and their malicious orchestration. Don't forget to look beyond the masks and the make-up so you can fully see the malicious mind of a corrupt messenger.

"Skippers" are occasionally instigators who keep people fighting each other because they realize that team unity will expose their stupidity, shadiness, and sleaziness. That's why they start rumors and take part in gossip. They are masters of *"he said, she said"* campaigns and will infect your closest relationships with doubt and venom. So, listen carefully to conversations because skippers will expose themselves when they talk. When others are talking about principles, skippers are usually talking negatively about people.

"Skippers" are manipulators who epitomize what it means to be a "fake friend." Because they are so good at trickery, it is easy to be deceived by them. They are extremely conniving and will have you questioning your own judgment, your experiences, and your sense of discernment. If that happens to you, don't feel bad. They have to baffle you. If they keep you confused, you won't be able to assess and evaluate their real character or uncover their deception.

"Skippers" are frauds who manufacture credentials, degrees, experience, and certifications. They didn't go to school, or at least not the school on their resume. They didn't attend the programs or complete the courses. They made it up. You don't believe me? Ask them a detailed question. You won't get a complete sentence, a workable suggestion, or a well-thought-out solution. You will receive simple soundbites because they believe that talking less will fool people. However, nobody is fooled; circuitous conversations make it easy to detect opportunists and charlatans.

"Skippers" are frauds, phonies, and top-notch fools who are unaware of the limited impact that they have in the world. They could be more, but they want to circumvent the process and do less. They are intelligently lazy and spiritually sluggish. Their immaturity is only eclipsed by their inability to notice that we "see" them, all of them, and their low-down, scandalous ways.

"Skippers" are always status-seekers who walk on the backs, heads, and toes of others to achieve their brand of success. There's nothing wrong with ambition. But when ambition is more important than integrity, there's a problem. When people will do anything, even sell their soul, for profitability and popularity, they will eventually fail and fail publicly for others to see.

Why do skippers behave in such unscrupulous ways? Because they didn't go through the process! They didn't develop the power, the perspective, or the proficiency that the job required; they skipped steps. Now, they have a position, but they are impotent! And their lack of competence has cost them what they need most to lead — RESPECT!

Soaring Solution: Don't rush to promotion. Learn. Leverage. Lift, and then, lead. When you know what you are doing, you won't need to deceive people, because you will be believed by people.

Remember: Growth happens from SMALL to BIG, not BIG to SMALL. I remind you again, be patient. You can't step into success. You must be groomed for greatness! And both grooming and growing take time.

Are you ready to grow and be groomed for your purpose?

Get ready. Get set. Go!

It's time to Soar!

23

SHORT-CUTS MAKE THE LONGEST JOURNEYS

In our hyper-fast culture, people are frequently looking for ways to get there quickly, wherever "there" is. They are looking for short-cuts, a fast road, a magic pill, or a quick path to reach their goals. What's ironic is that people will spend lots of time finding quick ways to earn money, achieve success, lose weight, find love... just to name a few. Yet, they fail to apply that same commitment to sacrifice, learning, discipline, and hard work.

But can we be honest? Short-cuts rarely work. All the by-passing, jumping, cheating, lying, and other no-effort schemes are seldom fruitful. And whatever advances are made in the short-term rarely last. For example, most people who lose weight quickly gain all of it back. And most add a few additional pounds to their girth, too.

What about people who inherit or win enormous sums of money? The research shows that most lottery winners, or people who inherit lots of cash, crash. Within five years, some are broke. Why does that happen? They received money too quickly without learning how to manage it. Winning or being given sizeable sums of money without learning how to manage it is a different type of short-cut, but the results are the same. Easy come, easy go!

The research is clear. Short-cut enthusiasts often find themselves right back where they started....at the starting line. And unfortunately, they end up back at the starting line with less energy, less time, fewer resources, and less credibility. And what's most unfortunate is that their quick-fix schemes often leave them feeling defeated, deflated, and of course, in debt.

Just so we are on the same page, I am not suggesting moseying along in life; pursuing your purpose requires a sense of urgency. However, committing to a no-work plan to circumvent the process will never prove beneficial. Without the process, you don't gain the wisdom and expertise needed to manage and maintain what you achieve. The journey is essential for mastery.

My friend, don't believe the hype. Becoming the best of anything takes time; quickness rarely produces quality. That's why you can't become a good doctor overnight. You can't become an exceptional teacher overnight. You can't become a great electrician overnight. You can't become an excellent lawyer overnight. You can't become a prominent brain surgeon overnight. You can't become an exceptional parent overnight. You can't even become a loving partner overnight. Becoming an overnight sensation is an illusion. So, take your time and learn what you need to master so you can pursue your purpose effectively and elegantly. And most of all, never forget that getting "there" first and fast does not mean that you will have the strength and the stamina to stay.

I am going to say it again for the people in the back. Most short-cuts make the longest journeys because most shortcuts squander your time, energy, and resources. And your purpose does not have time to waste.

It's time to Soar Higher!

24

ASK GOD TO TAKE YOU HIGHER EVEN IF YOU ARE SCARED OF HEIGHTS

Have you heard the saying that "every level brings a new devil?" The adage alone is enough to make you reconsider new aspirations, right? Ascending to your current level was hard enough. So hard that even thinking about going to a higher level in your life feels intimidating.

The truth is, every level will reveal a new devil because elevation makes you vulnerable. The challenges are bigger, the risks are greater, and the haters are deadlier. Make no mistake about it....as you rise in your career and in your purpose, you will encounter situations that will frighten and discourage you. You may even feel overwhelmed, under-prepared, and under-resourced to deal with the scrutiny or the saboteurs that will contest your very presence. Trust me, advancement is never easy or drama-free.

I had to learn the hard way that opposition was a part of elevation, and that opposition can sometimes be brutal. It can be so brutal that you may be tempted to quit climbing or even worse, you may settle for your current destination without ever knowing what you were capable of doing, being, and contributing. You may even feel so threatened that you just give out, give up, or go home!

So, what do you do when you are climbing up the ladder of success, and the height terrifies you? What do you do when you are being called to lead a social movement in a contentious environment and with little support? What do you do when you are being attacked and criticized for pursuing your dreams and for adhering to your values when people expect you to compromise? What do you do when you feel unable to produce, perform, or participate on a higher level because you are being hindered in ways that are beyond your control? What do you do when you feel all alone and too afraid to ask for help?

You breathe. You pause. You feel the emotions, but you do NOT quit.

When I met Sam, he had just been promoted to a leadership position in a big Fortune 500 company. He was well-respected and well-known for being an innovator and a risk-taker. His background in engineering gave him a unique perspective on problem-solving, and he was often called upon to improve manufacturing processes and devise complex strategies for a new robotic system.

Even though Sam had the education and expertise to perform the job, once promoted, his demeanor changed. He became terrified, and his fear prevented him from effectively leading his team. He wouldn't give direction, provide useful feedback, or facilitate productive meetings. He vacillated when making decisions and when developing plans of action. When he attended planning sessions with senior leadership, he froze. He stopped offering solutions, challenging ideas, or providing insights for growth. He lost his swagger and his voice. He stopped being "Confident Sam."

At first, it was difficult getting Sam to share. However, I could sense that he felt embarrassed and ashamed of his feelings and behavior. I was patient because I didn't want to risk emasculating him because he was already discouraged, and was doing his best to hang on to his fading self-esteem. I said, "Sam, I sense there's something happening in your spirit that's bigger than this job."

Sam initially didn't speak, but his tears let me know that his heart was heavy. "I don't want to fail. I prayed for this. I deserve this. But, I can't get myself to do the job. I don't want to mess this up. Everybody is depending on me. I feel embarrassed that I am showing up like this. I don't feel like a man."

My heart broke wide open. His pain and his predicament were familiar to me. I heard similar fears from my son and from other Black men. Heck, I felt the same way for most of my corporate career.

"Sam, what feels the heaviest for you to carry – the job requirements or everybody's expectations? "

"I know that people want and expect me to fail."

"What people?"

Sam gave me names and speculated why each person withheld support.

"Do you feel that you can do the job?"

"Of course, I do."

"Since you know you can do the job, how can you gather the support you need to thrive? Every one of your colleagues has sponsors and mentors; you deserve the same. Since the company won't provide them, what can you do to create your own personal board of directors to guide you, so that you don't feel so alone and unsupported?"

Together, Sam and I listed ways he could find support. We identified a mentor who could guide and advise him when needed. We discussed ways to lead his team by tapping into his gifts of motivation and innovation. We reviewed all of his successes and discussed how his experiences uniquely groomed him for his current position, and ultimately for greatness. During our conversations, we talked about his mind and the health of his spirit because success is always an "inside job."

What ultimately surfaced during our time together was that Sam had many deep-seated fears about what it meant to be a high-ranking Black man in corporate America. Throughout his life, and especially during his career, he had heard and witnessed how successful Black men were mistreated, and he had also experienced his own share of abuse. For example, he had been victimized several times while "driving while Black." He was constantly followed in upscale stores. He was always questioned when he paid for merchandise with his platinum American Express card. He was constantly monitored by his neighbors when he jogged through his neighborhood. He constantly had to modify his speech, mask his emotions, and manage his movements to accommodate his white colleagues. For Sam, being a successful Black man and being forced to deal with pervasive racism was mentally exhausting and sometimes, debilitating.

Sam and I had an honest conversation about systemic racism and historical injustice, and we talked about how those same unspoken, unfair practices continue today. We also tearfully discussed how powerful Black men are sometimes politically attacked and publicly maligned when they hold leadership positions; that conversation was demoralizing yet cathartic for both of us. Finally, we talked a lot about President Barack Obama. Watching how President Obama was publicly villainized, de-legitimized, scrutinized, and dehumanized was difficult, and at the times, unbearable to see. Watching the barrage of mean-spirited, unsubstantiated attacks was traumatic, and was enough to discourage any Black person from seeking career advancement, political office, or a leadership position. The attacks on President Obama were harsh, constant, and hostile, and just the thought of experiencing a similar fate paralyzed Sam.

To Sam, it almost seemed as though Black success and Black leadership brought out the worst in some white people. I agreed.

Sam had legitimate concerns, because let's be honest, America has a history of physically and politically emasculating and lynching Black men. In this country, Black men are constantly under attack and minimized by public systems, public servants, and clandestine serpents. That's why being a Black man in America can feel terrifying and be anxiety-producing. I am not a Black man, but even as a Black woman and a Black mother, I am constantly scared and stressed myself. For example, when my Black son goes to work, I fear that he won't return unscathed. The fear is real, exhausting, and soul-depleting.

There is no other place in the world I want to live but I must be honest: America is a great country, but it has many systemic disparities. America is not a perfect union, yet. Even in 2020, the county continues to grapple with equality, fair access, and diversity. Even in 2020, American is steeped in white supremacy, protected by white privilege, and insulated by white fragility. Even in 2020, the entire nation is viewed, controlled, and interpreted through a white lens, white "centering." Even in 2020, many people still don't appreciate how racism perpetuates violence, poverty, and destruction. Even in 2020, racism is still ravaging our national culture and rotting our collective souls.

Thankfully and prayerfully, America is evolving. Through blood, sweat, tears, and policies, America is working hard to practice and embody the values it espouses. But, America is still a work in process. Everybody still does not enjoy life, liberty, and a pursuit of happiness, yet. Radical shifts are still needed to make America a more inclusive, more equitable, and a more welcoming place for all its citizens.

Despite the state of our country, there is still hope. There is hope for Sam, and there is also hope for you. Despite what you have witnessed and experienced, you still can believe in yourself, advance your career, and pursue your purpose. You still have what it takes; you have a history of success and a wealth of experience that's undeniable. Your talent cannot be ignored. Your growth cannot be limited. And your light cannot be dimmed.

So how do you silence your inner critic and address the old narratives that try to hinder and terminate your success? First, you identify how you see yourself, how you are speaking to yourself, and what you believe about yourself regarding the goal. Do you see yourself as small, incompetent, or ill-equipped? Do you feel unworthy or undeserving of the position? Or, do you feel competent about the job, but just frightened about the environment?

Secondly, you must ask yourself some tough questions to identify the root of your doubt and fear. After you pinpoint what's robbing you of your ability to focus, function, and persevere, you can address the issues with love, compassion, and truth. Thirdly, you activate your God-given gifts. Remember, you already have what you need to rise to the occasion. If you were not qualified, you would not be in the room.

Finally, you analyze what's happening around you and you adjust your plans. You identify where you feel most vulnerable and most ill-equipped, and you hire support. Then, you arm yourself with a fierce determination because you know deep down in your heart that you are qualified; you are deserving, and you will rise.

Remember, your unique journey has equipped you with the insight, strength, and expertise you need for this specific moment. And, you have the internal fortitude to tackle and tear down any belittling bully or terrorizing thought that affects your performance. You can meet any challenge, and even if you have to stand on wobbly legs, you can stand. You were born great and to be great – don't forget that.

Thankfully, Sam was successful. He conquered his fears and delivered the automated system ahead of schedule and under budget. However, it was not easy because he was undermined by a few cut-throat saboteurs and also berated by his own inner demons. Just so you know…old trauma, old head trash, painful memories, and old childhood stories will always rear their sordid heads when you are most vulnerable or when you are attempting to destroy outdated beliefs. Even though you prefer ease, your former, familiar self won't give up its prominent position in your life without a fight. That's why you must constantly tackle your old, crippling beliefs with the truth or a new vision so you can access the strength, wisdom, and skills you need to execute your purpose.

Sam won some important internal battles which restored his confidence, and helped him win some important battles in his career. And my friend, you are just as talented and brave as Sam. You are just as secure and just as prepared because success is not new to you. You have slain other dragons, you have won other wars, and you have conquered other territories. You have a track record of success and you have evidence of your expertise. And most of all, you are God's child.

So, just like Sam, stay calm, stay clear, and stay open. Don't give up on your purpose, don't collapse under the pressure, and keep listening to the Spirit because you have what it takes to succeed. Remember that you are only tested by trouble, and adversity is just another opportunity for you to cling tighter to God.

My friend, yes, you are up high, but your purpose is calling you higher. So, step up! Step fully into your gifts. Step courageously into your power. Step faithfully into your wisdom. Step firmly into your values. Step completely into the experience. Step forward into the goodness of God.

You can do it! I believe in you.

You have a purpose.

It's your time.

Soar!

25

YOU CANNOT HAVE YEAH WITHOUT A LITTLE BIT OF YUCK

Have you ever worked on something that triggered all of your insecurities? I have. A few weeks ago, I was working on something that made me feel extremely frustrated and way out of my comfort zone. I felt so inadequate that I started doubting my own experience and expertise, and I started wondering if I was really following my purpose. I wondered, did God make a mistake? Was I really cut out for my calling? If you have ever felt over your head, and a bit out of your mind, you can imagine what I was feeling. Yuck!

I do not know why I felt so unsure of myself. But, for some reason, I did. I felt outmatched and outnumbered. I knew that I did not have the knowledge that I needed to do a thorough job, but that was not new for me. I was accustomed to operating on the edge of my experience and competence. In some ways, I am a bit of a daredevil, so not knowing everything doesn't stop me from taking action. Yet, something was different, and I felt lower than low. Yuck!

Despite my tears of frustration and my feelings of overwhelm, I was still somewhat lucid enough to know that I was being swallowed by FEAR. Life had taught me that when you are trying something new or doing something controversial, if you are not careful, fear will seep into your pores, hijack your agenda and steal your resolve. And trust me, fear is very sneaky because fear has many disguises. It shows up as perfectionism, procrastination, analysis paralysis, comparison, vacillation, wallowing, hypersensitivity, and closed-mindedness — or at least that is how fear visits me. Fear is like some of your crazy, loud-mouth relatives who come to visit you without calling and then have the audacity to overstay their welcome. I bet a few of your cousins come to mind, right?

Well, fear came and grabbed me away from what I wanted and needed most — confidence. And isn't that what fear does? It grips us, grabs us, and then guts us of our strength, creativity, and courage to move toward what we really want in life. To me, fear feels like being confined behind a gate while watching the life you desire march right past you like a slow parade.

Needless to say, I felt paralyzed, and I felt ashamed that I felt paralyzed all at the same time. And isn't that just like fear to create problems, on top of problems, on top of more problems? Fear multiplies your doubts and magnifies your insecurities.

Thankfully, my son Tariq came into my office and said, "Mom, just go to bed. You will get it tomorrow. You got this." Even though he didn't know what I was working on, his words were comforting and eased my anxiety. For some reason, I needed somebody – anybody – to remind me that everything would happen like it was divinely planned. So glad that my son gave me that reminder when I needed it the most. Yeah!

After a few more tears, I went to bed and consoled myself, knowing that if I did my best, God would give me grace. Yes, grace! I trusted that grace would fill in the gaps that my gifts could not fill, and there were many gaps because the work was honestly outside my sphere of genius and experience.

Thankfully, I finished the project. The results were good, but not great. I poured all of my energy, creativity, and know-how into something that I felt was acceptable, but not excellent. It was not as comprehensive as it could have been. To be honest, some information I just didn't know. And I also didn't know what I didn't know. I had conscious and unconscious ignorance. Now, that's a real dilemma!

Suffice it to say, that I gave my best but knew that the outcome was not up to me. And, isn't that just like life? We plant seeds, water the plants, but it is always God that determines the harvest and multiplies the increase. Remembering that God was in charge gave me the peace that my spirit craved because I knew that I didn't possess all the skills that were required to perform at a competitive level.

Praise be the God, I won the contract. I was not the most qualified and I had not submitted the least expensive proposal, but I won. I am no fool; it was God's intervention. My parents told me long ago that when you do your best and when you acknowledge your insufficiency, it gives God room to do the impossible and the unbelievable. To me, that room is called GRACE! Yeah!

The entire experience taught me a valuable lesson! I learned that when God gives vision, God gives provision, but the provision may be different from what you expect. The provision may be introducing YOU to your own dormant gifts that you don't use, or your own abilities that you forgot about, or your own tenacity to persevere, or the fervency of your own prayers, or the power of your own thoughts. PROVISION! Provision is a multi-layered, multi-dimensional, and multi-level gift that God grants us when we step out and step forward in faith. My elders were right. Faith will work if you work it.

Moral of the story: Success, however you define it, comes with lots of *"yeahs"* (good times) and a few *"yucks"* (challenging times). Those *"yeahs"* and *"yucks"* make room for grace. So, do your best and trust that God will do the rest because vision always precedes provision, and the provision may contain a few "yeahs" and "yucks" along the way.

Declare Today: All things, yeahs and yucks, work together for my good.

It's time to Soar.

26

YOU NEED ANOTHER SET OF EYES TO HELP YOU RISE!

The other day I stumbled upon a TEDx Talk and watched a surgeon talk about the power of coaching. Now, honestly, it never occurred to me that a highly skilled surgeon would be interested in coaching. I always associated coaching with athletes, actors, singers, or leaders. I never really considered how valuable coaching would be for other professions. Not sure why I didn't, but I didn't.

But then I had an *"aha"* moment and realized that coaching is not for specific professions; coaching is for ALL people because nobody develops alone. Nobody rises in silence. Nobody grows in isolation. Nobody reaches the pinnacle of their abilities through their own efforts. Nobody becomes their BEST self by themselves. Everybody needs another set of eyes to rise.

What is another set of eyes? *"Another set of eyes"* is that constructive critiquing, coaching, or consulting you receive from a person who is more skilled, more experienced, and more knowledgeable than you are. It's the courage and willingness to understand how another person sees you, experiences you, and assesses your ability. It is the humility to invite and welcome external ears and eyes into your reality so you can build your strengths, address your weaknesses, discover untapped talents, and identify blind spots that impede your success. It is the commitment to excellence, even if it means that you must unlearn, learn, and relearn skills and techniques to upgrade your performance.

But unfortunately, most people are averse to close inspection and critical critique. We live in a culture of fragile egos and being carefully observed and constructively scrutinized by third parties is seen as an indictment of our skills or an insult to our competence. So much so that we resist valuable feedback and, consequently, forfeit the insight we need to enhance our lives. We short-circuit our success, shortchange our divine callings, and settle for mediocrity.

Even if you don't want to admit it, you need feedback; we all do. Every high-performing, high-achieving person needs a trusted advisor to assess them to improve their performance. From the most prolific athlete to the most motivated lover, everybody needs additional discovery, understanding, and skill-building to maintain proficiency, contribution, and influence. The best stay the best for many reasons. One reason: They have several sets of eyes teaching them and tweaking them toward greatness.

If you are not experiencing or achieving what you want most in life, maybe you need another set of eyes to see what you are unwilling or unable to see. Remember, not seeing something does not mean that it does not exist; it just means that you are blind to it or blocked from it. And we all know that being blind or blocked from the truth can affect your ability to fulfill your divine assignment.

My friend, it's time to see your full potential, even if it means seeing it through the eyes of others.

Are you ready to see so you can effectively pursue your purpose?

Declare Today: I will see what I need to see about me so I can be all God has called me to be.

It's time to Soar!

27

A STUMBLE IS
NOT PRETTY, BUT
IT IS PROGRESS

Doing something for the first time is never pretty. Even when you feel prepared and equipped, you make mistakes. You say the wrong things, you go the wrong way, and you wear the wrong clothes. You do everything wrong, but you still feel victorious because you tried something new. You took a risk.

That's why we love watching babies learn how to walk. They crawl, they step, they fall, and they cry. But, they get right back up and try again. They wobble, they strain, and they stumble, but they keep stepping. They wince, they lean and then tumble, but they stay committed. Eventually, their determination pays off, and they walk and then run. Babies innately know that a STUMBLE is still a STEP. It's not pretty, but it's progress.

Writing my first book, *I Can Depend On Me*, was a public stumbling experience. Even though I researched how to self-publish, I still didn't know what I was doing. Yet, I wrote a book, had some friends edit it, took some cheap pictures, and slapped on a cover. I didn't even that know that I should have hired a make-up artist, wore different attire, and hired a professional photographer. I just did what I knew to do and tried my best to put together a marketable product.

Even though the cover was slightly boot-leg (not professionally designed) and the interior layout was not optimal, I was proud of my first book because it was my entry into the publishing world. Most of all, I accomplished my lifelong dream of becoming an author. Yeah, for me!

I Can Depend On Me was met with mixed reviews. Some felt that my book was too angry and polarizing. Others felt that my writing style was too churchy and preachy. A few said that the content of my book was inspiring, despite the low-quality book cover. The responses I received were all over the board, and I felt incredibly grateful for every review because people didn't have to read it or share their thoughts. So, to me, every book review was a generous gift. Even the harsh criticism felt like a tremendous honor to a novice like me.

My entrance into the publishing world was definitely a stumble; I made tons of mistakes. But I would rather stumble my way to greatness and excellence than to live on the sidelines with regrets. I don't care if I am not embraced by the masses or achieve what others define as mastery; I want to take a chance. Even if I don't accomplish my desired outcome, I want to give my dreams my best effort and an honest try.

My friend, progress is never pretty. Sometimes it's even painful. But who cares? When you are pursuing your purpose, you will stumble because you will be required to do things that you have never done before. You will make blunders, and some will be costly. However, nothing is more spiritually expensive than not pursuing your divine calling. And, regret is painful, almost tormenting. If you don't believe me, ask your elders about the pain of missed opportunities and the inner turmoil of living in the land of *"coulda, shoulda, woulda."*

If you have to limp, roll, crawl, fall, skate, drive, bike, swim, or catch a ride, keep moving forward toward your purpose. Your progress does not have to be pretty, just purposeful. Don't worry about what your haters or naysayers say about your journey either. They can't be too focused on their own lives if they are so busy watching yours.

Step and stumble! Step and stumble. Step and stumble. When you are doing what God has called you to do, even your missteps – your stumbles – will move you forward toward God's plan.

Declare Today: I will stumble and fall, but I have the faith to get up.

Let's Dare To Soar Higher!

28

CRITICISM IS NOT A CRISIS; IT IS A CATALYST

Have you ever said something that you thought was benign, but people were offended or just plain mad? I have. One day I shared my thoughts about equality, and the next thing I knew, I was public enemy number one.

Honestly, I was shocked by the speed of the retaliation. I didn't think what I said was incendiary or controversial, and I didn't say it loud enough for many people to hear either. But somehow, a few people heard what I said or what they thought I said, and were miffed, to say the least. Of course, they filtered what I said through their own biased lenses and then shared their exaggerated, embellished version that only contained a few kernels of truth. Granted, I did say a lot, but I didn't say a fourth of what they said I said. But what they thought I said and what was unfairly attributed to me, was enough, I became a pariah.

That painful experience taught me a lot about the power of

my voice. I learned that if you are a thought leader, a trailblazer, or anyone who challenges the status quo, critics will condemn you. The attacks will be swift and voluminous because, to some, dissenting opinions feel threatening. In fact, some people will be extremely terrified by your willingness to think outside of the box (their box), especially when you speak about injustice. And when people feel offended, most don't investigate, they retaliate. They malign you or manipulate your message to minimize your impact. Trust me. Most people don't respond kindly to free thinkers, truth-tellers, visionaries, change agents, or freedom fighters. History proves that.

So as you pursue your purpose, remember that you will ruffle a few feathers. Some people will be enraged that they can't control and confine you. Others will be intimidated by your ability and courage to think for yourself. Some will be irritated because they can't close your heart, close your mouth, or close your mind. Your most vocal dissenters will be annoyed that you are professing or proclaiming something that they didn't have the courage to say first. And since you are powerful and poised, the power brokers will be furious that they can't silence or suppress you.

Yes, any time you dare to challenge convention, call out injustice, or introduce something new, you will be criticized. But, don't let the criticism derail you because criticism is not a crisis. Criticism is common, so anticipate it. And anticipate that it will come from the most unlikely places, your so-called allies.

My pastor, Dr. Kenneth L. Samuel, is a scholar, a social advocate, and a modern-day prophet. He is an outspoken minister who courageously preaches and teaches about the radical inclusion of all God's people, despite their color, gender, age, nationality, economic status, educational level, income, sexual orientation, and gender identification. He also challenges the church regarding its complicity in the perpetuation of social injustice and its failure to practice the principles of Jesus. To some, my pastor is a religious renegade, but to me, he is a fearless reconciler who refuses to blindly follow rules and doctrines that fail to honor God's people, all of God's people.

Despite his message of love and his strong commitment to the community, he was fiercely attacked. Not just by the church community, but by people who claimed to support his message and mission. Even some of his staff ministers and church leaders who promised to personally stand by him publicly attacked him for going *"too far,"* as if going too far with love is even possible.

Dr. Samuel stood up for his beliefs and lost money, his home, community support, speaking engagements, the respect of prominent clergy, and thousands of members. Yet, he didn't waver in his commitment to do what God called him to do. Though severely ostracized and maligned, he didn't surrender his mission or dilute his message. And now the very pastors and leaders who tried to ruin and discredit him, call him for advice. Look at God!

Watching my pastor endure so much vitriol was painful. I don't know how he was able to withstand so much hostility and loss, but by watching him, I learned a lot about the power of purpose. I learned that external attacks are inevitable, but you must not let external criticism immobilize you or water down your message. You can't cower to the crowd or surrender to the herd. You must stand firm and refuse to let public criticism become a personal crisis.

So, what can you do to ensure that external criticism does not become an internal crisis? How do you leverage it but not be limited by it? How do you bloom from it and not be bullied by it? How do you stay committed when you feel emotionally crushed? How do you keep standing up when the venom of your haters feels like it's crushing your soul?

First, remember you are a person of purpose, and murmuring is part of every mission, message, and movement. Also, you keep one thing in mind: others may attack your idea, but your identity is under divine protection. God is protecting you and will continue to protect you when you are moving in God's will.

Will the attacks hurt? Yes, the verbal jabs will be excruciating, the comments may sting, the remarks may trigger old wounds, and your feelings will be hurt; you are human. But also remember that your opposition is using hurtful words as weapons; their comments are intentionally inflammatory to disrupt your momentum and to dampen your resolve. But don't quit!

Secondly, remember that what you are doing is essential, not optional. Your divine assignment is valuable, vital, and valued by many, even if people never speak up in your defense. Now, that's a hard pill to swallow because we all want people to support us publicly. However, be prepared. Some people will publicly support you, but others won't. But supporting and aligning with you is their decision and their option, not your concern. When you are walking in your purpose and changing norms, challenging assumptions, and critiquing policies, you must have the emotional and spiritual infrastructure needed to stand alone. The good news is that you won't be alone. The spirits of other change-makers and legacy builders will be standing and rising with you. Most of all, God is always there.

Finally, remember that harsh critique may contain pearls of wisdom. For example, the comments that initially wounded you can also help you win. I know it sounds crazy, but some of my best marketing campaigns, defense strategies, and sales systems originated from my haters. So, if you can listen to their attacks from the perspective of a warrior, you will see opportunities, potential, and new connections that you may have overlooked. Like my grandmother used to say, "when people throw lemons, make sweet lemonade, rest in the shade, because you have got it made." I don't know if all of what granny said is true, but her advice has served me well.

Dr. Samuel was resolute in his pursuit of purpose. Despite the heart-crushing attacks and the salacious backbiting, he always encouraged his followers to *be concerned but not consumed* by the mean-spirited campaigns aimed to defame his character and undermine leadership. He encouraged all of us to stay on the battlefield for God and to fight the good fight of faith.

What happened to Dr. Samuel may also happen to you;

answering your divine call may include some emotional bruises and sleepless nights. Though it may be challenging, remember that you are not in a crisis or having a crisis; you are being a catalyst. You are making a difference in the world, a world that is fiercely clinging to a model that no longer serves humanity or honors God.

My friend, welcome criticism because you are on the precipice of greatness. You are at the tipping point of change. You are on the edge of excellence. You are on the border of better. You are unlocking societal cages and rattling political fences. You are creating a new reality, and you are about to launch into a new stratosphere of success. A higher dimension of destiny is calling you up higher and higher.

So remember, criticism may not feel good, but you are doing *"good."* Know that in your soul so that criticism will make you better, not bitter and faithful, not fearful. Know that criticism is a small price to pay to transform the ethos of the world.

Dr. Samuel didn't give up, and he continues to be a voice for justice, inclusion, peace, and equity even today. And you should not give up on your purpose either, because the world needs you to say what God has told you to say. The world needs your message to motivate the masses and to create a movement – God's movement.

Are you ready to embrace your purpose with commitment and resolve?

I hope so because it's time for you to Soar.

FRIENDSHIPS: CALLED, COURAGEOUS AND CONNECTED

Success never happens in isolation; it happens by divine collaboration.

Let Your Purpose Pick Your People™

If not, your pain, your past, and your own perspectives will.

Declare Today: I will attract and surround myself with courageous people who will support me.

29

TITLES TAKE TIME

Lately, I have been thinking a lot about friendship. It seems that more than ever before people are seeking and yearning for loving connections. It seems as if people are starving, almost desperate, for communities where they feel nurtured, cared for, and cared about. They want to belong, and they want interactions that provide intimacy, In-2-Me -See. Do you agree?

I know that some people hoped that social media platforms would provide some sort of substitute for human connection. On some level, I hoped so, too. I hoped that Facebook, Twitter, and virtual communities would provide social bridges so that people could meet and mingle with like-minded folk. I hoped that internet groups, though imperfect, would fill a much-needed void so that people would feel less isolated and alone in the world.

But over the last ten years, I have become more convinced that virtual connections are not enough. They are helpful, but nothing replaces a hug when you are grieving or eye contact when you want to be seen and witnessed. Nothing replaces the touch and the tenderness of another human being when you crave companionship. Nothing replaces real intimacy when you grow weary of shallow or superficial conversations. Nothing replaces praying and worship with people when you crave depth, soul-satisfying, soul-enriching bonds. Nothing. Nothing replaces the joy and warmth of physical closeness.

Wanting meaningful relationships makes sense because we are wired for connection. We are social beings and we function better and live longer when we are woven together in healthy communities. Research even confirms that social connection boosts our immune systems, wards off depression, and lowers stress. And even the most difficult times in our lives are more bearable when we have supportive friends. Let's face it. We need each other—that's why God placed us in families, tribes, and communities.

But even though we need each other, bonding too quickly could be risky for our purpose. As a person of purpose, you need time to examine motives, assess compatibility, and uncover a person's true character. You need time to determine if a person's dreams and goals align with yours, so you won't get distracted and derailed from your divine assignment. You need time to *"learn"* people and learn about people before you bring them into the innermost sanctums of your world. Yes, you need time because it takes months, not minutes, to determine if a person is spiritually fit or emotionally mature enough to travel with you on your purpose journey.

I know I may sound like a snob, but I am not. However, I am a good steward of my energy and gifts, which means I must be selective about my environment and all of my "ships" — mentorships, sponsorships, fellowships, friendships, companionships, and discipleships. I must be rigorous and socially shrewd because even though I believe that everybody is valuable, only the right people are vital for my divine call, my purpose.

I wish I could say that I learned that lesson quickly, but I can't. Betrayal, embezzlement, and downright thievery taught me some expensive and painful lessons. Honestly, I can't even say that I didn't see the signs of deception and thuggery either. There were indications that some people in my life could not be entirely trusted. Unfortunately, I was so busy building a business, speaking on platforms, and writing books that I ignored suspicious behavior and discounted my intuition. That's why my pockets were being picked while I was preaching and speaking. I was climbing the ladder while they were going to the bank, with my money, might I add. What's sad is my advisors tried to warn me, but I wouldn't listen. It was a costly lesson, but I learned.

Just so you don't experience the same misfortune, please heed this advice: take your time. Yes, take your time because titles take time. It takes time to determine if a person has the courage, capacity, and competence to be and uphold the title of "friend." And it takes more time to determine how and where to position a friend in your life. Because we all can admit that all friends are not equal and therefore should not be treated equally. That's why as you are pursuing your purpose, some of the most important decisions you will make will concern people. Don't forget that.

As you are pursuing your purpose, you must identify if a person belongs to one of three groups.

The first group you must take your time to carefully identify is your "core." Your "core" is your smallest group; it usually consists of three or fewer people. These people must be thoughtfully selected because you "do life" with them. You spend time with them. You invest in them, and they invest in you. They are your peeps.

What makes your core so special is that they support you and are committed to your vision. They are not jealous of you; they don't compete with you, and they don't compare themselves with you. They have their own fulfilling lives; that's key.

People in your core also have the emotional intelligence and the spiritual maturity to see you and know you without your masks or social personas. They are not impressed by your highs nor intimidated by your lows; they are balanced and stable. That's why you can trust them with your flaws and fears. If you stumble, they won't judge you or become jaded which means they can be trusted to carry the weight of your success and the burden of your divine assignment without fear of defection.

Most importantly, core-worthy people are also open-minded and objective. They welcome healthy discussion and debate, which means that they are always looking for the best decision and will not co-sign your bad decisions. They want you to win because they like you and respect your gift. That's important because some people like your gifts but secretly hate your guts. Trust me, it is a painful thing when people who you thought were your core turn out to be opportunists who only viewed you as transportation for their elevation. It's unfortunate, but it's true.

The next group of people you must take your time to identify is your "circle." People in your circle may or may not personally like you, but liking you is not the goal of the relationship. Remember, you are not trying to "do life" with your circle, you are trying to "do work." The goal of the circle relationship is effective partnership, not close companionship.

People in your circle are important to your purpose because they provide resources you need and connections that you don't have. Since you share some values, a vision, or a desire for the same victory, you can effectively work with them because there is a commitment to synergy, synchronicity, and mutuality which makes for fruitful collaborations. However, don't divulge your deepest secrets or share too much, too soon. Focus on the mission and strategically share your time, talents, and your energy so all parties can grow and prosper.

My client Reese came to visit me because she had problems identifying what types of people had the mindset and the mastery to be in her core and in her circle. She wanted healthy connections, but she felt that she could not find people who cared about her as much as she cared about them. I asked her, "Reese, how do you determine who qualifies for your core and for your circle? And how do you pressure-test your decisions to make sure you have placed people in the right category?"

Reese was initially reluctant to answer the question. She said,

"I believe that everybody has good in them, and I don't judge people. Judging people doesn't feel good to my spirit. It's wrong."

For most of her life, Reese felt people had unfairly judged her because she was differently-abled. And because she constantly felt discounted and discarded, she was hesitant to assess people, even if assessments were for her own good. She also preferred that relationships develop organically because she believed organic bonds were more authentic and purposeful.

Just for the record: I believe in organic relationships, too. However, I also believe that being an effective steward of our lives means that we make wise choices about who we spend time with and who we talk to. Our friendships are critical; they affect our ability to fulfill our divine call.

I said, "Reese, I am extremely sensitive about prejudging people too. If we look at judgment as a way of discerning how to improve your life, what ways could you determine if you are spending time with people who are not just available, but are suitable for what you want most out of life?"

"I don't like the word suitable. I don't want to use people. I value people. I want people to know that I genuinely care about who they are as people."

"Reese, of course, you value people. Investing your time, money, and resources to become a better friend is a sign that you value people. So, when you think about valuing people and valuing yourself, what questions can you ask them and ask yourself before you give people greater access to your life? What can you observe to learn more about people and about yourself?"

Reese struggled with my questions because she didn't want to appear biased or dismissive. However, she finally accepted that evaluating a person's behavior and character before giving them access to her life was wise. Thankfully, her willingness to screen and assess people has helped her develop relationships where she feels seen, heard, and known.

The last category of people you must take your time to discern is the "crowd." The crowd is the group of people you "do change" with. They are not the ones that you necessarily hang with, but they are the ones you join forces with to transform systems, create movements, and disrupt norms. They are the people you unite with to start revolutions in the world so that the world is more equitable, more inclusive, safer, saner, and more reflective of a loving God.

My friend, on your purpose journey, you will face many crowds. Some crowds will publicly challenge you and attack you. Some crowds will love you, defend you and evangelize for you. Some crowds will love you until you say or do something that they disagree with. Some crowds will ascribe motives, beliefs, and comments to you that don't represent you or your character. Some crowds will try to co-op your message, image, and brand. As you pursue your divine calling, you will face many crowds and some crowds will even mutate into vicious mobs with no provocation or explanation. That's the truth.

As a person of purpose, you must manage the crowds, and be ready for the crowds that morph into mobs because you will simultaneously face both. And even though it's easier to accept applause from your crowds, the harsh critiques from the mobs will be equally helpful on your purpose journey. Why? Both attacks and applause provide the visibility you need to amplify your message, raise money, and recruit new followers. Of course, the rebukes may sting, but they also help you strategize more effectively. So be ready to listen and learn from both so you can quickly pivot and shift your energy and efforts to maximize the moment. I know it won't be easy but your faithfulness will be rewarded because God is always orchestrating circumstances for your highest good.

At the end of the day, how do you determine if a person is part of your core, circle, or just part of the crowd? Time! Only time can provide the information you need to determine how and where a person fits into your life. Only time can reveal if a person is an asset or an adversary, an assistant or an assassin, a supporter or a saboteur, a blessing, or a burden. Time!

My friend, take your time and be mindful of the titles you give to the people in your life. Prayerfully give the title of "core" only to those who deserve it and can spiritually embrace it. Work strategically with your "circles" and master, but don't get sucked into, the "crowds." Most of all, continually evaluate yourself to ensure that you are modeling the kinds of behaviors that attract the people you need to help you fulfill your divine assignment.

Remember, you need people, and people need you. You can't soar alone; you need a team, a squad, and a support system. So, take your TIME before conferring titles. And when you have the appropriate people in the right places in your life, you can pursue your purpose with integrity, with community, and with love.

Are you ready? Your purpose awaits.

It's time to Soar Higher!

30

REAL FRIENDS ARE CURIOUS; THEY ASK WHY BEFORE THEY ARE CRITICAL ABOUT THE WHAT

One of the highest compliments you can give someone is to ask them for their opinion. Asking a person about their point of view shows genuine interest, sincere concern, and great respect. It shows people you care about them and admire their insight. And we ALL need and want to feel cared for and highly regarded, right?

But even though asking questions improves the quality of relationships, most people fail to ask questions or to ask them consistently. How do I know? By observing how people speak to each other or sit together. In less than five minutes, I can tell that barriers have been built, boundaries have been crossed, needs have been ignored, and priorities have been misaligned. And most of all, I can sense what I call "soul-sadness," which happens when people feel chronically misunderstood, ignored, and hopeless.

If asking questions fosters healthy relationships, why do most people make quick assumptions? The truth is, most people assume they know EVERYTHING about you, even when they know very little about themselves. Yes, unfortunately, most people jump to conclusions about your beliefs and behaviors without the benefit of a conversation. They also make projections and judgments about *your* dreams, decisions, and destiny based on *their* abilities, values, and standards. Frustrating, right?

So, what can you do to ensure that you lead with curiosity and inquiry? What can you do to remind yourself that you are not an authority on all cultures, subjects, or interpretations? What can you do to remember that the facts you learned may differ from the actual truth? What can you do to remind yourself that there are complexities, circumstances, and challenges in a person's life that you don't understand and have never experienced? And even if you have had a similar experience, how can you remember that you may not have experienced the same event in the same way?

You ask open-ended questions that allow people to share fully, freely, and honestly. You ask clarifying questions to uncover cultural differences and language nuances that are outside your experience. You allow words to flow easily between you without constant interruption, judgment, or debate. You humbly inquire with grace, empathy, and sensitivity to show people you value them as people, even if you disagree with their perspectives.

When I think about all the problems in the world, I am confident that asking more questions, even if asked incorrectly, could bridge the racial, gender, cultural, and generational divide. Questions – deep, honest, reflective questions – could initiate so much healing, reconciliation, and global transformation. If people came to conversations with openness and a genuine desire to learn and understand each other, they would realize they have common needs, goals, and interests. And if people were more committed to creating space for difference instead of insisting on domination, the world would become a safer, more humane, and more loving place.

My friend, let's give asking questions a try. Let's commit to courageous curiosity so we can learn, unlearn, relearn, and grow together. Let's step outside of our silos of superiority, off our pedestals of arrogance, and away from our seats of judgment so we can gain wisdom, promote mutuality, and foster unity. Because once we do, we can SOAR together as the human family that God intended us to be.

Let's Dare to Soar Higher!

31

PEOPLE CAN WANT WHAT YOU WANT, BUT THEY SHOULD NOT WANT WHAT YOU HAVE

It's good to have people in your life who want what you want. If you want peace, prosperity, and a beautiful home, it's nice to find people who want those things too. Having people in your life who want what you want is a good thing. It breeds a sense of belonging, commonality, and community.

But, if people want what you have, that's another thing. When people want what's in your home and what's in your hand, you no longer have a loyal supporter; you have a conniving saboteur. You have a person susceptible to jealousy, betrayal, and manipulation, and those types of people are dangerous to your peace and destructive to your purpose.

But before you label someone as a saboteur, it is important that you first look inside of your own heart. Sometimes we unknowingly project our feelings onto others and accuse people of the very emotions that we hold in our souls. Just think about it. Maybe people don't want your stuff. Perhaps you are so insecure about your success that you are assigning motives to others because you feel unworthy of your accomplishments. Maybe you suspect others because you are not operating with integrity yourself. Something to consider, right?

But after you search your heart, and you feel that you are not projecting your feelings onto others, it is time to face what we don't want to consider: jealousy. I know it's uncomfortable to think that jealousy could affect your relationships; I get it. But here is the truth: some of your friends will not be able to handle your elevation. They may resent that you have a new car, a better job, a sexier spouse, access to the power brokers, more disposable income, or just more free time. My elders said it best when they said, "having M-O-R-E can make others S-O-R-E." Yes, your success can hurt your friends' feelings. It's unfortunate, but it's true.

At the end of the day, we all naturally struggle or have struggled with jealousy. Be honest. We all can admit that there was at least one time in our lives when we wanted something that belonged to someone else, right?

Just for the record: wanting somebody else's stuff does not make us terrible people. But, it does expose our need for continued self-introspection. Why? Feeling tempted to steal or covet is an important clue about our desires; it is a sign that we don't have what we want, we don't have what we need, or we don't have something in the form that we want it. Something to consider, right?

Again, people can want what you want, but they should not want what you have. So, be alert. Be prayerful and discerning. Identify motives because as you pursue your purpose, the last thing you need is to be surrounded by people who are haters and "coveters".

Do you hear me?

Let's Dare To Soar Higher!

32

YOU WILL HURT YOURSELF IF YOU CAN'T HUDDLE

In high school, I played on the varsity basketball team. I wasn't that good of a player, but what I really loved about playing basketball was being in a huddle. The huddle was where the players would get close to each other, put their arms around each other, and listen intently to the coach — the huddle.

Even the girls who hated each other and talked behind each other's back, at that moment, put their childish, cliquish issues aside, and joined in to listen to the game plan — the huddle.

There was a sense that even though we were different colors, different ages, and had different dreams, at that moment, when the game was on the line, we were one, a connected, unified group. We were a team — the huddle.

When we were losing, we gave each other strength. When we were winning, we cheered each other on. When players were selfish in a way that jeopardized us winning, we chastised them.

When players didn't follow the game plan, we corrected them-the huddle.

The coach's presence was irrelevant because we were committed to each other. Of course, our teenage commitment only extended to the length of the game, but we realized we had a common goal... winning. We wanted victory — the huddle.

The huddle was that sacred space where every player mattered. The superstars locked arms with the benchwarmers. The drenched, sweaty girls shared space with the dry girls. The black girls hugged the necks of the white girls and brown girls. We shared water bottles, sweat-soaked towels, high 5s, tons of tears, and energy — the huddle.

I could not explain it then, but I somehow knew that *"Huddling"* was empowering. I knew that those 30 and 60-second time-outs did something for our collective souls, and I knew it was spiritual — the huddle.

Huddling reconnected us, refocused us, re-energized us, and re-embolden us. What one player emotionally and physically needed was unselfishly given by someone else. We shared, we dared, and we cared — the huddle.

I graduated from high school almost 40 years ago, and I still remember those magical times more than I remember the games. I don't remember who scored, the names of the players, or the names of the schools we played, but I remember the tender moments of the huddle.

Do you have a huddle? Do you have people you nestle with in times of tribulation, tragedy, and trouble? Do you have confidants that make you feel safe enough to be open, honest, and authentic? Do you have teammates who can visualize with you, dream with you, and strategize with you? Do you have people who are so confident in who they are that you can genuinely be who you are? Do you have a tribe that is so committed to confidentiality that you can openly share your strengths, successes, and your sensitivities? Do you have people who cheer for you and celebrate you even when you are struggling to cheer for yourself? The huddle.

To have a happy and healthy life, you need "huddlers." It does not matter if you are in a family, a corporation, the military, a sorority, an organization, or on a sports team, you need people to huddle with you. You need people, and people need you because research confirms that people who have strong support systems not only live longer, but they live fuller and more meaningful lives. And isn't that what you desire and deserve? Don't you want a group who "gets" you and galvanizes you to greatness? Don't you want comrades, companions, colleagues, and collaborators who lovingly confront, celebrate, and correct you?

Find supportive people and huddle with them. Find your crew. Find your team. Find your sister circle. Find your brother group. Find your network. Find your peeps. Your life, your livelihood, your legacy, and your ability to love depends on finding people who share a common goal and who openly care about you.

Get some huddlers. Then love them. Nurture them. Motivate them. Be there for them!

Are you ready? Where are your *"huddlers?"*

It's Time to Soar!

33

A TRUE FRIEND COVERS YOUR WEAKNESSES; THEY DON'T COVET YOUR WINS

These days it seems as if all types of associations are masquerading as friendships. It seems that some people are so desperate for a sense of belonging and connection that they are quickly bonding with fakes, frauds, or fools. They seem to be emotionally needy, so needy that they are failing to ask critical questions to discern if a person's values, principles, and character qualify them for healthy relationships.

Just so we are clear, I am not suggesting that you and I are better than anyone else. But if you want to be successful, there are a few prerequisites that must be considered before granting someone access to your life. For starters, a true friend must cover you and not covet you.

Covering is an old term that I learned in church, and it is a phrase that seems to be quickly going out of style these days. To review, covering means being willing to shield or hide a friend's vulnerabilities and frailties. And don't we all need someone to shield us from criticism or humiliation when we make mistakes or experience a temporary bout of insanity? We all can think of at least one time in our lives when we lost our minds and behaved in ways that didn't reflect who we were. Everybody has experienced at least one time in their life when they lost their good sense and acted a fool.

Consider this. Unless you are committing a crime or acting in a morally reprehensible way, real friends don't broadcast or even discuss your flaws and failures in a public setting. Real friends protect you and discreetly manage information that would tarnish your reputation or make others question your character. When they have concerns, they come to you in confidence and "check" you privately. They may even chastise you, but they would never do anything to undermine or defame you overtly, not a true friend. True friends are loyal, honest, and faithful. And most of all, they understand the meaning of discretion and confidentiality. They love you and care about you even when others don't.

On the other hand, a fake friend covets your wins, which makes them untrustworthy and susceptible to betrayal. Since they secretly want your job, your house, or your spouse, they look for ways to weaken you. They devise strategies to exploit your flaws and failures in attempts to gain a competitive edge. On the surface, they look like devoted assistants and dedicated advisers, but they are really demonic, deadly assassins who plot your destruction.

Over the years, I have learned that fake friends who covet are incredibly clandestine, which initially makes them hard to detect. If you work with them, they will make your coworkers question your competence, second-guess your character, and undervalue your ideas. If you live with them, they will share sensitive information or broadcast your most embarrassing secrets to advance their own agenda. Even if the information is irrelevant or insignificant, they will make up reasons to "*spill your tea*" to sully and demolish your reputation.

Trust me. Fake friends are cunning and deceptive. They will politically cripple you and undermine your relationships without you even having a clue.

Why would people stoop to such low levels to jeopardize you, your life, and your livelihood? Because they are insecure, they feel inadequate, and they lack integrity. They are envious; they covet.

The saddest part is that fake friends who covet don't understand that their devious plot to slander you really hurts them. Stepping on your neck or undermining your agenda rarely bears fruit because successful people are usually wise and intuitive. Successful people have experienced their own personal attacks, endured endless criticism, and have suffered a few fools themselves and can quickly detect sabotage. Successful people know firsthand how destructive traitors, liars, and thieves can be. That's why high-achieving, spiritually conscious go-getters refuse to entertain smear campaigns or engage in defamatory innuendo.

Moral of the story: Even when fake friends conspire against you, don't get distracted. Stay focused on your assignment and don't get sidetracked. Once a false friend is exposed for the back-biter, backstabber, or betrayer that they are, doors will close, opportunities will dry up, and their access to influential people will be denied. Eventually, fake friends will fall into the very ditches that they dig for others. Karma is real; it's a spiritual law.

Let's be clear. You do need friends; purpose does not happen in isolation. But, take your time and carefully evaluate who is worthy of the "friend" title. Make sure that the person you select has the desire, maturity, and commitment to cover your weaknesses and not covet your wins because you are poised to have a tremendous impact on the world.

Are you ready?

It's time to Soar!

34

STOP ASKING PEOPLE TO TALK WHEN YOU KNOW THEY DON'T HAVE ANYTHING NEW OR INSIGHTFUL TO SAY

My granny used to say, "If you are not going to say something nice, don't say nothing at all." Her grammar was wrong, but her advice was right. And honestly, don't you wish more people adhered to that policy today?

I mean, really. Aren't you shocked and saddened by what people say about each other and to each other? Some of the vile, venomous, and vicious comments hurled in the public arena make my flesh crawl. Degrading names, inflammatory adjectives, unsubstantiated statements, fake facts, and personal attacks that defy human dignity are expressed so carelessly. To me, it's reckless to have such a disregard for others; it's downright dangerous. Nothing is gained by wounding people with words. All it does is injure people and incite them to respond in more dehumanizing ways. And do we really want or need to "out-mean" each other? Trophies are not awarded for being malicious, are they?

Yes, it bothers me when people use words to intentionally inflict pain. And it is equally bothersome when we invite pain in our lives. Yes, we invite pain when we seek advice from people who NEVER have anything positive or insightful to say.

Let's be honest. It is easy to identify people you should avoid. All you need to do is to talk about your dreams. Before you get the entire vision out of your mouth, naysayers will tell you that your idea is too big, that you are under-qualified, or that you will fail. Before you even finish your sentence, they will give you fifteen reasons why you don't have what it takes to prosper, progress, or produce. And please do not mention anything about being in love. Without even knowing the person, they will offer unsolicited advice about how to keep a relationship together even though they have been married four times themselves. You know the type. You have a few naysayers in your family.

Here's the problem: naysayers don't think for themselves, and they have nothing helpful to say. They have not read, researched, or reflected about anything long enough to develop their own perspective. They don't critique, consider, or contemplate; they only copy what everybody else has already said. So if you ask them a question, they will just parrot what's on the news, or what they heard somebody else say, or they will quote something from an Instagram post. They never offer an original thought or any new insight. They are regurgitators, not originators.

My friend, none of us benefit from asking narrow-minded, shallow-thinking, or negative-believing people questions. We can't ask them for opinions; they don't have any positive ideas to share. Listen. You are a person with aspirations, and it is not wise to invite people into your conversations when you know they don't have anything positive, insightful, or fruitful to say. You need wisdom to win, not foolishness.

What reinforced my commitment against inviting certain people to important conversations was my sessions with my client, Jackie. Jackie got pregnant in high school, and her religious community demanded that she marry the baby's father. She didn't love the father or really know him, and most of all, she didn't want to get married. But Jackie felt pressured because in her faith tradition, being an unwed mother was a sin. And if she refused to marry, she could get excommunicated from the only community she had ever known.

Since her parents supported the church's decision, she buckled under the pressure and said, "I do" even though her spirit screamed, "I don't." She even tried her best to be happy because her husband was a great father to their child. But gradually she found her marriage and her childhood town mentally too restrictive and her childhood religion suffocating. She had outgrown her limited life and was ready to embark on a fresh life filled with new possibilities and colorful experiences.

Even though Jackie's pastor never offered any encouragement for her budding dreams or expanding faith, Jackie would frequently meet with her for advice. The pastor would continuously extol the virtues of being a wife and a mother and condemned Jackie for wanting "more." One time, the pastor even called Jackie greedy, sinful, and immoral because she wanted to have a career and continue her education.

After every counseling session with her pastor, Jackie felt more discouraged about pursuing her dreams. She questioned her vision and feared that she would be resigned to living an empty, boring life. But, she wanted more and knew that wanting a bigger life didn't make her a sinner. She knew her desire to grow, explore, and experience life didn't make her selfish or corrupt.

When Jackie shared her dreams with her family, she received more criticism. Her family didn't understand why she wanted to live in a big, sinful city filled with heathens or why she wanted a career. To them, being a mother and a good Christian woman, based on their definition of Christianity, was righteous and admirable.

Because Jackie didn't believe in her own truth and trust her inner wisdom, she continued to share her thoughts and dreams in an attempt to find somebody who could validate her perspective. She desperately wanted somebody to rubber-stamp her views and endorse her decision to leave her childhood church and community.

I asked Jackie, "why do you need permission to proceed with your life? What's making you seek approval from others who consistently discount your vision and question your faith?"

Jackie quietly said, "I want everybody to be okay with my decision. If not, I may lose my family, and then I will be alone."

As she cried, I asked her, "Jackie, in what ways do you feel alone now? And, what does being alone at this moment mean for you or feel like for you?"

I encouraged Jackie to reframe and expand her thinking so she could imagine more possibilities. Jackie wanted a new life, a life that reflected who she was and what she aspired to be. She wanted space to grow and develop without being subjected to another person's brand of religion or being subjected to constant rebuke.

I quietly asked her, "In what ways will you continue to be lonely if you stay?"

Jackie cried, "I will be lonely because I will have nobody to understand me, support me or stand up for me. I will have no one, not even myself."

"What can you do to move forward in a way that gives you some of the support you need, but opens the door to receive more of what you want?"

"I don't know and I don't know what to do. I know I don't want to stay, but I don't know how to leave."

Jackie is like many of us. Honestly, it's human to want acknowledgment and affirmation; we all crave acceptance and belonging. But when we are desperate to be heard and known, we sometimes invite people in our lives who infect us with their toxic beliefs. And fear-filled beliefs affect our ability to make healthy, deliberate choices for ourselves.

My friend, your growth may threaten those closest to you. When you upgrade your identity and transform your thinking, your family and friends may reject you. Your newfound attitudes and opinions may even cause conflict and elicit negative reactions that bruise your soul and prevent you from thriving. That's why when you are seeking and trying to figure things out for yourself, you may not be able to share your thoughts with your loved ones. You may need to find or create new connections that are more conducive to nurturing and exploring your ideas and supporting the new you.

My advice may be hard to hear, but trust me, constantly hearing words of caution and doubt will stifle you. Being bombarded by anxiety-loaded comments can actually prevent you from pursuing and fulfilling your true calling. And you don't want to live with regret, get stuck in mediocrity, or miss your opportunity to shine.

So, what can you do to ensure that you consistently connect and converse with people who can inspire you to defy the odds and pursue your true calling? Ask yourself the hard questions like – why do I keep inviting certain people to my life-defining conversations when I know I will leave feeling crushed, condemned, or confused? Why do I discuss my journey with certain people when they don't possess the mentality or expertise to offer wisdom? Why am I inviting fear, doubt, and mayhem into my creative space when I know that I am growing and vulnerable? Why am I seeking approval from people who don't approve of themselves? Why am I casting my pearls before swine?

Those are hard questions. But when we routinely invite people into our lives who demean us and dismantle us, that's a clue that we need to heal. And, when we hustle to gain approval and permission before we make decisions, we risk becoming imprisoned by the views and the needs of others and we don't move forward.

Just for the record. I am not saying that people who don't offer wise counsel are not valuable. They are valuable, but they may not be vital to your purpose. Until they expand their minds and respect the new you, they can't help you become the best and highest version of yourself. They can only hold you hostage to your history.

So, be prudent. Don't invite destructive discussions in your life. Don't ask purpose-type questions to people who have not demonstrated that they know their own purpose or have their own perspectives. When you are a visionary, truth-teller, and change-maker, every encounter, and every interaction must yield something to make you better, bolder, and bigger so you can SOAR higher.

Hard advice? Maybe. But it's time-tested advice that can't be denied.

Let's Dare To Soar Higher!

35

FRIENDS ARE NICE PEOPLE, BUT NOT ALL FRIENDS ARE NICE

I like my friends, and I am glad that I have people in my life who are invested in my development enough to tell me the truth, even when the truth is not nice. Let's face it. When we are pursuing purpose, we need people in our lives and in our corner who love us and respect us enough to give us honest feedback so we can be better, bolder, and stronger. We also need people who are confident enough to question and challenge us to sharpen our thinking, expand our minds, and examine our paradigms. The adage is true: nobody becomes their best self by themselves. We need each other.

But here's the challenge. People can't tell you the truth if you are emotionally fragile. If you fall out, fall down, and fall into despair when people share their truth about how they experience you, you will never improve. Greatness and destiny will elude you, and you will find yourself stuck, ineffective, unproductive, and alone.

What we must remember is that successful friends are assets, and they are not interested in befriending us if we are only committed to comfort and convenience. No way. Mission-minded folks require connections that are built on confidence, courage, creativity, and healthy conflict. And they are not willing to downgrade their requirements or adjust their "friend" criteria to make the emotionally fragile and the spiritually weak content.

Here's the honest, but loving, truth. People who are walking in their purpose expect you to walk in yours too. And they will walk in their purpose with you or without you. They will not let your presence or your absence derail their destiny or hijack their agenda.

Please hear my heart: friends are necessary. Every dream requires a team, and every purpose requires partners. But it is up to you to receive feedback because your success depends on your ability to be corrected and coached, not coddled. Constant pacification prevents cultivation and elevation.

Remember this...people who only tell you what you want to hear are not true friends; they are just people-pleasers, puppets, or pawns who are not invested in your greatness. So, cultivate some true friends. Get the feedback you need to stay competitive, innovative, and relevant. Have the conversations you need to inspire your heart and stretch your mind so you can grow.

Oscar Wilde said it best when he said that "true friends stab you in the front." Mr. Wilde was right because true friends don't talk behind your back; they tell you what you need to hear to your face so you can soar higher!

It's time to Soar!

36

DON'T STAY TOO LONG AROUND PEOPLE WHO DON'T LIKE YOU BECAUSE YOU WILL RISK NOT LIKING YOURSELF

Have you ever been around people who didn't like you? Not the ones who tell you they don't like you, not those. The people who tell you to your face that you are not their cup of tea are honest. I am talking about people who smile in your face but secretly dislike you. You know who they are. They are your frenemies.

Frenemies... we all have them. They are easy to recognize because their sarcastic comments and their thinly veiled put-downs reveal their actual disdain for you. Just think about some of the folks you work with, live with, or pray with who are quick to give you backhanded compliments disguised as constructive critique. The ones who are quick to say "you look pretty TODAY" as if to say that you are ugly on the other days. Or make comments like "you were right FOR ONCE" as if to imply that you are consistently wrong. Or, the ones who make snitty remarks like "you didn't mess up THIS time" to suggest that you always make mistakes. You know the type. Just think about some folks you spend time with who rarely offer real words of wisdom, but never pass up an opportunity to throw verbal jabs that wound your soul, worry your mind, and wreck your confidence. You know who they are. Frenemies!

When frenemies behave negatively toward you, the most loving thing you can do for yourself is to sever ties. If not, their seeds of doubt, malice, and jealousy will be watered by their continuous flow of criticism, cultivated by their constant acts of sabotage, nourished by their perpetual bitterness, and sustained by their ill-intentions. Their toxic seeds will grow and will eventually suffocate your greatness, erode your genius, and choke your goodness. And their hateful comments will penetrate deeply into your psyche and spread to other facets of your life and leave you with nothing, just like dead meat. And, that's a pitiful, powerless place to be.

Yes, their seeds of negativity will infect you, and everybody attached to you. And, then, one day, you will look up and discover that you don't like yourself either. You will magnify every flaw, rehash every failure, and ruminate about every fall. You will cease to revel in your talents, marvel at your beauty, or celebrate your brilliance. The quality of your inner dialogue will suffer, and you will eventually lose confidence in who you are and what you are becoming. You will be left with nothing to successfully navigate in the world. No self-love, self-respect, or self-worth, nothing!

Yes, it may be hard now, but you must stop spending time with frenemies, or at least re-position them in your life. Hanging around haters will eventually make you hate yourself. That's a fact.

Remember, people don't have to like you. BUT, YOU MUST LIKE YOURSELF enough to surround yourself with people who affirm, honor, and celebrate you. And just for the record, your purpose demands fertile ground and a positive environment to bloom, too.

Did you get that?

It's Time to Soar!

37

IF YOU GIVE THE WRONG PEOPLE AMMUNITION, THEY WILL TURN AROUND AND SHOOT YOU WITH IT

Sometimes we talk too much. Oh, yes, we do. We talk and talk and talk without agendas, strategy, and intention. And when we do, we say too much, and we share information with people who are not emotionally and spiritually mature enough to handle it. You know those types of people. We all know a few folks who can't handle sensitive information. We all know people who don't know how to keep confidential information to themselves. As my granny would say, *"some people can't hold anything. Some can't even hold water with a cup."*

Since most people are careless with your secrets and your personal information, here's a WARNING...WARNING... WARNING... WARNING. STOP TALKING. Some people will shoot you with the bullets — the information — you give them, and some will do it deliberately.

Let's be honest. Betrayal happens, and it occurs when people become jealous of your ascension or when they become angry that they can no longer exploit you for their gain. And we all know underhanded people like that. We all have experienced the pain of deceit and endured the sting of disloyalty. We all have suffered because some of our private mistakes and exploits were made public by loose lips. We all know that betrayal bites.

Oh yes, betrayal bites, and the ache from betrayal can linger for days, and sometimes decades. And what makes betrayal so excruciating and deadly is that it causes irrevocable damage. It destroys families, your relationships, your reputation, and your livelihood. It also destroys your trust in others, and it makes you question your own judgment. I know because it happened to some of my friends and me.

Here is some advice. Be prayerful and cautious when sharing personal information. Qualify and vet people before you divulge sensitive data. And most of all, don't talk when you are angry. Heed the Biblical warning that says, "A fool vents all his feelings, but a wise man holds them back." (Proverbs 29:11, NKJV). My friend, you are too smart to be a fool.

Don't forget.... very few people can totally be trusted with your most sensitive information. When some people don't get their way or if they can benefit from disclosure, they will *"spill the beans and add some seasoning on top"* to decimate your character. And even if betrayers don't have any information about you, if it promotes their cause, they won't mind making up a few "facts." Let's face it. Some people are just low-down, dirty backstabbers and will stoop to unbelievable levels for a minute of fame or for a few measly dollars. It's tight, but it's right. You can say amen.

I hate to admit it, but throughout my life, I talked too much. I gave people ammunition, and they shot me with it when I was at my weakest. I almost lost my job, my standing in the community, my business, and my mind. Only through the grace and love of God have I recovered and been able to heal and forgive those who wounded me.

My friend, remember, you are on assignment! You have a purpose. The adage is true: loose lips sink ships and your mission is too important to sink. So, watch what you say and be mindful of what you share. Don't get shot by your own bullets. Trust me, "friendly" fire kills, too.

Declare Today: I will keep my mouth shut so I can soar.

Let's Dare to Soar Higher as we pray before we share!

38

BE SELFISH ENOUGH TO BE DRIVEN, BUT BE SELFLESS ENOUGH TO BE DEVOTED

Balancing all of the variables of your life is never easy. Even when you have carefully identified your goals, finding the right balance of drive and devotion is difficult. You plan. You evaluate. You reassess. You pray. Yet, there remains a constant tug-of-war in your relationships when you are pursuing your purpose that frays your closest connections.

I have to admit that I was caught off guard by the impact that my purpose had on my loved ones. When you pursue your purpose, nobody warns you that harmonizing and heeding the needs of family and friends can take a toll on your relationships. Let's face it. People want your time and attention, and their requests are understandable, but not always manageable.

Despite the difficulty, you try your best to juggle. But when you miss appointments, forget events or fail to give your family your full attention, you are often criticized for being selfish or self-absorbed. Your loved ones villainize and demonize you; their biting criticisms are relentless, and their insults cut deep. So deep that it's tempting to blame others or condemn yourself when needs are not met. It's also tempting to resort to name-calling and return some of the mean-spirited jabs that your friends and family unfairly hurl at you. Yes, ministers think about revenge too.

But after careful reflection, you realize that people are not needy, and you are not negligent. You realize that it's just hard to figure everything out; managing conflicting desires and competing demands is not easy. For example, your siblings want you, but you NEED you, too. Your family wants a vote in your life, but you have a vision for your life, too. Your children desire your time, but your dreams demand your time, talent, and treasure, too. Your parents want to talk to you, but you need quiet time, too. Your spouse wants to play today, but you want to plan for tomorrow, too. And so, you do your best to juggle multiple balls with unpredictable and inconsistent success; sometimes you catch the balls and sometimes you don't.

After years of working with visionaries, creatives, and leaders, I have learned that balancing the demands of life when you have a compelling purpose is analogous to walking on a tightrope hoisted high in the sky. It's tricky and complicated because your purpose, your WHY, never comes with instructions, guidelines, or a timeline. There's no detailed manual, no tried-and-true formula, and no well-defined pathway to do what you have been divinely commissioned to do. The HOW and WHAT of purpose are always unfolding, which makes achieving harmony and synergy difficult. And, how could you possibly plan effectively and accurately when you don't know what you don't know, and you don't know what's needed until it's needed? Remember, the steps of purpose are often revealed while in motion, not in inactivity.

So, what do you do? How do you achieve some semblance of balance in your life, so you are not tossed around like a rag doll? How do you determine if you are driven enough yet devoted enough to create something spectacular without disrupting the lives of your loved ones? How do you find peace when you are compelled to do one thing but concerned about missing out on something else? How do you plan your schedule without being controlled by everybody's agenda?

First, you scratch everything off of your agenda, and then determine what aligns with your divine assignment. If a relationship or activity moves you forward and aligns with your purpose, you make room for it in your life. If the activity or relationship moves you away from your purpose, you purge, prune, and reposition it to bring yourself back into alignment with your calling.

Your purpose must be your guide. It must be the deciding factor for everything you do because your purpose will determine your focus. Your focus will determine your flow. Your flow will determine how you flourish. How you flourish will determine your fulfillment. And, your fulfillment will bring you peace.

So, if restoring your balance costs you a few moments with your family members, don't beat yourself up. Learning how to integrate all the facets of your life is part of the purpose journey. Also, sometimes you may need to educate and include certain family members in the process so they can gain a deeper understanding of what you are doing and why you feel compelled to do it. Sharing your vision with them will help them contribute and not compete with your work.

My friend, God gave you drive and devotion. Both are God-given gifts to be used as you pursue your purpose. So, stay focused on your purpose and wisely allocate time for loved ones. Most of all be flexible because "balance" will look different based on the different seasons, stages, and circumstances of your life and their lives. And sometimes, you won't achieve balance; you will just become better at life integration, which I believe is more sustainable, anyway. Makes sense?

My elders always told me that I would find the right rhythm for me to rise. And guess what? You will too.

Are you driven and devoted? If you are a purpose-driven person, you are both. You just need to strategically and expertly integrate them both in your life so you can do what God has called you to do.

Are you ready to Soar? Let's go! Success awaits.

39

IF YOU WAIT TOO LONG, YOU WILL SAY TOO MUCH

Sometimes people cross the proverbial line. They post comments that feel degrading, they write letters that feel demeaning, or they share opinions that feel incendiary. It's not that you are overly sensitive, but some statements just defy human decency. But when people cross the line and offend you, it is your responsibility to speak up immediately or as soon as you can. It's a fact. When you wait too long, sometimes you will say too much.

I know we all can remember at least one time in our lives when we waited too long to address an offensive comment. Against our better judgment, we waited and waited and waited, hoping that our hurt feelings would automatically dissolve or that the relationship would repair itself. But our hurt feelings stayed around like old shoes. And since we never expressed our grievances, we eventually became extremely resentful and defensive. Sometimes we became so bitter that we launched preemptive verbal attacks at anyone who crossed our paths. Or, we exploded and said some pretty harsh remarks to some unsuspecting friends and loved ones. Because of our outbursts, we hurt our reputations and lost our most faithful supporters.

Of course, we apologized or at least tried to apologize, but we could never recall our words. Our verbal jabs were nasty, repulsive, and filled with years of accumulated vitriol. In our anger, we reverted back to our pre-enlightened or pre-church days to make sure that our words stung, too. Yes, we said too much.

Let's be honest. Even though we were hurt, we never really planned to say all of what we said. We were even a bit surprised when the words jumped out of our mouths. But now we have to face the consequences that our blunders and anger-filled tirades caused when we lost control.

I know. I wish people could un-hear what they heard, too, because apologies don't always glue relationships back together. And isn't it just like life that the people we need the most in the future are the very ones that we hurt the most in the past? Ponder that.

Yes, people will get on your nerves, I mean, your LAST good nerve. But often they don't realize that they have encroached on your boundaries because you never let them know that you were offended, crowded, or smothered. Remember, we all are wired differently. A gesture that is interpreted as an INVITATION to one person MAY feel like a VIOLATION to another person. We all experience and express support, love, and appreciation differently. And how could we not? We were raised and socialized in different cultures, in different communities, under different circumstances by different clans. The factors that influence our actions and responses are as varied as night and day. Don't forget that!

Because we are so different, when people hurt your feelings, speak up. Approach the conversation with a spirit of curiosity so you can learn more about their intentions and not focus entirely on the impact. After you understand their motives, then make an informed decision about the relationship. Don't be hasty and don't throw people away until you fully analyze the situation. Maybe you are angry at them for something that you failed to do yourself. Remember, perspective is everything so get all of the facts and assess all the feelings before you take action. As the Bible says — *"in all our getting, get understanding first."* (*Proverbs 4:7*)

Here's some more friendly advice. Talk directly to the person who offended you, and not twenty other people. Did you get that? Talk TO the person and not ABOUT the person. Often times, when our feelings get hurt, we talk to everybody else except the person who hurt us. And as a result, many relationships get damaged, organizations get undermined, churches get jeopardized, reputations get needlessly ruined, and the problem still never gets resolved. Trust me. I have seen much relational and organizational damage caused by a person's unwillingness to speak DIRECTLY to the person who offended them. So, be brave, be humble, and speak directly to the person who hurt you and speak to them quickly.

I will say it again! Speak up immediately; don't wait. And watch your words and your tone. Remember, you have a purpose. Don't let arrogance or ignorance ruin your relationships or weaken other relationships because the people you may need tomorrow will be the same people you mistreated yesterday.

Say what you need to say now so you won't say too much!

Are you ready?

Let's Dare to Soar Higher!

40

FINDING YOUR TRIBE REQUIRES THAT YOU FOLLOW YOUR TRUTH

Sometimes I feel extremely lonely. I feel too different for one group, too direct for another group, too disenfranchised for that group, and too distant from this group. Because I am a progressive, out-of-the-box thinker and a tradition-averse "liver", it is sometimes challenging to find people who understand me or want to understand me. As a visionary, change agent, and heart-centered leader, you probably have felt the same way, too.

But life has convinced me that when we LIVE our truth, people will find us. Why? Because people are also searching; they are also on a spiritual quest for their tribe. People are also looking for that special community that feels like their own definition of "home." Trust me. People are looking for you just as much as you are looking for them.

This is what I have learned: there are lots of wonderful people who are open enough and mature enough to love you just the way you are. There are amazing groups of insightful people who are not stuck or stymied by the status quo who can offer love and companionship in creative and life-affirming ways. There are many folks who are willing to explore the world with you because they realize that life could be bigger, broader, and more beautiful through the eyes of diverse perspectives and by combining disparate narratives. There are many hearted-centered communities that will welcome your every flaw, your every imperfection, and your every mistake because they know how to celebrate **all** of your humanity while they simultaneously appreciate their own.

Be encouraged. The people you need and desire to do life with are there. But you must live authentically so they can find you and align with you. You must be honest about who you are, what you believe, and what you want to contribute to the world so you can attract the right allies, stakeholders, and supporters to help you fulfill your life's mission.

My friend, be you and trust who you are. Shine as bright as you can. Speak from your heart and you will attract the right people who are willing to reflect back to you your own genius, your own brilliance, and your own truth. Live freely knowing that there are people who will understand your essence, believe your experiences, and honor your existence.

There are genuine people who are willing and waiting to live in solidarity and in solace with you—not wanting anything from you but love.

I know. It's my testimony too.

It's time to Soar!

41

EVEN IF PEOPLE TALK BADLY ABOUT YOU, DON'T YOU TALK BADLY ABOUT YOURSELF

Some people will talk badly about you. It does not matter if the facts are wrong. It does not matter if the events are lies. It does not matter if the information is based on a misperception, a misinterpretation, a mistake, or a misprint. Some people will talk, and their comments will hurt your feelings; their words may even hurt like hell.

But even though people are saying negative comments about you, don't you say those comments to yourself. NO! Don't parrot their poison. Don't contaminate your spirit with their chatter.

Don't ruin your regard for yourself because of their remarks. Don't let their words wound you. Don't voice their venom. STOP it!

Even if some of the remarks are true, you did the best you could at the time. As the late Dr. Maya Angelou would say, "when you know better, you do better." So, now you know better. Now you realize that you did what you knew to do. Now you recognize that your actions were based on the insight, the knowledge, and the self-awareness that you had at the time. Now you appreciate that what you did is not the substratum nor the sum total of who you are or what you are. Now you know.

Please, my brother or sister, honor yourself and remember that you are growing. Free yourself from the tyranny and scrutiny of an unforgiving crowd and walk confidently in your purpose. Hold your head up, not in an arrogant way, but in a way that acknowledges that you are a child of God.

Remember, your words, not their words, have power in your life and are the power for your life. So, let your words be the engine that propels you forward to do what God has called you to do. Let your words be the catalyst for change and contribution. Let your words be words you need to hear to inspire you when you are down and to sustain you when you are up. Let your words remind you of your giftedness, vision, and mission.

Speak life over yourself. Speak peace to yourself. Speak goodness about yourself.

Speak because your purpose is calling you higher to a new place of contribution and influence.

Let's Dare To Soar Higher!

42

LET YOUR PURPOSE PICK YOUR PEOPLE

As a visionary, I believe that expecting new things in our lives — joy, success, fulfillment— has everything to do with PURPOSE! Purpose! We all have one. We all arrived in this world fully loaded — wired, formed, and equipped—to make a difference in the world. We all have been divinely designed to do something that only we can do.

But our purpose can only be fully realized through the help of the right people. Just like winning sports franchises draft players to help them dominate their sport, your purpose will require a similar selection process to ensure that you have the right people in place to strategically implement your vision. In other words, your purpose must pick your people.

When your purpose picks your people, it demands specific criteria, which are time-tested qualities. I refer to these qualities as the Indispensable 5 "Cs" — the qualities your purpose needs to thrive and survive. Of course, there are more qualities, but these are the five that your purpose cannot do without, especially if you desire to fulfill your divine call.

The first "C" that your purpose demands is CHARACTER. Regrettably, many leaders don't carefully evaluate a person's character until it's too late — after the damage has been done. But the first factor that must be assessed is a person's character — who they are on the inside and what they do when no one is looking. So what do you look for? You look for qualities like honesty, discipline, fairness, resilience, and dependability. You consider how people make decisions, how they rebound from failure, and you carefully observe their habits. You ask questions to better understand their motives, beliefs, and ethics. And most of all, you watch how potential teammates treat other people who have less power, less status, and less money. What I have learned over the years is that nothing reveals a person's true character more than how they treat people they *think* they don't need, or how they treat people they feel superior to. Nothing!

Just for the record, a person's character is sometimes hard to assess. But be patient and be diligent. Do your homework, look for clues, and conduct a thorough background check. Ask critical questions to uncover their values, their self-esteem, and their self-awareness. Meet their relatives, former colleagues, and friends to observe how they behave in different settings. Remember… you can't judge a book by its cover. You must carefully scrutinize who you invite on your team to ensure that your PURPOSE is not jeopardized by people who have tons of charisma but are devoid of character.

The second "C" that your purpose demands is COMPETENCE because your purpose requires more than proficiency; it requires excellence. Remember, excellence produces the fruit that people desire, enjoy, and expect. That's important to keep in mind because people will not pay a high price for low quality work for too long. No sir! So, don't get lazy, don't take people for granted, and don't become complacent. Keep your standards and performance high because what you produce or provide will significantly serve the world.

Now, to ensure that you attract and employ competence, surround yourself with people who know how to get a job done! But here's the key: you need competent people who complete you and NOT compete with you. That's not always easy, especially when you are working with highly-skilled people. But finding people who complement your strengths and who can cover for your weaknesses is not only wise; it's strategic and will position you for greater success. That's why it's so critical to consistently invest in yourself to strengthen your leadership skills because competent leaders will attract other competent leaders. Trust me, high performers are repelled by willful ignorance, deficiency, and mediocrity. So maintain your competency and constantly evolve as a leader to attract the talent and wisdom that your purpose requires to contribute at the highest level.

The third "C" that your purpose requires is CHEMISTRY. In my 30+ years in corporate America, I have learned a painful truth: competence without chemistry produces fatal explosions, not fruitful collaborations. Am I right? We all have worked in toxic environments where people didn't like, value, or have respect for each other. We all know how demoralizing it is to work with people who have bad attitudes, short tempers, and negative energy. So, ask yourself, have I selected the right talent with the right temperament for the right task? Those three important questions will help guide you when making staff decisions.

Just so we are clear: chemistry is never an excuse *not* to have a diverse team. You need a multicultural, multiethnic team. You need people who don't look like you, love like you, live like you, think like you are, pray like you, believe like you, or vote like you on your team. Your purpose needs people with different perspectives, various personalities, several talents, diverse identities, and varied backgrounds to provide insight, illuminate blind spots, and optimize strategies. Your purpose also requires a positive atmosphere that can birth fresh approaches, exchange disparate ideas, and develop creative solutions. If your purpose is going to serve the world, your team needs to look like the world, too. It must be inclusive of all God's children.

Listen. You have a job to do. Your purpose is too vital and valuable to be limited by homogeneity or inner conflict. So, consider chemistry and let your purpose pick people who are willing to cheerfully collaborate, openly respect differences, and authentically share their unique talents with humility. It's a fact: when people enjoy their work, feel like they belong, and feel celebrated, productivity soars. People are more innovative, committed, and invested which will help you execute your purpose more effectively in a complex, changing world.

The fourth "C" is CAPACITY. I define capacity "as the ability to remain resilient and anchored despite negative and detracting influences." After years of coaching leaders, I have learned that capacity is one of the hardest concepts for leaders to embrace because it requires agility, adaptability, and a high degree of emotional intelligence.

Here's the key. On your journey to purpose, you will face personnel issues, financial issues, competitive changes, legal issues, spiritual issues, and your own personal struggles. Your ability to balance and juggle competing demands while staying optimistic, focused, and strategic will determine how far and how fast you SOAR.

Of course, you can't anticipate every change or have all the answers; most changes are outside of your control. But when change is needed, can you shift and pivot? Are you flexible enough and adaptable enough to unlearn, learn, and relearn people and processes to remain viable and relevant? Are you willing to restructure and recalibrate your resources to evolve so your purpose can be expressed and executed with more potency and veracity? Your ability to respond, withstand, and leverage changes will ensure your sustainability, and ultimately contribute to your long-term success.

The final "C" is Courage. To me, courage is the ability to proceed in the face of fear and uncertainty. And make no mistake about it; as you pursue your purpose, you must possess courage. A purpose walk is an ever-winding journey of highs and lows; it's a bumpy ride. Without courage, you won't have the inner fortitude to survive setbacks, transcend adversity, or take the risks needed to move your mission forward.

More importantly, as the leader, you must also possess the courage to "en-courage" the people who your purpose picks! You must continuously model it. You must speak about it. You must educate about it. You must embody it. Courage is important because history proves that even chickens can SOAR like eagles when led by a courageous leader.

The late Dr. Maya Angelou said it best, *"Without courage, we cannot practice any other virtue with consistency,"* and my friend, your purpose will require consistency because your purpose is your baby. God gave you the vision, and it is your responsibility to bring the vision to fruition. And even if operationalizing your purpose is difficult, with courage, you can internally access exactly what you need to do what must be done.

The good news is that you have been divinely born and built for your purpose, and you have a wonderful future waiting for you. So, let your PURPOSE PICK YOUR PEOPLE® and let your purpose use the 5 Cs — character, competence, chemistry, courage, and capacity — to ensure that you are equipped for your journey. Yes, there are other qualities, but remember, these Indispensable "Cs" are foundational. You need them to build and blossom into the powerhouse that God has called you to be.

I know that none of us will live forever. But what I know for sure is that our PURPOSE may not give us more time, but it will give us more life. Your PURPOSE will stimulate your mind, speak to your heart, soothe your soul, and help you leave a legacy for generations to come.

Today, Let Your PURPOSE PICK YOUR PEOPLE®. Why? Because it is time to Soar!

43

DON'T CONNECT WITH PEOPLE WHO CAN'T SEE WHAT YOU CARRY

On your purpose journey, you will meet many people. Some people will enter your life to support you, to celebrate you, and to challenge you. They will encourage you to take risks, pursue your dreams, and execute your vision; they will be your allies. You will also meet people who will not see who you are or who you are destined to do. They will invalidate you and dismiss you, which will make you question your purpose and your ability to pursue it. It's unfortunate, but it's true.

So, as you are making friends and cultivating relationships, it is essential that you quickly recognize and connect with your allies – people who truly see and honor you. If people come into your life and refuse to acknowledge your gifts, talents, beauty, and brilliance, and cannot see that you have a divine calling on your life, you must immediately sever ties. If not, you will waste your precious time and energy trying to earn their love and to prove your worthiness. You will be tempted to jump through emotional hoops and climb through emotional tunnels to win their approval and validation. And as a result, you will physically exhaust and spiritually deplete yourself trying to convince them of your ability and value. That's dangerous! Hustling for acceptance is detrimental to the psyche and to the soul.

Sister, if a person does not accept and honor what you carry, you will spend too much of your creative energy being in warrior mode. You will always find yourself defending your dreams, explaining your goals, and protecting your vision. You will waste valuable mental energy trying to anticipate their thoughts, answering their distortions, and second-guessing your actions. You will constantly weaken and disregard your discernment, which will leave you defenseless against predators or cut off from your intuition, your inner witness. Most importantly, you will become unanchored from your truth and drift away from your true essence.

As a person of purpose, people in your life must be convinced of the call on your life and about the gifts you carry. They must know that you have a divine mission, and they must possess the emotional maturity and intellectual horsepower to hold space for you as you pursue it. If not, you will risk losing your confidence, shrinking your identity, downsizing your goals, and jeopardizing your health. You will risk losing momentum and you will mismanage life-defining moments.

My friend, I want to remind you again. If people don't appreciate and accept the gifts and talents you carry, don't connect with them. It does not matter if it is your mother, father, lover, spouse, child, employer, client, business partner, or childhood friend. You must release them, or at least, loosen the ties so you can rise and step into your destiny.

Hear me today. You are carrying something, and the world is waiting to see what God had in mind when God created you. So, only connect with people who know what you carry. That way you won't get distracted by doubts, get unfocused by fears, get mired in mediocrity, and miss out on the joy that God has waiting for you.

Are you ready?

It's time to Soar!

SECTION VI

SELF AWARENESS: THE JOURNEY TO ME

Everything you have been through was a training ground to prepare you for your purpose. Everything. Every experience, every season, every relationship, every failure, every struggle, and every success helped you see you, know you, love you, and fortify you for your divine path.

Declare Today: My truth will set me free to be who I am called to be.

44

YOU CAN'T FLY
FAR IF YOU DON'T
KNOW WHO YOU
ARE

We all want to SOAR, and we all were created to SOAR. We have all been endowed with skills, talents, and abilities that God has encoded in our DNA to help us contribute to the world. We were all uniquely made to be persistent and proficient in our pursuit of purpose.

But when we don't know who we are, we don't ascend. When we cannot identify and remove the labels, the societal stickers, the paradigms, the expectations, the conditioning, and the other constructs that conceal our true essence, we limit ourselves. We play roles. We become shape-shifters. We become chameleons. We become people pleasers. We use all of our energy and magic to accommodate what people want and expect from us, and we abandon who we are. And as a result, we are left depleted, defeated, and sometimes spiritually drained.

But when you know who you are, your truth, you feel grounded and rooted in your being. You accept that you are favored and flawed. Strong and sometimes weak. Loving and sometimes low down. Generous and sometimes greedy. Magnanimous and sometimes mean. Disciplined and sometimes distracted. Honest and sometimes hypocritical. Supportive and sometimes shady. Principled and sometimes petty. Clear and sometimes confused. Sassy and sometimes silly.

You accept ALL of you. You don't hide, defend, or protect yourself or your opinions; you own all of you. You embrace your true nature and your divine essence. You no longer ask for permission or validation to honor and express yourself. You don't fear retribution, ridicule, or rejection for defying the "shoulds." You don't imitate or mimic others to be included in the clique or to be invited to the club. You don't lower your gaze or lower your voice to make others comfortable. You refuse to acquiesce, accommodate, and alter who you are to be accepted and respected by people who don't like you or even like themselves. You refuse to be tamed and tricked into slowly giving pieces of yourself and your soul away in exchange for fake belonging.

You stand firm in your commitment to embracing all of YOU, even the parts of you that have been mocked, maligned, and mistreated. You accept your individuality and originality, and you acknowledge your duplicity. You reclaim those parts of you that were buried in fear, suppressed by shame, and compromised by conformity. And so, you fly unencumbered with the weight of expectations, demands, and rules that previously kept you confined to a sea of sameness, powerlessness, and hopelessness.

When you boldly define who you are, without apology or approval, you fly and fly and fly and fly. You fly high and far because you know what you were divinely called to do, cultivated to produce, customized to perform, and created to be. That's power! That's potential! That's unlimited possibility. That's purpose, YOUR purpose.

Hold fast to who your Creator designed you to be. Embrace and cherish your uniqueness because you will indeed fly FAR when you know who you are!

It's time to Soar Higher!

45

SAYING NO IS EASY WHEN YOU K-N-O-W

Saying "no" used to be difficult for me. Even though "no" is just a two-letter word, the word "no" used to make me so uncomfortable that I would occasionally go against my best judgment and agree to things I didn't have time to do or even like to do. Unfortunately, going against my best judgment left me feeling overwhelmed, out of alignment, and full of bitterness. Honestly, knowing that I was not honoring myself or my truth literally sucked the joy out of me.

I am not the only one who struggles with the big N-O. Even though "no" is just a little word, most of us still have a lot of fear or at least some discomfort appropriately and courageously using it. Our concern is understandable because, as children, we were taught to abandon ourselves and not heed our wishes. We were punished, rejected, or cast aside for saying the dreaded two-letter word when we wanted to assert ourselves. Since we wanted to avoid punishment, conflict, and criticism, we acquiesced; we backed down. We surrendered our desires and needs to please people, to prove ourselves worthy of love, or to be a part of a group. Suffice to say that we caved under pressure and said "yes" to others even when our souls screamed "NO," and sometimes, HELL "no!"

Here's what I know for sure. When you are clear about your divine assignment, it is easy to reject everything that contradicts and undermines your God-inspired purpose. Trust me. Saying no is empowering when you K-N-O-W that your Creator has orchestrated a path for you to fully actualize and activate your divine gifts. When God whispers your mission in your ear and speaks to your heart, "NO" becomes a welcomed boundary, a compass, and a declaration that keeps you focused on your purpose.

How do you courageously say "no" with clarity, courage, and conviction?

You...

1) Know who you are
2) Know your purpose
3) Know what you need
4) Know what you want
5) Know how you are wired to win
6) Know what success looks like for you
7) Know what self-care means to you
8) Know your priorities
9) Know that your time is valuable and irreplaceable
10) Know what gives you energy, power, and peace
11) Know how to LOVE yourself
12) Know a person's happiness is not your responsibility
13) Know what types of people you want in your life and why
14) Know what you are willing to do to SOAR
15) Know your values and your moral compass
16) Know the sound of your own internal voice
17) Know what beliefs and behavior weaken you
18) Know what is good for your overall health

19) Know what ignites you and what fights you

20) Know how you learn and process information

21) Know your history and heritage

22) Know who fills you and who drains you

23) Know how to deal with fear

24) Know how you want to be remembered

25) Most of all, KNOW GOD for yourself

If you don't know the answers to these questions, pause. Spend time alone to get to know yourself more intimately. Wrestle with a few concepts and precepts. Peel back all of the false identities and widen the narrow constructs that society imposed on you and the ones that you forced on yourself. Reflect. Listen. Interrogate the answers until you feel that sense of peace that only comes from knowing that you K-N-O-W. Then, relax in that knowing trusting that your sacred "no" provides the space for your holy "yes."

If you want to pursue your purpose and SOAR, and I know you do, make sure you KNOW what you need to know so you can say "no." Did you get that? That was a mouth full.

It's time for you to SOAR.

46

GET STILL, BUT
DON'T GET STUCK

Are you stuck? No judgment. I have been stuck too!

Truth be told… sometimes it's hard getting unstuck. When you know a decision must be made about a relationship, a business partnership, or a career change, but you don't know what to do, it is tempting to hesitate and procrastinate. Sometimes delaying a decision gives us the illusion of relief, especially when the stakes are high.

So, what do you do when you MUST make decisions that have life-altering consequences, which all of our important decisions have? What do you do when you don't have experience or when there's no history or precedent? What do you do when you have to choose between the right choice and the best choice? What do you do?

You get still. You slow down. You get quiet. You analyze the data in your mind. You process the wisdom in your heart. You commune with the Spirit in your soul. You sift through the information with every part of your being. You also discuss the circumstances with your advisors because the Bible reminds us there is safety in the counsel of many. Then, you wait. You wait to hear what your SOUL says because your strength lies in your soul, your "knowing" lies in your soul, and your power lies in your soul.

While you are reflecting, keep asking yourself and the Spirit......

- Who am I?
- What do I want?
- Who do I need to be to achieve this goal?
- What do my dreams and goals need me to do?
- What is my purpose calling forth?
- What do I really care about, and why?
- What innate gifts and talents can I activate to support me today?
- Who do I need to become in this season?
- What do I need to let go of?
- What's trying to be birthed in me and through me?
- What needs to be healed, explored, retrieved, and released?
- What needs to be said?
- Where do I need to create more space for what I want in my life?
- What has God given me to share with humanity?
- What values do I need to express more bravely to fulfill my purpose?

Ask the questions and then wait and listen. Remove all distractions so you can access the deepest recesses of your soul and hear your intuition — your inner witness. The answers will come.

As you pursue your new path and create a new narrative, more of your true nature will unfold. The newness may initially cause you some internal angst but don't be alarmed; that's just a sign of growth. You may also find yourself in the "messy middle"

— you are too far away from your past but have not arrived in your future. That may be uncomfortable too, but trust the process because you are on your way. You are in the midst of an incredible, zigzagging journey on your way back to YOU so you can carry out your divine mission, your purpose.

Remember, as you progress on the path to purpose, questions will come to test your resolve and to refine your mission. Questions like... What if I miss the mark or make a mistake? What if I get off course or make a wrong turn? What if I fall on my face or misinterpret God's voice? What if I get stranded because I lack resources? What if? What if? What if? The questions will never end because the questions are there to expand your mind so you can see potential even in the bleakest times and places.

My friend, blazing a new path triggers insecurities and often fills us with doubt. That's to be expected. Just know that whatever action you take will be an important part of your journey. If you accomplish your goal, you will get a positive result. GREAT! If you do NOT achieve your goal, you will get a great lesson. GREAT! Both outcomes are valuable and will provide wisdom for the next steps of your journey.

The good news is that when it comes to discovering and uncovering your purpose, there is no such thing as failure. Everything that happens provides greater clarity about your life's work, your purpose.

So get still and then get going!

You can do it. I know you can. It's my testimony too.

It's time to Soar!

47

DON'T LET
WEARINESS
MAKE YOU WEAK

Have you ever been so tired that you started making dumb decisions? I mean tired, bone-tired, so tired that you committed to something because you didn't have the energy to negotiate or explain your "no." I mean tired, so tired, that you forgot to pick up your child from daycare, forgot to pay the water bill, forgot to put gas in your car, and forgot to eat dinner. TIRED!

As a single mom, I wasn't just tired; I was weary. I was so emotionally fatigued trying to be all things to all people that I actually forgot to be something for myself. I was exhausted, so exhausted that I shuffled to work, dragged myself home, begged myself to cook, bargained with myself to exercise, and pleaded to God to help me endure another day. I willed myself to smile, I pushed myself to listen, I pressured myself to care, and I "shamed" myself to give away what I didn't have to give. I was a manipulator, and I constantly manipulated me. I was weary.

As a Black woman in corporate America, I wasn't just tired; I was weary. I was spiritually exhausted trying to assimilate into a culture that professed diversity but practiced division. I was tired of the color-blind comments, the affirmative action tirades, and the reverse-racism claims that were used to invalidate my experiences and nullify my existence. I was dog-tired of the white fragility that quickly surfaced when I shared examples of the mistreatment I endured at the hands of biased managers. I was tired of the white-centering that was used to neutralize my contributions and comments when I called attention to racist slights. I was tired of being characterized as insensitive, touchy, colorful, or aggressive when I challenged unfair practices or when I just had an innovative idea for a marketing campaign. I wasn't just tired; I was weary.

Yes, I was weary, not just tired, weary. Weary is beyond being physically fatigued. Weary is when you are so spiritually dissatisfied and emotionally frustrated that your strength is sapped. Weary is when you are so mentally depleted and spiritually numb that you become immobilized and paralyzed. Weary is when you are so out of alignment, out of sync, and so out of your mind that you cease to thrive. You exist as a fraction of who you really are. Weary!

I was weary. Here's the sad part. My chronic weariness made me weak, and it made me desperate. I was so desperate for help that I allowed people to rob me. I was so desperate for love that I allowed people to abuse me. I was so desperate to be seen as a competent professional that I accepted assignments that jeopardized my health and threatened my ability to parent my son. I was so desperate to keep up the façade of being a superwoman that I let people pile more responsibilities on my plate even when I was already overwhelmed, over-committed, and over-extended. I wasn't just tired; I was weary, but I never said a word.

During those painful periods of my life, I wish I could say that I was courageous and confident enough to stand up for myself, but I was not. I wish I could say that I dared to stop the over-committing, over-functioning, over-performing, and over-everything, but I did not. Fortunately, my body did what I could not do. My body stopped; it gave out. It said NO, and no more. My body refused to go on. It started a revolt.

My body's revolt was frightening. The protests forced me to be a patient at a few hospitals because my cardiac arteries spasmed and refused to calm down. It seemed as if my blood vessels even objected to the crazy, chaotic life that I was living, and they didn't care what type of medicines were prescribed to pacify them. My arteries wanted and needed rest. They were worn out by the caffeine-induced highs, the adrenaline-loaded pace, and the insomnia-filled nights. My body was weary, and it was going to have the last word. Rest or die.

I had to learn a hard, but life-changing lesson. I had to learn that weariness can make you weak. Weariness can make you vulnerable to temptations and make you defenseless to seduction, particularly when you don't feed and heed your soul. Weariness can also encourage you to compromise your integrity because you are starved for rest, a rescue, or a respite. It's sad to say, but weary people can't be trusted. Not because they are malicious, but because they are exhausted.

Weariness makes you weak and keeps you weak when you cram your life with meaningless activities and trivial tasks in a feeble attempt to avoid the truth. What was my truth? I was unfulfilled and frustrated. In fact, I was miserable. I had created a life that did not represent my true nature, values, or morals. I wasn't living; I was masquerading. I was impersonating a woman that I didn't even like or know. I was lost.

I am not sure when or how I got so off track; pretending to be somebody else was so gradual that I cannot pinpoint the start of my detachment or decline. What I know for sure is that I had lived my life trying to prove to the world that I mattered. I tried to convince the world that I was smart, that I was capable, that I belonged, and that I was desirable. I tried to prove to the world that I was not a stereotype, a statistic, a second-class citizen, or a slut. I tried to prove that I deserved a seat at the table only to realize that I was on the menu. I was on the hit list to be slaughtered and sacrificed for somebody else's gain. I was weary.

Trying to prove my worth made me weary. It made me weak. It made me a wreck. It made me a whiner. It made me wither. It made me wallow. It made me feel worthless in ways that dishonored my soul. I was weary.

I had to learn that the only way to heal the weariness was to be honest. I had to acknowledge that I carried burdens that were not mine. I created problems that were not mine. I catered to people who didn't matter, and I cared about things that were outside of my control. In my effort to show my worthiness, I tried to rescue, revitalize, and restore people and situations that were not my responsibilities, and outside of my divine assignment; I had to accept that I was not God! But most importantly, I had to admit that I needed to heal those deep wounds that motivated me to behave in dysfunctional, self-loathing ways. I had to admit that the emotional scars from years of institutionalized racism and societal bullying had driven me to extreme exhaustion and almost to the brink of death. I had to admit that I was living to "prove" my potential and not living to pursue my purpose. I was weary.

When I released people, their problems, and their perceptions, I started to heal. When I finally accepted that I only had to love me, love my son, and love God, I released the guilt that left holes in my soul. When I realized that I had nothing to prove, nothing to defend, and nothing to protect, I started to slow down. I got out of the rat race and stepped off the corporate roller-coaster. And thankfully, I began to sleep.

After resting my fatigued soul, I started a journey, a healing journey. Thankfully, my journey introduced me to the POWER OF PURPOSE, and I learned that purpose is what gives life. I learned that purpose is what gives meaning, provides joy, and results in fulfillment. Purpose is what energizes your soul and stimulates your mind. Purpose. I learned that purpose is God's work.

I realized that I was weary because I was not in purpose. I was not doing what I was born to do. I was just hustling and trying to be something that I was never meant to be. I was chasing the carrot on a stick, but the stick could not give me what I needed—soul satisfaction, meaning, and "mattering."

I also learned that I was spiritually dying because living a lie had ruptured my soul, and left a hole, a God-sized hole. And that hole created a gaping wound that I tried to fill with profits, popularity, and perks. And the challenging part was that I wasn't aware that I created the wound that was killing me. Me. I created the internal turmoil because I thought success was external; I was convinced that success came from others. I didn't know that true happiness only comes from within. So here I was working overtime to gain the whole world, and in essence, I was losing my health and traumatizing my soul.

This is what I know for sure: if you are doing something that is outside of your power and out of your purpose, release it. Put it down and walk away. If something or someone does not serve your highest good, your purpose, give yourself permission to make a different choice. If you are dating someone who is shrinking your goals, blurring your vision, or controlling your mind, let them go. If you are working for a company that is "aggressing" and oppressing you because you are "packaged" in a certain body, race, sexual orientation, or gender, create an exit strategy. If you are holding on to "shoulds," definitions, and traditions that you have outgrown, drop them now. Release them so you can rest.

Remember, you are not bound to the behaviors and beliefs of your past. You are not responsible for the needs, desires, or expectations of others. It is only your divine duty to use your time, talent, and treasure to find and fulfill your divine assignment, your purpose, your calling, your God-agenda.

My friend, you can't win when you are weary. But when you are honest about what you want, what you need, and what you have been destined to do, you will rest. Your energy will be restored, and your faith renewed. Your body will be rehabilitated, and your spirit will be revived. Your imagination will return, and your joy will reappear.

You don't have to be weary. You don't need to hustle. You don't have to struggle. You don't need to jeopardize your health in exchange for status and success. Just be the person your Creator designed you to be, and you will have peace, a peace that the world didn't give you, and can never take away.

Declare Today: I will embrace peace and pursue my purpose.

It is time to Soar!

48

FOLLOW YOUR HEART ONLY AFTER YOU KNOW WHAT'S IN IT

Has anyone ever told you to follow your own heart? The advice would be useful if more people actually knew what was in their own hearts. The truth is that most people don't know what they feel or why they feel what they feel. They just have emotions without investigation or reflection.

But what if what's in your heart is not your truth? What if your desires are really not your own or inconsistent with your true nature? What if you are only choosing what you have seen, heard, or been taught? What if you are selecting something that feels close or "almost right" but are left hoping, yearning, and desiring for more? What if you are just picking what's safe because your heart's desires are unpopular, unorthodox, or too polarizing to admit? What if you are altering and adorning yourself to make yourself more likable and palatable? What if you are blending and assimilating but are leaving pieces of your soul behind? What if your heart holds ideas that have never been seen or shared before? What if?

There are no guarantees that following your heart will definitely lead to your exact purpose, but following your heart is still the best way to uncover your true desires and live your dreams. Even if your heart sometimes leads you down the wrong path, following it will still help you learn a lot about yourself. Let's face it. Nobody likes detours, but sometimes being wrong leads you to what's "right" for you. Trust me; being wrong can provide valuable insight to get you back on track when you feel confused, misaligned, and overwhelmed by life.

If you want to feel more confident about following your heart, take time to get to know yourself. Peel back the layers of pain, expectations, and social programming to identify what YOU want and desire. Discover what aligns with you, what activates you, and what awakens the deepest parts of your soul. Sift through all of your experiences to identify what subjects delighted you, ignited you, and excited you. Examine your unspoken interests and your secret needs to see why they have not been expressed or cultivated. Visualize what fulfillment and flow look like and feel like for you. Question every aspect of your life and critique your deepest beliefs. Then wait and listen. And, slowly but surely, the innermost parts of your heart will slowly be revealed, and you will know yourself in a more intimate, profound way.

Remember, you must be patient. Knowing what's in your heart may not surface quickly. Heart discovery is often a long-layered journey, but it is worth the trip because knowing your heart will help you build a life that aligns with who you are. It will help you be congruent so you don't live in hypocrisy, duplicity, or regret. Most of all, knowing your heart helps you stay connected to your sacred self – your inner knowing – so you can live your values, live your vision, and live in victory.

When I first met my client Bea, she was a high-powered

attorney who worked in a competitive law firm. She was the "go-to" person when legal cases became contentious because she was an effective negotiator. She had a reputation for being calm, being fair, and being able to find common ground even in the most hotly contested cases. She was extremely gifted in seeing opportunities for compromise and collaboration.

Despite her success and acclaim, Bea was exhausted not only from her workload but from acting. Yes, Bea was acting like she loved her career, but secretly she was bored and burnt out. She never had a heart for law, but she felt compelled to go to law school because her parents were lawyers, and her siblings were lawyers. Most of all, she disliked the constant combative nature of her job. The constant back and forth drained her energy and filled her with angst. She wanted peace and wanted a profession that allowed her to use her skills for peaceful reconciliation and racial healing.

When I asked Bea what was in her heart, she said she didn't know. However, she was quick to share all of the reasons why continuing as a lawyer was the best decision for her. She talked about status, connections, and money. Her list was long and detailed. Even after constant questioning, she continued to rationalize her decision to stay at the law firm despite the impact that it was having on her health and soul. Just for the record. I called her on rationalizing because to constantly rationalize really means to tell *"rationale lies."* You know, rationale lies – the excuses that masquerade as logic that persuade us to stay stuck in painful situations.

With the skills of an effective litigator, Bea tried to convince me or really convince herself that changing her profession would be financially irresponsible and selfish. I said, "Bea, I heard from your head. If your heart had a chance to speak, what would it say?" Silence. Slowly tears flowed, which were followed by deep soul-purifying sobbing.

Bea said, "My heart would say that I hate my job, that I am living my family's dream, but I don't know what to do now. My heart will say that it's scared to leave, scared to stay, scared to make a wrong decision. My heart will say that I am totally disconnected from myself, and I don't know what to dream or how to create my dream. My heart will beg for peace."

During our time together, Bea and I took a deep dive into her heart to uncover what she really desired for her life. We explored her childhood, identified her gifts that made her unique, and discovered what types of settings brought her peace and joy. Little by little, Bea was able to let go of her old definition of success and an old identity that kept her trapped in a profession that was stealing her joy and preventing her from doing what she felt called to do, reconciliation work.

Bea's experience and responses are not uncommon. There are millions of people living lives that don't resonate with their hearts. Each day millions of people drag themselves to jobs they hate and spend eight to ten hours a day feeling disconnected from their souls and disenchanted with their careers. Some people have felt hopeless for so long that they have resigned themselves to living in perpetual sadness and chronic defeat. They have not only settled, but they have also sunk, and they keep sinking and floating farther away from who they are.

During our time together, Bea discovered what was in her heart, and she revamped her entire life. She quit her lucrative, but soul-draining job. She started a company and used her exceptional negotiation skills to help organizations transform conflict into creative decision-making. Truth be told, growing her business has not been easy. Bea is still working long hours, but she is not exhausted; she's engaged, enthusiastic, and energetic. She feels as though she is making a difference that will not only help companies but also help people engage in conflict in healthier ways in their personal lives.

It was not easy for Bea to change her life, and it may not be easy for you to change yours either. But changing your life becomes less complicated when you understand what's in your heart. Remember, your heart knows more than your mouth can articulate, and more than your mind can comprehend; your heart knows the truth. So, search and study your heart. Then, follow your heart after you know what's in it. That way, you can ensure that you will live more harmoniously, authentically, and courageously in the world and experience true fulfillment.

Remember, you can't follow what you don't know. But when you know what you know, you will have peace, joy, and prosperity.

Check your heart.

It's your time to Soar!

49

YOU ARE NOT DONE UNTIL YOU'RE DEAD

The other day I received a message from a distraught client who said, "I am too old to start all over again." The entire email lamented the challenges of getting older. She sounded incredibly defeated and resigned to spending the rest of her years in apathy, loneliness, sickness, and sadness. In her opinion, there was nothing to look forward to or to live for anymore.

The email message resonated with me because our culture is so obsessed with age that sometimes I wonder if I missed my moment too. It's not that I feel "old," whatever that's supposed to feel like. But, some days I wonder if it is too late, or if I am too elderly to do something amazing. The truth is, every now and then, I wonder if my age disqualifies me from greatness, happiness, or genuine joy. I sometimes even wonder if I still have enough energy to pursue my dreams like I did when I was younger, or if I will be forced to settle for being a "has been," an old prune, a relic, or a blast from the past. Does that ever happen to you?

My opinion about aging developed from observing the mothers in the church, you know, the ones who sit in the front pews and wear the big hats. As a child, I closely watched the church mothers and got the impression that at a certain age, you stop living and you happily retire. Old age, being over 50, was a time for you to sit down, shut up, take your teeth out, dye your grey hair, put on your good wig, wear dresses that look like potato sacks, babysit your grandkids, volunteer at hospitals, and regularly attend funerals.

Now that I am in my mid-50s, I am not interested in taking out my teeth; my teeth still look great. I am not interested in making funerals my primary source of recreation and social contact. I am not interested in wearing shapeless clothes; I work out too hard not to display my bulging, yet feminine muscles. I am not interested in sitting down or doing "old people" stuff, whatever that is. I don't want to relax and just become invisible, dispensable, and disposable. I don't want to sit around and wait to die. Who wants to do that? I don't want to retire from life, maybe from my job, but not from living. I want to live honestly and openly once and for all. I don't know about you, but I still want to contribute to the world. My tank is still full.

Yes, my tank is still full because I have more potential, more dreams, and more wisdom in me. I have not maxed out on my ability and desires. I have not exhausted all of my talents and gifts. I have not said everything I need to say. When I reflect on my life, I realized that I have not fully lived, yet. I am just beginning to learn about the value and the joy of life.

I have not fully lived yet because when I was younger, I made most of my decisions based on what was socially acceptable or what was deemed "culturally appropriate" for a Black woman like me. I unknowingly narrowed my life down to the status quo, and I didn't even attempt to do anything outside of the norm. I stayed in the box and in my place. Of course, I had all types of goals and aspirations, and most of my goals were within my reach and my skill set. However, I held back and never discovered what I was fully capable of doing, being, or creating.

When I was younger, I think I was just too scared, felt too invisible, and was just too tired from battling naysayers to bloom. I was resilient, but after three decades of fighting for a seat at the table, I was worn down and worn out from the trauma of working in corporate America. For over thirty years, I fought battle after battle, trying to navigate a system that not only had glass ceilings but systemic barriers that prevented my ascension. And I didn't even know that creating my own opulent table was even an option until I was forty. But that's another story.

But now you and I, we, are at a new phase in our lives. We know without a doubt that we have MORE in us. We know without a doubt that we can do what we have dreamed about, thought about, and prayed about. We recognize those old paradigms and decades of inequity didn't squash our hopes or kill our dreams. We now know that those boxes, closets, labels, stickers, and categories that reduced and restricted us were inaccurate, manufactured, and oppressive. We know that those expensive purchases and walls of credentials we earned didn't make us feel as good as we thought they would either. We know a lot now. Those first five decades of our lives provided valuable insight about ourselves and the world. Now, we know what we want and we created our own definitions of happiness. We earned our wisdom the hard way, and we have the battle scars and years of success to prove it.

My friend, we ain't done or dead yet. We are in a beautiful, exciting season in our lives that offers unlimited opportunities. We have extensive knowledge; our experiences alone give us a head start in our pursuits if we tap into and leverage what we have learned. Just think about it. We now know not to chase shiny objects because we have learned that everything that glitters ain't gold. We now know not to judge people by outer appearances because expensive clothes can never conceal a poor character. We are now less concerned about flashy, fast cars because we know that fast cars mean nothing if you don't have spiritual direction. We no longer need to chase love because we have learned to deeply and courageously love ourselves. We are not trying to keep up with the Joneses because we know that the Joneses are broke, busted, and broken. We now know not to believe everything people say because we have learned that humans are inherently flawed, fickle, and sometimes emotionally feeble. We now realize that some of the lessons we learned as children were based on fear and false narratives. We now know that we don't have to follow a particular religious doctrine because we know how to practice our faith in a way that connects us to God. We now have wisdom, life-changing wisdom, that can alter the trajectory of our lives. We are now uniquely positioned for greatness and genuine success.

My friend, everything we have been through has equipped us to contribute to the world in a significant and meaningful way. So, who cares if we are not as adept at technology? We don't need as many gadgets; we have guts that can only be gained through experience. Who cares if we can't run as fast as we used to? We don't need to run as fast; we can walk with intention because we finally know where we are going. So what if our eyesight has dimmed? We now know how to walk by faith and by the sound of our intuition, God's voice.

Listen to me: you ain't done or dead yet. Stop sitting at home waiting for the hearse to pick you up. Do now what you didn't dare to do when you were younger. Wear what you want to wear. Love who you want to love. Be fabulous, be carefree, be illuminating, be playful, be flexible, be adventurous, and be daring! Immerse yourself in creativity. Dance on the table. Write a book. Share your vision. Go back to school. Open your mind. Do whatever you want to do to feel energized, excited, and sexy for a change. Be free! Don't worry about what others think. You spent enough decades trying to make everybody happy. Do what pleases you and feeds your soul. And, most of all, pursue your purpose.

My friend, you are not done or dead yet. The game is just beginning. It's prime time, and it is your time. It's time to reclaim your dreams. It's time to revitalize your calling. It's time to renew your spirit. It's time to rehabilitate your heart. It's time to review your finances. It's time to rediscover your passions. It's time to re-prioritize your life so you can experience all of the riches that life offers.

You still have a purpose because you are still alive. You still have a divine assignment, which means that you have more living and giving to do. You are not done because you ain't dead, yet. So, get up! Burn out, but don't rust out. You don't have time for remorse, resentment, or regrets. It's your time to Soar!

50

IF YOU PUT A LOW VALUE ON YOU, THE WORLD WILL NOT INCREASE YOUR RATE

One day one of my friends, let's call her Sue, told me, "You act like a discount diva." If you know me at all, you can imagine that I didn't respond well. I felt shocked by her opinion, and her willingness to say something so hurtful to me in such a casual way surprised me. My face got hot, my mouth got dry, and my body stiffened. I instantly felt an adrenaline rush and my fight-or-flight response kicked in; I was ready for war.

Thankfully, I had lots of experience and training in conflict management, and so I didn't initially become too defensive. I was irritated, but I didn't show it. I was calm, professional, and articulate, or at least I thought I was.

I peacefully and patiently explained to Sue why her perception of me was totally inconsistent with how I navigated in the world. I was confident that my explanation provided the insight she needed to change her view of me. Because, based on how I saw myself, she was wrong, dead wrong!

When my carefully constructed explanation failed to change her mind about me being a discount diva, I intensified my argument. I had to. Something inside of me felt threatened, insulted, and frustrated by her assessment. Her views were inconsistent with my track record. But despite my rebuttal, she didn't budge. In her mind, I was a discount diva.

You can imagine that her unwillingness to agree with me angered me. Honestly, I was outraged. My ego went on overdrive, and I started enumerating my accomplishments. I reminded her about my degrees, my promotions, and my credentials. For some reason, I felt compelled to change Sue's mind because being called a discount diva was offensive, belittling, and mean. Most of all, her assessment hurt my feelings.

Despite my persuasion and a little manipulation, Sue did not waver, and she was not intimidated by me either. I continued to challenge her hypothesis by listing every award, every achievement, and every accolade again. I thought she must not have heard me clearly the first time because her opinion hadn't changed. You see, I was on a mission to change her perception and honestly, deep inside my soul, I felt like a 6-year-old child who was having a tantrum. I wanted to yell, "I am not a freaking discount diva. I am a queen, darn it." I wanted to use the other word, and knowing me, I probably did.

When Sue refused to recant her comment, I stopped trying to convince her, and I started yelling. I mean, I literally had a meltdown. I got emotional, aggressive, and a bit weird. I slowly unraveled, and without me even realizing it, hot tears started rolling down my face and I just lost it. The pain had cut me deeply, and I was emotionally overwhelmed. I was a hysterical mess.

I was obviously distraught and my friend's indifference to my feelings angered and saddened me. I thought to myself, "how could she be my friend and be so blind to my accomplishments and my professional prowess? How could she be so dismissive and apathetic about my position?" We both knew that I was a top performer, and I had the guts, the goods, and the genius to prove it. I was amazing, right? I was impressive, right? I was all that and a bag of chips, right? I mattered, right?

My "tell, sell, yell" strategy didn't faze her. My crocodile tears, runny nose, and quivering chin didn't move or influence her either. She didn't sway in her assessment of me, and for some reason, I started to weep loudly and uncontrollably. I cried from the depths of my soul even though I didn't know why I was so affected and offended by her assessment. It was just her opinion, not a scientifically-proven fact. She didn't have data to substantiate that I was a discount diva. She wasn't an authority on "divahood." But if she did not have a Ph.D. in "diva-ology" or wasn't a diva expert, why was I so hurt?

After my emotional meltdown, we sat silently because we didn't know what to say to each other. We were both bewildered by the exchange and didn't know how to proceed. Who knew that one comment would create such an emotional tsunami, and a public one at that?

After about twenty minutes, I regained my composure and was able to reflect on her words. Being called a "discount diva" jarred me so much that it made me wonder if she was telling the truth. I wanted to dismiss her opinion, but I couldn't. She was my friend. I knew she loved and cared about me. She had proven her friendship and commitment to me for over twenty years. So, I could not just disregard or ignore her perspective. I wanted to dismiss her, but I could not let my arrogance rob me of an opportunity to learn and grow. My friend was a reliable and fair truth-teller and was always one of my biggest supporters. She had earned the right to challenge and critique me.

After I apologized for my uncharacteristic outburst, I asked her how she experienced me. She gently and generously shared her opinion about my energy, how I easily detached from people, how my busyness was a defense mechanism, and how I was a people-pleaser. Wow! Her remarks were hard to swallow, but I stayed present, realizing that she was giving me a gift.

She shared examples of my behavior and offered solutions. Her feedback was thorough and revealing. Even though hearing her perspective was painful and sometimes embarrassing, my intuition told me I could believe her insight. Her words didn't feel vindictive or cloaked in jealousy. In fact, her words were laced with love, concern, and mutual respect.

That evening, I listened and learned a lot about myself. I wasn't able to capture and digest everything she said; it was overwhelming, to say the least. But I took notes as best I could so I could review what she said to ask questions later. Her courageous and thoughtful assessment of me was eye-opening. Her assessment pulled off my protective mask, uprooted some hidden insecurities, and illuminated some deep fears in my soul. I felt exposed. I felt small. I felt stupid. I felt angry. And I felt numb, probably because numb felt better than accepting how she viewed me and had perceived me for years.

I didn't sleep well that night. I tossed and turned because truth has a way of piercing holes in your emotional armor and breaking down your defenses. It left me feeling naked, scared, and vulnerable. I didn't know what to do or how to process all of her revelations, but I knew that I had to peel the proverbial onion to get to the truth. My veneer of success, confidence, and self-love was shattered. I had to go within to see what beliefs were influencing the self-sabotaging behaviors that were obvious to my friend but hidden from me. I had to see myself with new eyes if I wanted to address old behaviors that were not serving me.

After a few months of therapy and introspection, I finally had to admit that I was indeed a discount diva. Yes, I finally accepted that I was not valuing myself and that I didn't require others to honor me either. Of course, that realization was painful. I also realized that for years, I hid my feelings of insecurity and inadequacy behind a polished persona. No, I didn't hide on purpose; I was an unconscious chameleon. I was a shapeshifter, and I was proficient at it, so proficient that I could put on and take off personas in seconds without even knowing it. I was a masterful actress who performed but honestly hustled for acceptance and belonging because that's what I wanted most – to be loved.

After months of hard, healing work, I acknowledged the truth. I admitted that I regularly allowed people to violate my boundaries. I did not protect my time, my intellectual property, my finances, or my emotional health. My floppy boundaries had proven to be fatal, yet I had failed to adjust them to support my sanity, livelihood, and legacy.

I accepted that I tolerated abusive treatment. I allowed people to disparage me behind my back, lie about my intentions, embarrass me publicly, ridicule my dreams, give harsh critiques without provocation, laugh when I felt hurt, discredit my opinions, send me emotionally crippling messages, and disrespectfully talk to me with no repercussions.

I admitted that I didn't demand respect because I didn't want to be perceived as mean, entitled, or uppity. I had to painfully acknowledge that I dreaded rejection and abandonment, the same fears that plagued me as a child. I also had to confess that my childhood trauma was driving my life into a ditch.

Regretfully, I had to accept that even though I was successful that I was hiding my real talents. I had to acknowledge that I had been socialized, colonized, and ostracized out of my brilliance by people who didn't look like me or respect me. I had to admit that I downplayed my giftedness, under-shared my ideas, and did just enough to get by and to get along. I had to own that performed, smiled, and sometimes stooped to "step-and- fetch-it-like" behavior in a way that dishonored me.

The revelations were crippling and debilitating, and for days, I was emotionally paralyzed. For months, I deeply reflected on what I discovered, and everything inside of me wanted to resist the truth. But the truth does not need to be acknowledged or accepted to be true. Truth can stand alone, and it was my responsibility to stand under it. And, I had to stand under it; I had no choice, especially if I wanted to learn how to stop giving my power and dignity away. If I wanted to understand why I was minimizing, compromising, and sacrificing myself to accommodate others, I had to tell the truth, so I could heal enough to create a better reality. I had to allow my friend's truth to penetrate my heart so I could challenge the dysfunctional ways I engaged with others and abandoned myself.

I must admit that therapy felt like surgery, and in some ways, it was surgery. It was open heart surgery because I was forced to look inside my heart to see my unresolved trauma, my struggles, and my weaknesses. I had to see how I undervalued myself, how I undercut myself, and how I underappreciated myself. I had to admit that I accepted what people gave me even if they only offered crumbs of approval, friendship, support, or compassion.

The emotional surgery was excruciating, but I was committed to cut out and cut away every cancerous cell of self-loathing and self-hate so I could heal. I wanted, but really needed, to reclaim my true identity and resuscitate those dead parts of me that had been suffocated and silenced in exchange for belonging. I knew that I deserved love and acceptance, but the path to both started by loving the person in the mirror, ME.

Being called a discount diva was emotionally agonizing, yet it was purposeful. It made me realize that if I put a low value on me, my work, my presence, and my contributions, the world would not willingly increase my rate. The world would let me settle for a dime of love, support, and success even if what I offered was worth a dollar. News Flash: accepting dimes for dollars is a guarantee that you will remain broke, broken, and busted.

I learned more about myself in six months than I did in ten years. I realized that I was not thriving, but only surviving in the world because I was playing not to lose, instead of playing to win. With that awareness came the ability to make changes and choices—to be my own best friend and my fiercest advocate. And, boy, did I make changes. I mustered all the wisdom, courage, and strength that I had and created a new reality. I pruned. I planned. I prepared. I re-positioned. I deleted everything that did not support who I was and who I was becoming in the world.

After coaching hundreds of clients, I have learned that my experience is not unique. Throughout our lives, all of us have believed or behaved like we were discount divas. We all at one time in our lives have put a low value on ourselves because of our past, our pain, or because our programming convinced us we were not worthy of love, joy, peace, and abundance. But we are not desperate discounts; we are divine designs. We are premium packages. We are priceless gems worthy of God's goodness and grace.

Over the next week, spend time with yourself. Think about how you engage with others. Consider how you treat yourself and how you allow others to treat you. Are you allowing people to discount you in ways that may be eroding your self-confidence and self-worth? Are you stepping over dollars of compassion and accepting dimes of criticism because you feel guilty, unworthy, or inadequate of your success? Are you accepting crumbs of toleration when you are worthy of a crown of celebration? Here is the hardest question: Are you willing to make choices to increase your value in your OWN eyes?

Remember…you are valuable! You are vital! You are valued! So set your own rate. Embrace high standards. Navigate from a high place, a royal place. Require that respect be a prerequisite to engage with you.

My friend, you have a purpose, and your purpose requires an evolved, positive self-perception. How you see yourself will determine how high and how fast you soar. So, are you ready to see yourself through fresh eyes?

Declare Today: I am royalty and I will own who I am and celebrate my value because I have a purpose.

It's your time to Soar!

51

YOU CAN'T MAKE "BUILDING" DECISIONS FROM A BROKEN PLACE

A few days ago, Jenna (not her real name) told me she was getting married. Getting married? What? You just met that guy.

Just for the record, I believe in love at first sight, and I believe in soul mates. I also believe in marriage counseling, patience, and vetting because love decisions that are made quickly rarely end well. Quick passion can turn the best of us into quick fools.

Since I know Jenna's history, I inquired about her sprint to the altar. I was not judging her, but I was concerned. She had been married twice already, and neither one of her marriages lasted more than a year. So why the urgency? Why was she making a mad dash to the altar again?

I won't pour all of her tea, but I believe that Jenna was using marriage to help assuage her feelings of worthlessness. Having a man, even one she barely knew, made her feel attractive, valued, and desired. As my son would say, Jenna was "thirsty." She was so desperate for love that she was willing to forgo her due diligence. She didn't do a background check or check his credit score, which, if you asked me, should be a prerequisite for marriage. She didn't even know if the man she was engaged to even had a job, possessed integrity, had any ambition, or knew God. Jenna felt so worthless that she traded her good sense for a mystery man. And he was a mystery; nobody knew anything about him, and neither did she. All Jenna knew was that he a pulse and was breathing and unfortunately, that was enough for her.

It's easy to judge Jenna and her hasty decision. But should we? We all have made some foolish decisions in our lives, especially when we felt unloved, unheard, unsupported, and unfulfilled. That's why some of us are in emotionally draining, soul-sucking marriages today. And picking the wrong partners is not the only crazy decision we have made. Let's be honest. If some of our irrational decisions and scandalous misdeeds got plastered on social media, some of us would go into hiding, never to be seen again. I know I would because when I was wounded, I did a few things that would make you clutch your pearls. That's why I tell so much of my business today because I want to share my mistakes before somebody else shares them. At least if I admit what I did, I can provide context to explain my flawed reasoning.

Jenna's inexplicable sprint to the altar reminds all of us of something that we must remember in our own lives; you can't make building decisions from a broken place. It's impossible to be strategic when you are scared, thoughtful when you are toxic, deliberate when you are doubtful, or fruitful when you are fearful. It's impossible to see options and possibilities through the lens of inadequacy, intimidation, and desperation. You cannot build on brokenness. Brokenness not only destabilizes you today but jeopardizes your purpose tomorrow.

So, what's a building decision?

Building decisions are decisions that improve, bolster, and

elevate your life. They are the decisions that ensure that you consistently practice self-care, participate in self-development, and engage in relationships that support who you are and who you are becoming.

Building decisions are also decisions that align with our destinies, our visions, and our unique spiritual S.H.A.P.E.S. (spiritual gifts, heart, abilities, personalities, experiences, and strengths). They are vital, calculated, God-directed decisions that we can only execute when we have healed enough to see past our pain. Until our old wounds are addressed, we can't fully access our internal wisdom or rely on our internal infrastructure to challenge our stories, sever toxic relationships, and activate our courage. Let's face it. Building decisions require us to be emotionally strong, bold, and grounded because building decisions shape and position us for the future and prepare us for our purpose.

So, before you make a decision that can affect the trajectory of your life, honestly assess where you are emotionally, mentally, and spiritually. Assess if you are in a healthy place. Determine if you are too broken to clearly see your current reality, and if you are emotionally sober enough to think deeply about your long-term goals. Determine if there are slight cracks in your spirit, mind, or heart where your strength and self-respect may be leaking out. Ask yourself if your self-worth and self-value are seeping out of your soul and leaving pockets of pain that are destabilizing you. Consider if you have old narratives that need to be examined, so you don't succumb to your old conditioning and cycles of victimization that keep you trapped in dysfunction and mediocrity.

Remember, there is no shame in being or feeling broken. And just for the record, brokenness is never your permanent identity. Brokenness is a temporary condition that can be changed through healing, coaching, and community. And, admitting and addressing your brokenness is an admirable act of courage and self-love because nothing expands your life more than healing and "skilling" your brokenness.

I admit that throughout my life I made many life-altering decisions from a broken place. There were times when I was too depressed, anxious, and afraid to choose what was best for me. And guess what? My ill-advised choices only intensified the turmoil that already existed in my life. I dated more liars. I mismanaged more money. I neglected my self-care. I also did a few other things that I am too embarrassed to share. That's why I know for sure that you cannot make long-term, life-sustaining, career-building decisions when your head is cluttered, and when your spirit is troubled, and when your confidence is shattered. No way.

Even though I am emotionally healthy now, I still have areas of my life that are shaky and require support. Sometimes I still get triggered and say and do things that defy reason. I still feel the urge to numb myself with food when I am lonely, over-commit when I feel invisible, and isolate myself when I feel embarrassed. I am a work in progress. If we are honest, we all are under construction in some aspect of our lives.

This is what I know about you: You have dreams, goals, and a divine purpose for your life. You are equipped with talents you have never leveraged. You have ideas that you have never developed. You have love inside of you that you never shared. You have songs that you never have sung. Am I right?

What I know for sure is that it's time for you to build and rebuild so you can have the internal infrastructure needed to courageously pursue your purpose. And the building starts from the inside out. It begins with developing your character, identifying your values, choosing supportive communities, and improving your decision-making. Building anything that can last for decades starts with a durable foundation.

My friend, here are a few factors to consider during the building process.

1. Building requires that you develop your prayer life and develop a relationship with your Creator, so you are fortified against private adversity and public attacks.

2. Building demands that you develop coping skills so you won't be swayed by public opinion or distracted by people-pleasing.
3. Building insists that you rise to the highest version and vision of yourself so you can withstand the stresses of success with grace, gratitude, and generosity.
4. Building challenges you to learn to hear your own voice above the voices of others.
5. Building requires that you know yourself so well that you can detect when you are gradually shifting away from your core.
6. Building requires that you become accountable for your choices and dreams.
7. Building demands that you become your fiercest advocate so you can create what you desire most.
8. Building requires that you are a life-long learner so you have the knowledge to lead yourself and lead other leaders.
9. Building requires that you take calculated risks and live outside of your comfort zone.
10. Building demands that you keep healing your past, keep exploring who you are today, and keep developing into who you desire to be in the future.

Thankfully, Jenna came to her senses and didn't get married. After some encouragement, but really nudging, she discovered that her husband-to-be was already married to two other women and had a baby on the way with an out-of-town girlfriend. Can you imagine how marrying a cheater and liar would have reinforced every negative belief that she already had and held about herself? Marrying that guy would have further chipped away at her already fragile self-esteem and diminished her self-worth. She would have lost more confidence in her ability to make decisions that aligned with her highest good.

Jenna finally accepted that she needed healing more than she needed a husband. Just like Jenna, we all need healing more than we need anything else in the world. We need healing so we feel liberated enough to question what we have been taught and told about life. We need to be healed enough so we can step outside and step away from belief systems that contribute to our calamity and distress. We need to heal so we can create a new narrative about who we are, who God is, and what we were created to do. That way, we won't waste so much energy trying to acquire what society defines as meaningful, acceptable, and rewarding. We can embrace and exemplify our own values, be who we authentically are, and create our own definition of success that makes us feel aligned and fulfilled.

Jenna is healing now; she's in the building phase. She is confronting her fears, shattering old beliefs, creating new relationships, investing in mentoring, practicing self-care, challenging her childhood stories, eliminating distractions, severing toxic ties, accumulating skills, and prioritizing her energy. With her newfound courage, she is building a future of abundance, adventure, and growth. She is developing and solidifying a foundation that can support the life and legacy that she feels called to create and destined to live.

I am in the building phase, and I bet you are too. So, what do you need to build and rebuild to propel you into purpose? What do you need to build to be who God created you to be? What do you need to unlearn and unleash to build the best YOU?

Are you ready to build a blissful life as you pursue your purpose?

I hope so because it's time to soar!

Declare Today: I am building what matters to me and to God.

Let's Dare to Soar Higher!

52

PRETENDING IS NOT SELF-PROTECTION; IT'S PROBLEM-PERPETUATION

Some people love to pretend. They like to act as if they are not hurting, not offended, or if they are not suffering. They love pretending, and they expect you to pretend with them.

But pretending does not protect us from our internal demons, inner critics, and inner hatred. Pretending does not protect us from our past, our pain, and our pathology. Pretending does not protect us from external insults, social injustice, and political intimidation. No, pretending only ensures that our personal and public issues continue to create chaos in our lives and in our communities.

I had to learn the hard way that pretending only traps you

into cycles of self-sabotage, self-loathing, and self-minimizing. How do I know? Because throughout my career in corporate America, I did a lot of pretending and one of my best pretending performances occurred early in my career. It's sad to say, but I pretended so well that I could have won an Academy Award for Best Actress Of The Year.

Here is what happened. After a successful year of sales performance, I interviewed for a job that I felt confident about getting; however, I didn't get it. When my sales director asked me if I was upset about not getting the promotion, I did what was acceptable in that corporate culture. I gave a politically correct response; I told them what they wanted to hear. I said, "I am fine, and I am happy for the person who got the job." I gave an obligatory smile and feigned graciousness. Even though most people and I believed that I was the most qualified for the position, I pretended to be unbothered by the glaring slight. What I didn't share was that the interview for the promotion shattered my confidence, undermined my humanity, and made me question my self-worth.

That interview experience was something that I will never forget. As soon as I entered the room to interview, I sensed that I was in trouble. From the look on the hiring manager's face, it was obvious that he had limited experience and had little interaction with women and people of color. He appeared disgusted or insulted that I was even in the room. Trust me, his caustic reaction was one that I was very familiar with. I had frequently experienced racism and sexism, and so his obvious disdain for me was not new for me. I wasn't shaken by his ignorance, arrogance, and his thinly veiled hostility. I was accustomed to swimming in toxic water with vicious sharks.

During the interview, his questions were humiliating, offensive, and totally rude. When he used improper English and bragged about having Black friends, knowing how to speak "jive" (his words), and about being cool, I was floored. When he asked me why a smart "gal" would attend a black college, I was mortified. I could not believe that such a biased manager was interviewing me for a corporate position. I had to bite my lip to contain my anger, conceal my exasperation, and to control my tears. Moreover, I could not believe that none of the other interviewers tried to intervene to stop the bigoted tirade. The degrading questioning continued, and I was humiliated. I felt publicly demeaned, and as if the entire room was laughing at me. Maybe the hiring manager was trying to put me back in "my place," who knows? All I knew was that I was furious, shocked, and outraged. I wanted to cry, cuss, and cut all at the same time. I thought to myself, is this really happening?

For years that interview experience haunted me, and I could not shake the feelings of embarrassment and shame. Public humiliation and degradation are hard pills to swallow, especially since I felt that I was already selling my soul by constantly censoring myself to fit in. I was already paying a high admission price to have a little, broken, invisible chair at the corporate table. I already endured gut-wrenching slights and endless microaggressions in order to climb a rickety corporate ladder. I paid with the gradual erosion of my self-worth, self-esteem, and self-respect. I paid with the constant destruction of my identity, the subtle and not-so-subtle assaults on my personhood, and the pervasive atmosphere of contempt. I paid by the need to be hypervigilant and by being on constant surveillance, which filled me with endless anxiety and extreme paranoia. I paid with public, plastered smiles and endless code-switching that made me feel schizophrenic and confused. I paid dearly.

Yes, the corporate jungle was treacherous. The constant racial slurs, the continuous stereotypical tropes, and the persistent gaslighting were relentless, and nothing in my experience prepared me for such vicious, unprovoked attacks. I was at a loss. I didn't know what to do. I had no allies. Nobody was willing to jeopardize their corporate career to help me or even stand up for what was moral and equitable. No one would admit that the mistreatment and misogyny that I endured were even unethical, illegal, and downright disgusting. Nobody said a mumbling word. I was on my own, and I had to find a way to protect and heal my bruised soul while still producing at a higher level than my white peers. Most of all, I had to find a way to hide and contain my rage that was simmering and threatening to explode at the most inopportune times.

The only way I knew to survive was to pretend that I was unfazed and unbothered; I had to emotionally detach from the environment and from my truth. I had to feign amnesia and willfully act as if I didn't know that fairness was just an illusion. I had to pretend as if senior management was fair, inclusive, and welcoming. I had to imagine that the men who witnessed the degrading interview forgot and respected me as a professional. I had to fantasize that there were no glass ceilings or institutional barriers for women, especially Black women. I had to convince myself that the toxic environment was healthy, equitable, and nurturing. I had to persuade myself that I wasn't constantly tokenized, trivialized, and traumatized. I had to make believe that the daily humiliating interactions didn't erode my confidence or my self-respect. I had to pretend that my colleagues accidentally forgot to invite me to dinner, forgot how to pronounce my name, and forgot to inform me about meetings. I had to pretend that oversights were not deliberate, malicious, and strategic. I had to make-believe that stealing my ideas was an alternative form of acceptance, validation, and collaboration. I had to pretend that my performance evaluations were fair, that developmental opportunities were equally distributed, and that nepotism didn't exist. I had to pretend to survive.

I always pretended, but one day I could not fake anymore because I was too broken and devastated. I was emotionally whipped, spiritually fatigued, and slowly sinking into depression. I was sick of all the compromises and concessions that left me distraught and perpetually embarrassed. I grew tired of smiling to hide my tears, laughing at insulting jokes to appear less threatening, and listening to KKK-like rhetoric that undermined my dignity. I was weary of the affirmative action tirades and *"I can't find qualified people"* conversations aimed to invalidate the talents, diminish the education, and discount the contributions of Black people. I grew disgusted by the sexual innuendos that made me feel dirty, fetishized, and just plain yucky. I was tired of dodging political bullets, removing political knives from my back, and accommodating racist attitudes. I was so drained by the non-stop abuse that suicidal thoughts gripped me and daily called my name.

Thankfully, I had enough sense to recognize that I was at a tipping point and was able to put my joy-sucking job in perspective enough to regain my agency and sanity. I told myself, "You can get another job. But you can't forget who you are. You are not a rug for people to walk on. You are God's child! You deserve better." My soul had to convince me of something that my mind no longer believed because my colleagues' toxic words and assessments of my worth felt truer than the word of God. I was dying.

Why would I pretend for so long? I am always asked that question, which honestly makes me feel small, inadequate, and ashamed. But, I have to speak out because there are many women of color who have also been shamed by their experiences in corporate America. There are other women who have been bullied and then blamed for the abuse they have suffered. There are other women who have been exploited to satisfy diversity initiatives but then vilified for wanting to speak and participate in meetings. There are other women who wanted to admit that corporate life felt like solitary confinement or a spiritual black hole but knew that their cries for empathy and help would be ignored. There are other powerful women who could not speak out because their families and communities depended on their salaries for food, shelter, and health care. There are other women who wanted to tell the truth but feared being ostracized and being kicked out of the very boardrooms that they suffered, sacrificed, and struggled to get into. And since they can't speak out, I will. Despite the stigma, the judgment, and the "why didn't you just leave" comments that fail to acknowledge the painful conundrums for women of color in corporate settings, I will tell the truth. I will share my truth and the truth of other powerful women who continue to be freedom fighters in corporate boardrooms and on corporate battlefields even today.

So, why did I pretend?

First, I pretended because the truth of how I was being treated was hard to accept, and I was embarrassed that I endured it and embarrassed that I allowed it. I pretended to protect myself from the judgment of my loved ones because my friends and family thought I had "made it," and I didn't want to lose their respect. I pretended because I was making more money than my parents combined and didn't believe that I could generate the same level of income in another industry. I pretended because I was socialized to tolerate injustice and expect discrimination, and as a result, I had a high "take crap" threshold. I pretended because I knew that systemic oppression was woven into the hearts, minds, and visions of most employers, and that injustice was the norm. I pretended because most companies didn't hire many people of color, and I knew that the "last hired and first fired" policy was prevalent and practiced throughout the industry. I pretended because I was warned as a child that being talented and educated would not insulate me from racial discrimination and sexual harassment. I pretended because I was socialized to live, accept, and navigate in racially unsafe environments. I pretended because I didn't trust human resources and leadership to hear me, help me, or support me. I pretended because navigating power dynamics and engaging in political gymnastics left me feeling worthless and impotent. I pretended for years because I felt that I didn't have a choice.

The truth is – I overestimated my emotional ability and my capacity to withstand the barrage of constant insults, racial slurs, and unfair marginalization. I actually thought I could quiet and pacify the internal demons that harassed me and further shamed me when I failed to advocate for myself. I also underestimated how destructive and disorientating racism was on my mind, body, and soul.

I hate to admit it, but for years, I pretended. But none of my pretending worked, and all I did was ache inside. And my pretending gave several biased managers ample opportunity to severely wound and traumatize other women and people of color for decades to come.

Thankfully, I no longer pretend. I now accept that I have a moral obligation to challenge injustice, biased policies, and oppressive behavior. I now affirm that I have a spiritual responsibility to challenge comments that demean and degrade me and others. I no longer pretend that systemic, historical, and corporate trauma don't exist and don't affect me or you. I no longer pretend that radical change and real progress will happen organically. I no longer pretend that controversy and agitation are bad words. I no longer pretend; I participate and disrupt "white" peace to promote change. If something violates my humanity and the humanity of others, I attempt to fix it, heal it, share it, protest it, finance it, talk about it, and garner support for it because pretending only results in problem perpetuation, not problem cessation. Now when I see a good fight for justice, I jump in it. I launch forward, fortified by God's word and God's promise for liberation and justice.

So, when you are hurting, face the problem, and fix it. Even if you need to maneuver politically, confront your fear, and conquer it. If you have a divergent opinion, own your perspective, and speak it. If something is not working, identify the cycle and break it. If somebody is unfairly labeling you, dismiss the label and discard it. If something is threatening your self-worth, acknowledge it, and address it. If people are not listening, amplify your voice and repeat it. If the problem is too big for you, find support and attack it. Don't pretend.

I had to learn the hard way that pretending that a problem does not exist will not make the problem go away. Pretending only guarantees that the problem persists, and ensures that biased policies, inequities, and violence will continue to hurt us, all of us, for generations to come.

My friend, don't pretend because you deserve better! You deserve to speak your truth without fear and retaliation. You deserve to be treated with dignity and respect. You deserve to be protected and supported. You deserve access and fairness. You deserve justice!

So, what do you do now? First, forgive yourself and be proud that you survived the experience and can share your story to help others. Secondly, release any shame that you feel about not speaking up. Systematic oppression was and still is a formidable opponent; you didn't create it, and you could not have single-handedly dismantled it even if you had reported the abuse. Next, forge a new path with the wisdom and strength you gained. You now have additional knowledge and insight that can help you navigate in new places and in more strategic ways. With that new understanding, you can reclaim your true identity and effectively mobilize, collaborate, and agitate for change. Finally, pursue your purpose. Regain your joy and passion by doing what God has called you to do.

Sis, (and Brother too), you don't have to pretend anymore because you have everything you need to win in life. You are gifted. You are anointed. You are loved. You are worthy. You don't have to surrender your soul by pretending to be less than you are and less than God created you to be.

Are you ready? The world is waiting for you, and so am I. It's purpose time!

It's your time to Soar Higher!

53

RAGE RUINS!

In my late twenties, my therapist told me I was "emotionally raging." My reaction was: "Emotional raging? What's that? Who, me?"

I didn't know what emotional raging was. The only rage that I was familiar with was road rage and my behavior was nothing like the crazy things I heard "road ragers" do. No, not me. I wasn't irrational, aggressive, or angry. I was professional, poised, polite, and polished, or at least I thought I was. So, as you can imagine, my therapist's perspective didn't land well on me.

Of course, I debated with her even though I didn't even know what emotional raging was. Her assessment just didn't feel right; I could not own it or "lean into it" as we say in the coaching world. But eventually, I paused to reflect on what she said. It was not that I didn't believe or accept her viewpoint; I valued her observations. She was thoughtful, wise, and insightful, but something about her rage diagnosis didn't sit well in my spirit. Her diagnosis challenged my sensibilities, and it felt as if she was undoing or unraveling my years of hard, tear-jerking, soul-searching work that I had done to cleanse myself from my painful past. I also felt that she was questioning my spiritual maturity, emotional growth, and self-awareness. And of course, my fragile ego could not allow that, not then. I was barely holding on to my re-emerging confidence and self-worth by a thread, and a thin one at that.

Needless to say, I questioned myself for days. How could I be raging if I were successful? I wasn't out of control, impulsive or reckless? What did she see or sense in my behavior and energy that I was not aware of? What was emanating from me that announced that I was raging?

I didn't sleep well for weeks after our session because I wanted to learn more about raging. I looked everywhere for information, but researching was difficult because in those days there were no Google or internet search engines to help me. There was little research about the topic, or at least I could not find much literature about emotional raging at the library. But for some reason, I could not dismiss her conclusion. On some level, her "raging" diagnosis resonated with me, but I didn't know why.

When I embarked on my rage finding mission, the first thing I learned was that rage and anger are not the same things. That was a big revelation for me because I used the words interchangeably. Here's the difference. Anger usually results from a current event. For example, if something happens or if somebody offends you, you feel as if you have the ability and power to successfully address it; you have control and choice. You can tell them off, leave the situation, protest the injustice, sue for damages, or have a conversation. You can address the real or perspective insult, issue, or indiscretion with hopes of resolution. That's anger.

"Raging" or rage is different. "Raging" is when there is a build-up of anger because you feel that you have been unfairly abused, dehumanized, and traumatized, but lack the power to defend yourself without experiencing severe retaliation, pain, or loss. Raging is that deep fear, extreme sadness, or excruciating pain that gets embedded into the crevices of your body which causes damage to your career, relationships, and soul. Rage is that soul-crushing ache that never gets resolved, expressed, or acknowledged, and so it builds, explodes, and burns up everything you desire, hope for, and dream about. Rage is that immeasurable suffering that disrupts your life, steals your joy, and robs you of your ability to live in peace. Rage ruins!

But here is the challenging part. Sometimes we don't easily identify rage because, for some of us, especially people of color, rage has been passed down from generation to generation. It was bequeathed to us. It was transferred to us. It was imposed on us. Rage became an unwanted inheritance to manage and an unfair burden to bear. And can we be honest? For people of color, there's much to rage about.

For starters, people of color in America were born into an oppressive system of hate, degradation, and colonization and often felt too powerless to challenge injustice. And so, our ancestors did the only thing they could do to survive in a culture of pervasive violence; they suppressed their feelings. They shoved their emotions down, deep down, into their souls in attempts to silence their shame, conceal their frustration, and bury their feelings of helplessness so they could exist. They didn't fully live. Didn't fully love. They were just alive, existing in an environment of emotional and physical cruelty. And unfortunately, their children and grandchildren had front row seats to witness their unmeasurable pain, humiliation, and suffering. Rage!

Yes, rage is abnormal, but it feels normal because, for some of us, it is normal. When you have been suffocated and silenced by brutality and trauma, rage is everywhere. It is seen, modeled, lived in, and practiced daily, without discussion, without acknowledgment, without explanation, and without restraint. It is so pervasive that it gets etched into the fabric of your physical, spiritual, and emotional DNA, and ingrained into your culture and traditions. It gets immersed, imprinted, and infused into every facet of your life. Rage.

Rage.   Seething   Rage.   Silent   Rage.   Simmering rage! Generational Rage. Societal rage. Political rage. Historical Rage. Sexual Rage. Mental Rage. Economic Rage. Religious Rage.

Intellectual Rage. Emotional Rage. Collective Rage! Exhausting Rage. Holy Rage. Righteous Rage. Communal Rage. RAGE! I was raging! And I didn't know it.

I am not alone. Some of us have been raging since our childhoods, and we don't even know it. Some of us are MAD as hell because we were molested, raped, abused, or violated by those we expected to protect, defend, and love us. We were ignored, not cared for, or not cared about by parents or caregivers who were too broken, too unavailable, too unstable, or too immature to make us feel visible, valued, or valuable. Out of necessity, sometimes, we were given too much responsibility too soon, and we grew up feeling overwhelmed, overburdened, and unsupported, which cultivated feelings of inadequacy, doubt, and escapism. Out of frustration, our overworked and undervalued caregivers hit us, yelled at us, called us names, and blamed us for things that were outside of our control and not our fault. Out of ignorance, they reinforced "Massa's" value system, which made us despise our hair, detest our color, dislike our bodies, and deny our intelligence. Rage!

Some of us are raging because we were demonized by uneducated, untrained, and misguided clergy and hate-filled faith traditions for being who God uniquely designed us to be. Some of us are raging because we were educated in school systems that discounted our history, glorified our extermination, and bastardized our contributions. Some of us are raging because we were forced to endure public humiliation and continuous gaslighting that punctured holes into our collective souls. Some of us are raging because we have deep wounds we can't touch, historical pain we can't access, and past-life memories we can't fully remember. Rage!

Rage! Some of us are raging. We are raging because we have been silenced by sexism, demonized by homophobia, colonized by enslavers, compromised by poverty, discounted by tribalism, manipulated by policies, exploited by illiteracy, denied by poverty, trivialized by history, abused by the law, tokenized by corporations, minimized by white supremacy, fetishized by perverts, victimized by the government, brutalized by police, pathologized by scientists, dehumanized by unregulated capitalism, vandalized by extremists, criminalized by psychologists, patronized by liberals, monetized by sports teams, scandalized by religion, marginalized by politics, plagiarized by conniving artists, and sensationalized by the media. We are raging. Collective rage, community rage, clan rage, and cultural rage! Rage!

Rage became a permanent, but unwelcomed, resident in our minds, hearts, and souls. Its presence hindered us, haunted us, and hardened us all at the same time. We did our best to outrun it and ignore it. We earnestly tried to numb it with alcohol, sugar, drugs, sex, religion, spending, gambling, and other forms of escapism. Honestly, I tried my best to quiet my rage by consuming unbelievable amounts of food. I ate whole chickens, family-sized bags of chips, whole cakes, and boxes of cereal, but my rage would not be silenced. It demanded my full attention.

Rage!

We unintentionally let rage live in our homes, in our places of worship, in our communities, in our perspectives, and in our expectations. Even though it degraded the quality of our lives, we felt powerless and ill-equipped to release it, dismantle it, or at least analyze it. As a result, we unconsciously colluded with it and created more of it. Rage.

Rage became our most constant companion and our most formidable opponent. Rage was an unwanted birthright and an unwanted birthmark on our lives. Rage was an uninvited visitor who would not leave. Rage!

Rage ruins!

I had to face it. I was raging, and rage was bubbling up and bubbling over in my well-manicured, well-orchestrated, and well-put-together life. I had to admit that I was ANGRY! I was furious! I was enraged! I was infuriated! I was frustrated! I was livid! I was resentful! I was beside myself. I was furious, and I had been furious for years, DECADES!

Rage was a draining, persistent, undesirable energy in my life.

I saw it. I felt it. I lived it. I ate in it. I vacationed in it. I worshiped in it. I went to school in it. I navigated through it. I maneuvered in corporate America through it! I WAS MAD AS HELL! As HELL! HELL!

My rage was slowly and silently killing me because it had leaked into my career, relationships, and self-love. It was unconsciously ruining me, robbing me, and restricting me of my joy and my peace. My rage was diminishing me, swallowing me, and it was impeding my ability to walk courageously into my divine assignment and step into my God-ordained purpose. Rage.

I don't recall exactly when, but I reached a tipping point, and I realized I had to do something about this bottled up rage. Something triggered me and I immediately started writing all the things I was angry about and kept writing and writing. I told my truth for hours, as I wept uncontrollably. I cried and wrote. I wrote and cried. This expressive writing was gut-wrenching and powerful. The emotions and tears continued to flow as I wrote. I didn't try to be practical or polite; I just wrote. I unloaded my over-burdened soul; the list was over twenty pages long! And then I violently threw up as if my body had a visceral response to what I revealed, and it needed to purge all the mayhem, madness, and misery that I had endured. Rage.

Thankfully, after decades of calming my rage, I made peace with it. I could no longer forget about its impact, numb its voice, hide from its threats, or minimize its influence. And I could no longer disown it, reject it, rationalize it, or ignore it. I had to ask my rage questions, listen to its voice, trace its origins in my life, and halt its growth. I could no longer contribute to its presence or allow it to marinate in my spirit. I could not co-exist with it because it was rotting me from the inside out, and it was running away the very friends, love, and resources that I needed to heal. Rage!

Thirty years later, I would love to say my rage is completely gone, but that is not true. As the African proverb says, *"wisdom does not come overnight,"* and my rage will not lessen overnight, but it's gradually diminishing. It is losing its power and prominence in my life as I learn to release it by forgiving myself and forgiving others. As I learn to look at the world through lenses of more compassion and less condemnation, with more hope and less hatred, and with more love and less lamentation, it's loosening its grip on my life. And as I learn to let my feelings flow from my heart, out of my mind, and to my pen so that my feelings can land on paper so I can look at them, my rage is dissolving in my soul.

Your journey to healing your rage may be difficult too, but the good news is that it can be healed. But if you haven't started addressing your rage, what can you do to squelch the raging inferno in your soul? How do you release the wounds so you can become healthy, happy, and whole? How can you transform your life from victim to visionary? How do you become more aware of its influence in your life? How can you address the devastating and damning impact it has had on your life and your community?

First, you start by remembering (re-membering) and reclaiming parts of yourself that got tucked away when you were trying to survive. You re-introduce yourself to parts of you that were never affirmed and cultivated and extend your love. You accept all aspects of your experience and personality, even those parts that feel embarrassing, unlovable, and unworthy, so you love them back to wholeness. Then, you embrace and care for those parts of you that were hurt, abandoned, and compromised and lovingly nurture those parts with compassion and understanding. Finally, you forgive and let go of those parts of you that no longer serve you or your highest good so you can thrive, not just survive, but richly live.

Yes, I know that the forgiving part may not be easy, but it is essential because, without forgiveness, you can't move toward your higher calling. Without forgiveness, you can't express and experience gratitude for the lessons learned, the wisdom gained, or the peace that's waiting for you on the other side of your healing journey. Without forgiveness, you can't liberate yourself from the toxicity of yesterday or release the pain of today in ways that allow you to SOAR tomorrow. Rage!

Why am I so diligent and disciplined about addressing rage? Because I want you to SOAR! I want you to use your rage as fuel, as a source of empowerment to liberate and mobilize you. I want your rage to help you identify every gift, skill, and talent that you have and use it to make something of yourself, for yourself, and for others. I want you to use your rage to rise above and beyond all limitations so you can create something unique, innovative, and useful in the world. I want you to use rage, so it no longer uses you.

The bottom line for me is this: my goal is not to live forever, but I desire to create something that can last forever. I desire for my loved ones to believe that they have the potential to challenge what ails them, and what ails the world. I desire to leave a legacy for my son, my grandchildren, and my great-grandchildren. I want them to inherit everything that I am and everything I have, except for my rage. Rage.

My friend, I want to say it again for those in the back. Identify your rage! Own your rage. Expose your rage. Heal your rage! Do what you need to do to engage your rage. And then, use your rage to reform your life and every life connected to you. Use your rage to repair everything that is broken in the world because your purpose is waiting for you. We are waiting for you. You are waiting for you.

It's time to SOAR higher!

Blessings!

54

IF YOU WANT A WOW, YOU MUST FIRST LISTEN TO THE WHISPER

So often in life, we want magical moments; we want miracles, and we want memories, but we won't move. When our spirit tells us to act, we don't listen. We allow fear, doubt, and failure to cripple us and paralyze us. We let the lack of resources, relationships, and revenue distract and disappoint us. But if you want a WOW, you must hear and heed the whisper. The Whisper is your guide; it is your "go," and it is GOD.

So, what is the whisper saying to you? What is it reminding you about your purpose? What is the whisper calling you to be? What is the whisper guiding you to do? What is it stirring up in your soul? What is the whispering warning you about? What is it explaining to you? What is the whisper challenging you to do, be, and to say?

The Whisper!

One of my clients shared that as a little girl, her parents wanted her to be a debutante. She wasn't interested, and so she resisted because, in her mind, she was not debutante material. She hated ballroom dancing, wasn't interested in etiquette training, and didn't care for the over-the-top fluffy dresses that irritated her skin.

But even though she wasn't fond of evening attire and the structured dancing, something in her spirit quietly said, "do it," and so she agreed. At first, she was uncomfortable; nothing in her upbringing prepared her for the dance practices or the formalities she had to learn. The pageantry was a bit extravagant and seemed too indulgent for her modest taste. She wanted to quit, but the whisper said, "do it" and so she continued.

For weeks she felt like a fish out of water. The dance moves felt mechanical, the high-heeled shoes hurt her feet, and her escort could not stay on beat to save his life. Yet she stayed, trusting that her spirit would provide the lessons she needed for the next stage of her journey.

Over a few weeks, her WOW was slowly revealed. Through the highly choreographed dancing routines, she learned the importance of partnership, teamwork, and synchronicity. Through her speaker training, she learned how to deliver speeches with clarity, poise, and precision. Through her frustration with the process, she learned how to persevere and exist outside of her comfort zone.

As a teenager, the lessons she learned didn't seem too important because she didn't initially see the value or the utility of the classes. Yet, the lessons she learned are the exact lessons that have catapulted her career today. Everything she gained in the debutante experience proved to be a great launching pad for her life as an entrepreneur, public servant, and coach. That slight whisper that she almost ignored became the foundation for her future WOW.

What's a WOW? A WOW is that quiet, indescribable feeling, that inner knowing, and that calm assurance that you are on the road to destiny. A WOW is that epiphany that illuminates possibilities and elevates your creativity in ways that defy your experience and expertise. A WOW is that still voice within that intensifies your intuition and helps you make wise decisions when you are confused. A WOW is when you finally know who you are and how you want to use your gifts in the world. A WOW is the super-natural stamina that fuels your passions and propels you into a different stratosphere of excellence. A WOW is that sudden awareness that you have been healed from your past hurts in a way that liberates you to create and contribute to the world. A WOW is that reservoir of faith that helps you see God's plans even in the midst of a chaotic reality. A WOW is when you realize that your experiences were orchestrated to equip you with the knowledge and the know-how you need to soar.

Your WOW is a Way of Wonder. It's God's voice. It's the voice that your soul longs to hear.

The Whisper. Do you hear it? The Spirit is speaking so listen! Pray! Heed! Ask! Do!

Success is waiting. People are waiting. Abundance is waiting. Your purpose is waiting. The highest version of YOU is waiting.

God gave the WORD. It was a WHISPER! Now, go get your WOW and go be a WOW!

It's time to Soar!

55

HEALING IS A JOURNEY, NOT AN EVENT

It was almost twenty years ago, but I can still vividly remember the pain of seeing my son's frightened, battered face. There he stood with tear-stained eyes, a look of bewilderment, and swollen lips. Seeing him bruised and bloody was painful, almost unbearable. His six-year-old vocabulary was too limited to fully express what happened and how he felt, but I knew. Just imagining his slight frame being hit, pushed, and kicked by 4th and 6th -grade boys while trapped in a bathroom stall made me wince because I knew. I knew, and just knowing how powerless he must have felt as fists pummeled his face made me feel as if I had been punched, too. I knew. My God, I knew.

As I watched my son cry and sniffle, I became angrier and angrier because I knew that being punched and slammed to the ground had been excruciating, belittling, and humiliating. Also tasting his own blood after being jabbed in the face had to be horrifying. My God, he was six years old. How was I going to explain to him why this happened? I didn't have words, and I knew that his experience would be a defining moment in his life. I didn't want to know, but I knew.

My initial response had to seem rather odd to the school officials. I stared at them, but I was really looking through them and straining to look into my son's soul. I was also struggling to make sure I was awake because parts of me thought I was dreaming. I hoped that I was dreaming, or maybe having a flashback, or having an out-of-body experience, or something. Was I hallucinating? Any experience would have better and less painful than the truth was staring back at me.

Seeing my son's injured face was agonizing. I wanted to touch it, but I couldn't. I wanted to clean off the dried blood, but I didn't. Since I really didn't know what to say, I just grabbed my son and hugged him as tight as I could. I wanted him to know that he was safe; mommy was here to protect him. I wanted to take the pain away. I wanted to erase the terrifying event from his memory. I wanted to give him my strength. I wanted him to feel loved. I wanted revenge. I wanted my Mommy. I wanted so much, but most of all, I didn't want my son, my only child, to hurt now or suffer later. I wanted none of that.

The school officials tried to explain what happened. I don't really remember what they said, because it didn't matter. They tried to give me some sort of explanation for my son's injuries, but any rationale was insufficient. Let's be honest, what could a six-year-old boy have done to deserve being brutally attacked in the bathroom while he changed his clothes? What could a six-year-old boy have done to warrant being jumped by a gang? What could a six-year-old boy have done to provoke such a vicious attack? What? And why did the teacher think it was okay not to immediately notify me about the assault? How could a teacher, an educated adult, be so callous toward a wounded, bloody child and so apathetic about his emotional state? How could school officials justify sitting my battered child in a room for hours by himself with no love, care, and comfort? How?

The school officials had no reasonable answers, and none of the school's politically correct I-don't-want-to-get sued statements contained any empathy or concern. The principal and his staff just didn't care, and none of their pre-packaged, non-caring explanations made any sense. My son was six, a first-grader. Nothing he did could have led to such an attack. Nothing he did could have warranted him being hit with so much force that this bloody face was so swollen that it looked like he had a mouth full of rocks. Nothing!

My son wasn't a bully. He was not part of a gang. He was not devoid of love, home training, or parental support. I made sure that he had the best, the best of everything, especially the best of me. What could have motivated a group of boys to use my son's body as a punching bag and to use his face for boxing practice? Were the bullies just looking for a victim, and my son was simply their unfortunate patsy of the day? What?

The sad truth was that my son was assaulted because he was Black. Yes, he was a Black male child with an Arabic name in a white, Christian school that supposedly promised and promoted love. That was his offense; his color. His color made him a target for home-bred hate. His color marked him for abuse and humiliation. His color made him vulnerable to a heartless school system. Yes, it was a color issue; my son was victimized because he was Black. That's the truth. But of course, that's not the truth the school acknowledged.

Despite knowing how risky it could be for my son to be the only Black child in a predominately white school, I trusted the Baptist Christian School to educate and care for my child. I trusted, but really prayed, that my son would have teachers who showered him with love and acceptance. I wanted, but really needed, his educational experience to be fun, and joyful, and not full of fear, humiliation, and isolation. I prayed so fervently because I wanted my son to thrive academically and to feel included; I wanted what all parents want for their children.

I prayed and prayed because I knew the risks and the dangers of integrating predominately white schools because I had integrated a few myself. I knew how being different and feeling invisible could erode a child's self-worth, self-concept, and self-esteem. I knew how destructive it was to learn false histories and belittling stories about your identity and community. I knew the consequences of not having enough affirmation and validation to bloom. Sadly, I knew the horrors of harassment and the lifelong effects of childhood bullying. I knew it all because it was my experience, and that's why I prayed that my son's experiences would be different. I didn't want him to follow in my footsteps. Hell, I spent decades in therapy healing from classroom and educational trauma; I didn't want that for my child. That's why I did everything in my power to research schools and interview teachers to ensure that he would be safe so he could thrive.

After I recovered from the shock and anger, my son's recovery process became my priority. I withdrew him from the school, purchased some school books, and I taught him myself. I didn't know exactly how to teach, but I was determined that he would learn, and learn in safety. I was not taking any more risks or jeopardizing my son's emotional health.

Being a single mom, homeschooling my son, and working a demanding job was difficult. I was in the pharmaceutical industry and my job required me to travel sixty percent of the time. Since I had to financially support us, my son traveled with me. If I could afford two plane tickets, he would fly with me to meet with customers. But if not, I would sometimes drive more than fourteen hours a day to fulfill my job obligations. It was a risk because having him on the road with me violated company policy. But I had no choice, so I devised creative ways to conceal my son's presence from my manager and peers.

For months, I worked and drove, and drove and worked. Keeping up the charade was exhausting, but what could I do? I was not leaving my son in a racist environment that masqueraded as a Christian community. No Way! And I didn't have any family support.

Eventually, the hiding, driving, and working took its toll on me and I could not take it anymore. I was so physically tired and emotionally drained that my lucrative consultant job lost its appeal. One day after driving six hours through Tennessee, I decided that I wanted to be done with the duplicity, grief, and constant dread; I wanted out. I could not take another day of juggling a demanding job, while homeschooling a child, while dealing with his post-attack nightmares, while driving six to eight hours a day, with no support. I just could not do it, and the constant anxiety of hiding my son while being on the road affected my mental health. One day, I had enough, and I decided that I was moving back to Florida. I was out of Kentucky. I hated it, and my spirit needed rest; it demanded calm and peace.

I told my manager what happened to my son. I shared bloody pictures and provided graphic details. However, senior management refused to transfer me because the company had just moved me to Kentucky the year before. They issued me an ultimatum; stay in Kentucky, or resign. I was fine with those options; I was moving. My son's safety and my health were not negotiable; my sanity was at stake. When I announced I was leaving, they agreed to transfer me if I financed the relocation.

What senior management didn't realize was that I didn't need, nor was I waiting for their permission. I had already updated my resume, contacted my clients, put my home on the market, and researched new schools for my son. No one was going to determine my son's future; I was the parent, and I was the provider, not a company.

My move back to Florida was difficult. For over eleven months, I had two mortgages which drained my savings. But money was the least of my worries; I had a traumatized son who was extremely distraught and was having nightmares. He was acting out; he was hurting. I didn't blame him at all because he was grieving, humiliated, and angry but did not understand how to process it all. And how could he have known? There is no rulebook that outlines how a child should heal after being assaulted. And why should a six-year-old child ever need to know how to recover from a hate crime, anyway? Heck, even adults have trouble healing after experiencing or witnessing hate crimes.

After we moved back to Coral Springs, Florida, my son started asking me questions that I could not answer. I didn't know what to say because how do you explain to a six-year-old boy that being Black was the reason that he got punched and kicked? How do you explain to a six-year-old boy that his last name gave a few fools a license to violate him? How do you explain to a little boy that adults colluded and protected the abusers, with little concern about his well-being? What do you say?

Thanks to the advice of some wonderful therapists, I learned that you explain as much as you can so that your child does not hate himself or hate others. You don't say too much, but you provide age-appropriate explanations and you tell the truth. I told my son the truth and sought support to rehabilitate his soul, mend his heart, and soothe his mind. And slowly, my son began to heal.

The healing journey was painful (yes, healing hurts), and I learned three powerful lessons about life.

1) Always do what is best for you. People love to offer advice without knowing or appreciating the variables of a situation. So, you must listen to your soul, and don't forget that it is YOU who must deal with the consequences of your decisions, not the advisors. Yes, listen to wise counsel, but always make the final decisions in your life. Don't abdicate authority to others. It is YOUR life; you have to live it for you.

2) Always listen to your intuition, which I know is God's voice. I must admit that hearing your soul is not always easy, especially when your ego screams while your soul whispers. But listen! Get quiet and get still. God will speak to you. God will use words, signs, people, and dreams to direct your path.

Sadly, I didn't listen to my intuition, and my son suffered. My intuition said, don't move to Kentucky; stay in Florida. My ego said, accept the consultant position in Kentucky; build your resume. My intuition said, the school does not feel right; Blacks are not welcome. My ego said, you are just being dramatic; stop being a wimp. My intuition said, your son is not being treated fairly; make an unannounced visit. My ego said, you are overacting; the world is not as racist as you think. My intuition said, honor your gut; Tariq is not safe. My ego said, focus on your job, make money, and advance your career. My ego was loud, and it muted the quiet, still voice from my soul. I didn't listen to my soul and my son suffered.

3) Forgive yourself. My son suffered, and I felt extremely guilty because it was my careless decision that put him in harm's way. And boy, the guilt was unbearable. I was so guilt-ridden that I stopped parenting him; I stopped disciplining him and preparing him for life. I checked out because I felt so ashamed. I felt unfit to be his mother, and at times, the guilt was so intolerable that I wanted to die.

But, I had to forgive myself because I wanted to be whole again. I didn't want to continue to doubt and hate myself. I wanted to reclaim my power and agency so I could function with confidence and grace. I wanted to restore my self-trust so that I could make sound decisions for my son and for me. I yearned to liberate myself from the gut-wrenching guilt so I could free myself from the inner demons and gremlins that were emotionally dismantling me from the inside out.

I didn't want to forget my son's bloody, tear-stained face, but I no longer wanted the image to haunt me. I wanted to move on, grateful that I learned a powerful lesson, and hopeful that I would never make decisions that endangered him or me again. I wanted to start over, and I wanted to parent my beautiful son again.

Dealing with my son's attack was one of the hardest times of my life, but I made it. Even when I was drowning in despair, too ashamed to ask for help, and too overwhelmed with my son's care, I persevered. Some days I struggled, but quitting was never an option because somehow, I knew that everything I needed for our healing journey was within me. I'm not sure how I knew, but I knew.

My son's attack was traumatic. It changed him, it changed me, and it changed our relationship. We grew closer, wiser, and stronger. We grew spiritually, and by God's grace, his attack did not cause irreparable harm to his spirit or soul. Sometimes he still has flashbacks; we both do. And every now and then, the guilt and the resulting grief grip me, and I weep. I weep for the old me, who felt so broken, invisible, and insignificant that she chose a career over what mattered most, her son. Just thinking about that dreadful decision still makes me cry today.

What does this experience have to do with purpose? I believe our pain equips us for our purpose. I believe that our pain stretches us and strengthens us to prepare us to serve humanity and to answer our divine call. I believe that our pain purges us, refines us, and fortifies so we can face Goliaths without wavering. Our pain softens us, so we never become so conceited, so arrogant, and so financially wealthy that we forget what matters most, people. Our pain is a reminder to stay humble, to stay open, and to always trust in God.

If you have made decisions that negatively affected a loved one, I understand. The guilt can consume and cripple you and make you feel as if you are not worthy of your purpose. But, you are worthy, and you still have something to contribute to the world. God still has something for you to do that only you can do. You have not been disqualified or pushed aside. You are still wanted, needed, and loved so please don't be so generous with judgment and stingy with grace; mercy suits your case.

My friend, the healing process is a journey, not an event. And with prayer and support, you will make it to the other side. You will heal. I know you can do it because it is my testimony too.

Your purpose is waiting for you. Use the wisdom you gained and let it help you win! You got this!

Blessings to you!

It's Time To Soar!

56

EVEN THOUGH GOD CAN SEND DOWN MANNA FROM HEAVEN, YOU MUST STILL PLANT A FEW CROPS HERE ON EARTH

I believe in miracles, and I have experienced many miracles in my own life. I have witnessed immediate healings, divine interventions, and supernatural shifts; miracles are real. They are transforming, stupefying and mind-mesmerizing events.

But I also believe that miracles are for emergencies and for dire situations, not for everyday use. To me, we should not expect daily sea-parting miracles from God, especially since God has generously given us resources, talents, and divine intelligence to do a few things for ourselves. Remember, God has encoded miracle-making capabilities in our divine DNA. We can do stuff, earth-altering stuff, when we are aligned with God's will and when we surrender to God's way.

I know my perspective is unpopular, and honestly, some religious people are quite perturbed by my position. I don't really understand why because if we are taught that faith without works is dead, asking God for something, and doing nothing just seems irresponsible to me. We just can't pray and idly sit by and wait for God to do everything. We must earnestly participate in our prayers and allow God's power to flow and operate through us so we can affect change, dismantle unfair policies, and care for the "least of these." We must be faithful action-takers, instigators, and implementors.

I know that God could do everything for us. I get that. God could send down manna from heaven right now. But if God always sends us manna from heaven, how would we ever learn how to plant crops here on earth? How would we learn how to exercise our faith, or develop our faith muscles, or access our heavenly wisdom to accomplish our divine call? How would we ever learn how to gather with two and three people (as the Bible instructs) to solve problems and to work as a team to address the ills of our communities? How would we ever realize that we are more than conquerors and that we could defeat our personal and political Goliaths if God didn't let us fight some battles? How would we ever know that we could resist the devil if God always made the devil flee? How would we ever learn how to expand our minds and explore the depths of our God-given gifts if God gave us everything on a silver platter?

As a minister, I believe that we MUST graduate from always expecting a *spiritual handout* (manna) to understanding the value of a *divine hand-up* (planting crops). I believe that divine hand-ups are essential because they provide opportunities for us to activate and acknowledge our God-given resources. Most of all, divine hand-ups activate our champion-like faith.

Just for the record: divine hand-ups are not new. Throughout the Bible, people were always challenged by divine hand-ups. For example, when a multitude needed to be fed, Jesus told the disciples to survey the crowd to find food. After the disciples brought back five loaves of bread and two fish, Jesus did his part. He blessed the food, multiplied it, and then fed the multitude. And what about the lame man at the pool? Jesus asked the lame man if he wanted to walk. And when the lame man said yes, Jesus told him to pick up his own bed and walk. Don't miss that! Jesus did His part, and people participated because they knew that Jesus would do what they could *not* do.

My friend, you are a person of purpose, and you have a divine calling. God is expecting great things from you and God will send you **manna** – relational, financial, political, intellectual, and spiritual manna – to assist you as you pursue your divine call. But just like in the Bible days, you must do your part. You must plant crops, which means you must go to school, study the market, get the training, start the business, strengthen your family, build a team, prepare the community, invest your money, produce services, read the lesson, take some risks, develop the strategy, and plan for the future. You must talk about your faith but also show your faith through your commitment and consistent actions.

So, how are you using your talents to plant your own "crops" in the various fields in your life? How are you taking action and enlisting others to support you as you plant seeds in fertile ground? How are you preparing the soil and watering the "proverbial" field so you can reap an abundant harvest? How are you working the land knowing that God has given you the grace to do what you can do, and promises to fill in the gaps for things that you cannot do? How are you cultivating and activating your prayers?

Rest assured that on your path to purpose, God will feed you; God always has. However, God will expect you to use what you already have to get more of what you need. So, after you pray, plant some crops; do your part. And then trust that God will send down manna from heaven to fill every gap and to meet every need you have on earth.

Are you ready?

Let's Dare To Soar Higher!

57

IT'S HARD TO SEE OPPORTUNITY IF YOU ARE FEAR-SIGHTED

Do you ever think about how you see the world? I didn't really think about how I saw the world until last week. After a sleepless night, I went outside, and the sky looked so gloomy and dark that I thought it was going to rain. Since I am extremely affected by the weather, I immediately started feeling tired and melancholy, and said to myself, *"This is going to be a long, draining day."*

It wasn't until I walked for about four minutes that I realized that I had my sunglasses on. I had put them on in the house to make sure that I wouldn't forget to bring them with me when I took my morning stroll. But when I got outside, I forgot to remove them. That's what multitasking does for you. It scatters your attention, but that's another story.

Thankfully, I realized that my sunglasses had affected my

perception, and consequently, influenced my mood. What a revelation! Even though my quick "aha" moment was not exactly brain surgery, it reminded me that our lenses determine how and what we see in the world. Our lenses shape our reality, undergird our understanding, or warp our judgment. And here is the kicker: most of the time, we are totally unaware of the lenses that govern and inform our lives. Sometimes we don't even realize that we are evaluating our worth, assessing our potential, and seeing our abilities through the lenses of cloudy conditioning, hazy histories, and distorted images. But just imagine how we could transform and elevate our lives if we remembered that our vision and our "I-Sight", how we see ourselves, are influenced by our unconscious beliefs, old narratives, and outdated paradigms. Can you imagine what a difference we could make and what we could create if we saw ourselves without cultural or societal filters?

Throughout the day, I made a list of all the lenses that affected my life. And boy, I had lenses around my race, sex, ability, size, marital status, weight, financial status, and age. And those are just the lenses I recognize. I am sure there are more lenses that are encouraging me to play small, and there are probably a few lenses that are skewing how you see yourself, too.

That day I analyzed how I viewed the world and realized that my lenses had a common theme: fear. Yes, fear is what hindered me from thinking broader, believing bigger, and stretching wider to courageously pursue my dreams. Fear is what made me retreat into relationships that were too small, reject dissenting views that felt too threatening, and relapse into old behaviors that I fought so hard to overcome. Fear is what prompted me to lower my gaze when obstacles looked too big, quit when my dreams looked too unattainable, and hide when opposition looked too intimidating. Fear is what silenced me when my soul begged me to speak up for my own needs, desires, and truth. It was fear that trapped me into "what was" and tricked me into giving up "what could be." Fear!

I had to tell myself the truth: I was fear-sighted. Yes, fear had blurred my vision, dampened my resolve, crippled my imagination, cluttered my mind, dulled my creativity, and distorted the truth. Fear had somehow blocked and hindered me from doing almost everything that I had been divinely called to do.

Just so you know, identifying fears can be tricky because fear hides under logic and is sometimes embedded in our childhood programming. But I am committed to rooting out fear because I don't want to be handcuffed to mediocrity and I don't want to live a monotonous life. I don't want my fear supporting debilitating narratives or perpetuating the oppressive status quo. And I don't want my life confined to what's Familiar, Easy, Acceptable, and Rationale. I want to operate at a higher level of truth so I can build the life that I was born to build, a life that includes stripping away the residue of racism, sexism, toxic individualism, and elitism so that that world reflects the all-inclusive love of God.

Here's the bottom line: We must always examine our lenses. We must identify our fears and all of its disguises, so we don't become fear-sighted. And if we are fear-sighted, we must create strategies to ensure that our fears do not jeopardize our calling, feed our dysfunction, or confine us to victimhood. And we must continually defang our fears so we can stop the cycles of collective destruction.

So, how do you ensure that you don't become fear-sighted? You ask yourself the following questions:

1) What lens am I looking through that is shaping my perspective?

2) How can I change my vision so I can see myself and the situation differently and accurately?

3) Who can help me see better and farther than I can see by myself?

4) Where do I see additional options or possibilities outside of my purview?

These four questions will help you convert your fear into fuel and provide the courage and clarity you need to make pro-destiny decisions.

My friend, it's time to fulfill your purpose. It is time to address your fears and correct your vision so you experience exponential growth, have massive impact, and enjoy a level of success beyond your wildest dreams. It is time to be a light in dark places, to liberate minds, and to transform hearts. It is time to bend societal expectations and deconstruct narratives that keep you safe but unsatisfied. It is time to build a legacy of unity that will provide a foundation of hope for generations to come. It is time to harness the courage, conviction, and faith you need to revolutionize the world. It is your time!

Are you still fear-sighted? I hope not because the world is waiting for you because it is your time to soar.

Let's Dare To Soar Higher!

58

KILL THE PESTS BEFORE THEY MAKE A MESS

When I was young, my parents would say to me, "Stop being a pest. And go sit down somewhere!"

I was a talkative, inquisitive child, and I was always asking questions that were considered inappropriate. Questions like: "Is that your real hair? Why you got that dress on? Why he can't read? Why white people always get to be the boss? Why is God a man? Why the boys don't have to wash the dishes?" I had questions for days.

My questions rarely landed well, but to me, my questions were fair. They were reasonable, my tone was respectful, and my intentions were pure. I wanted answers because so much of life made no sense to me. My entire existence was confusing, inconsistent, and full of nuances that my immature mind could not understand.

Despite continually being scolded, my inquiries continued. So much so that I was commonly known as THE PEST. Not SharRon, just THE pest. Yes, I was THE pest. I was the middle child who had a reputation for being a nosey nuisance who got on everybody's reserved nerve, the last good one. Yes, that was me.

As I matured and became more aware of social inequities, my pestering escalated. I always asked "why," totally oblivious to the impact my constant queries had on those around me. I didn't even realize that the tone of my questions was offensive and judgmental until one of my elders pulled me aside. She said, "Child, you up here asking questions like we just sat around doing nothing. We had questions, and we wanted answers too, but most of all, we just wanted to stay alive. Now, go over there and sit yourself down somewhere and act like you got good sense." In other words: be quiet and stop making people uncomfortable with your inquiries, you pest!

I knew a little about my history, but I didn't realize that some of my questions were accusatory and belittling. I didn't know that some questions were even too dangerous to ask, and some were even too risky to think. There was an entire historical context that I didn't understand because I had not lived long enough. I have not lived through the dehumanization of Jim Crow, the horror of lynching, and the degradation of segregation. I read about the experiences and indignities; I knew a few facts, but I did not know that emotional trauma sometimes got trapped in the body or lodged in the mind. I didn't know about the long-term effects of racialized and historical trauma that got inherited by offspring. I just didn't know, and I was too naïve and immature to understand that I was asking questions in a way that minimized the wounds, struggles, and sacrifices of my elders. My elders had endured many injustices and atrocities, and my line and tone of questioning, although innocent and sincere, were triggering, insensitive, and insulting to some of them.

As I got older, I asked questions with greater sensitivity, careful to honor the experiences of the "seasoned saints." I wanted and yearned for information that was omitted from the history books. I craved additional insight that provided a more honest account of what happened to my ancestors. I wanted to understand the horror, but also the resilience that fueled their commitment to their families and communities amid unfathomable odds. I wanted to enter their world of inexplicable tenacity that stabilized their spirits amid verbal, emotional, political, and physical beat-downs, and intellectual put-downs. I wanted to tap into that reservoir of endless hope and faith that nourished and fortified their souls in ways that defied reason. Whatever my elders had and knew, I desired and needed. I too wanted to survive in a world that was hell-bent on holding me down on and holding me back.

Thankfully, Mother Ann, a senior mother at the church, said, "Baby, keep asking questions because some people don't know the answers, and some don't even understand your questions. Some people have blocked stuff out and don't want to remember and understand. But don't worry about that, you keep asking until you get what you need. You are on to something."

Mother Ann's advice continues to inspire me today. And to ensure that I don't succumb to old crippling traditions and beliefs, I created a system called **P.E.S.T.S.** Yes, I named it after my childhood nickname.

What's **P.E.S.T.S. ™?**

P.E.S.T.S.™ is a framework that reminds me to interrogate rules, challenge labels, and pressure-test beliefs so I won't trap myself in conformity, numb myself into mediocrity, internalize false narratives, or base my life on dehumanizing cultural beliefs. It ensures that I identify and name visible and invisible barriers that attempt to keep me broke, burdened, blamed, and broken. It is a system that I developed to ensure that I stay "woke" so I can win even when the odds are stacked against me. And in America, many odds are stacked against people who are colored or "othered."

So, what does **P.E.S.T.S.** stand for?

The "P" stands for passed-down beliefs. Passed-down beliefs are ancestral, inherited, generational and cultural ideas, myths, and concepts that we all learn when we grow up; it is how we are socialized. Growing up, some of your passed-down beliefs were positive; they developed your imagination, cultivated your integrity, and nurtured your independence. But for people of color or those considered as "other," many of passed-down beliefs were destructive. For example, some passed-down beliefs encouraged us to follow demeaning rules, stay in our prescribed lanes, abide by the status quo, close our mouths, abandon our dreams, and surrender to authority. And of course, the authorities never looked like us.

Passed-down beliefs were everywhere; they were constantly taught by others or were caught by watching others. They defined our lives, determined our views, and built our worlds. They informed our values, shaped our desires, and structured our relationships. Passed-down beliefs touched every aspect of our lives, and they were enforced too; we were rewarded for obedience and punished for defiance. That's why some of our passed-down beliefs are still etched into our minds, hearts, and souls and influence how we believe and behave in the world today, sometimes to our detriment.

Honestly, I never really considered the impact of passed down beliefs until I became an entrepreneur. For example, it wasn't until I started flexing my entrepreneurial muscles, that all of my passed-down beliefs about money reared their ugly heads. When I started my personal training studio, I realized that I unconsciously believed that I needed a white man to help me grow my business and clientele. When I challenged that misconception, I realized I believed that rich people were evil and greedy. When I finally tackled that myth, I realized that being successful meant that I was materialistic and selfish. When I debunked that theory, I noticed that I unconsciously believed that being wealthy meant that I was a sell-out. When I untangled myself from that insanity, I recognized that I had crowned myself the financial savior for my family. When I threw away that heavy guilt and unfair burden, I noticed that I always didn't seek advice when I needed it. After I lost about $250k in a shady business deal, I realized that I held tremendous embarrassment about not knowing and not developing the financial literacy I needed to navigate in financial circles. When I healed from that humiliation and recovered from that financial loss, I realized I had still harbored extreme fear and trepidation about taking the risks I needed to build a financial empire. As I mentally processed that financial anxiety, I let envy, resentment, and vitriol from power brokers cripple me at negotiating tables.

Friends, I had some passed-down money beliefs. And the more money I made, the more my issues surfaced. And the more my money issues surfaced, the more money I lost. And the more money I lost, the more embarrassed and unconfident I became. It was a torturous cycle, and I almost gave up because I could not quickly reel in my pride to get help. I lost thousands of dollars, lost my confidence, and practically lost my mind. I almost threw in the towel and gave up on my dream to be an entrepreneur.

Thankfully, I got help and started unraveling all the beliefs, thoughts, and myths I had about money and wealth. Even though I started the unraveling process over twenty years ago, I am still unraveling and unlearning thoughts that are deeply buried in my subconscious. What I am also discovering is that sometimes it's not until people face unfamiliar terrain, explore fresh opportunities, or until they are triggered by pain that passed-down beliefs surface. That's why we must intentionally question anything and everything that affects our ability to dream, trust our own inner wisdom, take calculated risks, or activate our full potential because passed-down beliefs are always lurking in the crevices of your mind, ready to launch a surprise attack when we pursue greatness. They are always present without your consent or permission.

But here is the good news: Four critical questions can liberate you from the grip of passed-down beliefs.

The first question: Why do I believe this theory or view?

Second question: How is that belief supporting, empowering, or transforming me today?

Third question: How is that belief honoring me — my

thoughts, my dreams, my vision, my gifts, my wisdom, and my purpose?

Fourth question: How would believing something different alter my life?

Four critical questions can open you up to alternative possibilities and provide more room for you to find your way to your purpose.

The "E" stands for societal expectations, or what I call "shoulds." And let's face it; we live in a world of "shoulds." From the stifling status quo to the cage of conformity, we are often "shoulded" on because "shoulds" are woven into the fabric of society. They affect and infect us with shame, guilt, and onerous obligations that suppress our identities, dash our hopes, and if we let them, smash our dreams And, if we are not courageous enough to challenge them or if we don't know how to assert ourselves, we acquiesce and wither into a fraction of who we really are. Eventually, after years or decades of being "shoulded" on, many people, unfortunately, give up and settle for living a "good enough" life. They stay in "almost loving" marriages, "almost gratifying" careers, and "almost believed" faith traditions. Many people just resign themselves to "almost" living and never experience real fulfillment or inner peace. In essence, they exist in "should."

What I know for sure is that living your life based on the expectations and "shoulds" will leave you feeling exhausted and resentful. All of the pretending, performing, and producing to make others happy will eventually sap your strength and cancel out your dreams. All of the smiling, caring, and acting will erode your confidence and corrupt your conscience. And all of the sacrificing, subjugating, and struggling will deplete your soul and rob you of your agency to make choices to honor your needs. How do I know? I treated societal EXPECTATIONS as if they were God-given mandates for decades, and as a result, I lived a myopic, mediocre, and meaningless life. My life was "shouldy."

As a coach, it is easy to see the devastation caused by societal expectations. This was definitely the case with Trudi. Trudi was a 53-year-old lesbian who had married a man when she was in her early twenties. Even though she never wanted to marry a man or have children, she eventually had five children and stayed in an abusive marriage for over thirty years. When Trudi's children graduated from college and left home, she mustered enough courage to leave her abusive marriage. She was excited and felt that for the first time in thirty years, she could live her life based on her own desires and needs.

When Trudi was finally ready to embark on her new life, her mother was diagnosed with dementia. And of course, being the only girl, Trudi was expected to drop everything to care for her ailing mom. Her brothers didn't even consider helping with her mother's daily care. According to her brothers, caring for THEIR mom was a woman's job, and providing financial support was the manly thing to do. Here's the kicker: Trudi had been estranged from her mother and family for decades. In fact, she always had a complicated, tortuous relationship with her mother and her family. But because of her upbringing and religious beliefs, her "shoulds," Trudi again put herself on the back burner and surrendered her life to make her estranged siblings happy. She eventually took care of her mother until her mother died.

Trudi's experience may sound extreme, but it's not uncommon. I frequently meet people who have abandoned their dreams, hopes, and peace to do what is expected. I have witnessed people literally waste their lives people-pleasing, ladder-climbing, status-chasing, butt-kissing, image-staging, and "keeping up with the Joneses" while they silently die inside. But with awareness and support, I have also seen people shake off "shoulds," resist expectations, courageously revamp their thinking, and make their own rules too. No, it has not been easy, but it happens. When people can untangle themselves from stereotypes and adamantly oppose being caged and incarcerated by soul-depleting, joy-robbing expectations, people soar.

Fortunately, despite initially being saddled by passed-down beliefs and social expectations, Trudi refused to be bitter. She didn't let her age convince her that her life was over or that she was too old to create a new reality, either. Sure, she had regrets, but she didn't waste more precious time lamenting her past. Trudi thrived, and she continues to live her life today without apology, guilt, and concern for the cultural expectations that kept her trapped in a life that was not her own. Way to go, Trudi!

As you pursue your purpose, it is wise for you to watch out for subtle and overt expectations, too. Anything that sounds like or feels like an unspoken agreement, a cultural assumption, an implied social mandate, an understood religious decree, a historical suggestion, or a gender norm, should be examined. Remember that you have the right and the power to reject any belief that limits or compromises your ability to be fully at peace with your soul.

The "S" stands for systemic influences. Systemic influences are the structural, ideological, and institutional roadblocks that have been created, reinforced, and legalized to ensure that the privileged few stay in power. Systemic influences are invisible, but they are pervasive and prescriptive. They affect your health, where you live, the quality of your education, employment opportunities, death rates, police brutality, sentencing, voting accessibility, wealth building, health care, waste removal services, clean air, access to transportation, food availability, homeownership rates, taxation, life expectancies, and more. Systemic influences touch and taint every aspect of your life; they even determine if you experience the fullness of your humanity, live with dignity, and enjoy all of the benefits of being a citizen.

Most systemic influences are oppressive and immoral; people suffer, especially people who are "colored" and "othered." Why? Because systemic influences perpetually marginalize, tokenize, dehumanize, brutalize and victimize those who Jesus called "the least of these." And they relegate them to the margins of society. In essence, systemic influences are societal, political, and economic thieves. They steal joy, they steal hope, they steal opportunity, they steal justice, they steal protection, they steal fulfillment, and they steal dignity.

Even though America is a culture built on inequality, sustained by oppression, and steeped in injustice, we don't have to succumb to victimhood; we have power. You and I were born powerful, and we have the power to dismantle systems that subjugate us. No, it won't be easy, but when we understand and identify the institutionalized hurdles, the economic challenges, the educational roadblocks, and the political walls that were designed to confine and frustrate us, we can strategize. We can create legislation, protest unfair laws, and make vital choices to catapult us over the heads and beyond the hands of people who wish to intimidate, incarcerate, and immobilize us. We can courageously pivot, shift, and maneuver around and through societal barriers so we can do what God has called us to do. Remember, we are change agents, truth-tellers, and freedom fighters. And even though most of our societal structures are rigged and stacked against us, we still can confront systemic inequities, inspire hope, demolish legalized restrictions, and create change. If you don't believe me, just ask our ancestors because they have testimonies. Despite the consistent horror, disenfranchisement, and the collective abuse they endured, our elders pushed forward, and we can push forward too.

My friend, even though I am optimistic, I don't want to minimize the impact of systemic influences because oppression is suffocating, painful, and dangerous. It is a cancer that has affected and infected America for over 400 hundred years. But though oppressive, I refuse to give up or to give in; I will fight. I will always raise my voice and use my hands to advocate for truth and justice. I refuse to restrict how I move in the world; I will stand up for myself and for people who look like me. I will always call out and challenge systemic influences in all of their forms — patriarchy, white supremacy, and white privilege. And I will always remain committed to partnering with my white, brown, yellow, red, and black brothers and sisters to dismantle systems that hurt people, not only now but for generations to come.

Family, we must never forget that we all must hold America accountable so that its conduct reflects the constitution, its policies are consistent with its precepts, and its deeds align with its creed. It is up to us to ensure that we leave a better, fairer America to our children, grandchildren, and our great-grandchildren. It is up to us, you and me.

The "T" stands for Trauma, and let's be honest; we all have faced some pain in our lives. We all have endured, struggled, and suffered something that we are still trying to process and manage even today. We all have even been wounded in ways we don't even understand, yet, and in some ways, we are still being wounded. Though some people like to minimize or downplay its effect, trauma is real, and it influences how we think, what we think, what we do, and what we say. Trauma profoundly impacts our lives because it simultaneously affects the mind, body, and soul.

What I frequently see in my coaching practice is that many people try to hide and numb their trauma. They use food, sex, religion, achievement, busyness, education, alcohol, drugs, avoidance, under-functioning, and over-functioning to soothe and quiet their internal agony. Some people successfully numb their pain for years until it becomes so unbearable that they are forced to seek help to transform their lives.

I know for sure that healing our trauma is one of the most loving, transformative gifts that we can give ourselves. When we heal those fractured parts of our hearts and souls, we become well and whole. We get to see and know our true essence. We get to explore and activate our gifts, talents, and wisdom. We learn to trust our intuition, listen to our inner sage, and become our internal cheerleaders. When we address our trauma, we blossom, build, and become bold in how we function and engage the world. We get to see our worth, step fully into our worthiness, and experience God's love for us.

My friend, individual, and inherited traumas are real; both are destabilizing and devastating because trauma hides the truth, our truth. Most of all, unhealed and unacknowledged trauma causes death – the death of our dreams, our goals, and our souls. But when we heal it, deal with it, and skill it in ways that are culturally relevant, consistently fair, and individually effective, we can overcome its debilitating effects and rewrite, restructure, and rehabilitate our lives and flourish in ways that satisfy our souls.

I won't spend a lot of time talking about trauma here because, throughout *Deciding To Soar 2*, I share stories about people who have healed their broken places and fortified their fractured souls. I also share how old trauma often rears its ugly head when we are pursuing our dreams or freeing ourselves from destructive habits and toxic relationships. But I will remind you of this one thing: your trauma is your responsibility. Job trauma, relationship trauma, childhood trauma, societal trauma, religious trauma, marriage trauma, environmental trauma, racialized trauma, historical trauma, inherited trauma, ancestral trauma, corporate trauma, or any other trauma that prevents you from being your total self and from functioning at your optimal level is your responsibility. It's your project, it's your issue, and it's your act of self-love. Even if your healing journey requires support, time, and money, healing anything that weakens you is worth the investment because addressing trauma can enhance, expand, and prolong your life.

Finally, the "S" stands for stories – the narratives, thoughts, theories, and/or lies that we create about ourselves and others to help us navigate and bring order to an ever-evolving, technologically-obsessed world. And you and I create stories about everything. For example, we create stories about why somebody doesn't love us, why a person doesn't appreciate us, why somebody looked at us differently, why we can't be authentic, why we can't self-actualize, or why we can't commit to your dreams. We all consciously and unconsciously make up stories in an attempt to bring order to a world that becomes faster, more complicated, and more contradictory every day. Or we make up stories to compensate for our feelings of powerlessness, hopelessness, or unworthiness. Or we make up stories to conceal our fears and to hide our doubts. Or we make up stories to escape our reality and to give us an illusion of safety. Or we quickly create stories or draw conclusions because we fail to question the veracity of what we believe or conjure up in our minds.

Yes, dear family, we are all story-makers, and the stories we create shape our identities and our worldviews. The stories also seduce us into living misaligned and joyless lives. That's why we must remember that the stories we create are mere guesses, not the gospel. They are simple fantasies, not scientific facts. They are our deeply held thoughts, not the universal truth. Family, our stories are just fractions and fragments of our understanding of reality; that's all!

Here is a simple solution: just stop. Stop making up stories. Stop telling yourself lies. Stop making assumptions. Stop jumping to easy conclusions. Stop generalizing. Stop playing follow the leader. Stop looking for simple answers to complex questions. Stop trying to read people's minds. Stop using your standards of understanding as benchmarks for the world. Stop accepting everything you hear. Stop believing that you are privy to all of the facts. Stop thinking you know the full context of a situation. Just Stop!

When you have a feeling or thought, ask questions. Ask questions about people, places, and things before you determine what they mean. Ask questions about the hypotheses you create about beliefs, behaviors, and burdens. Ask questions about the biases you believe, the opinions you follow, and the perspectives you defend. Ask questions about the values you were taught. Ask questions about everything that enters your head before it leaves your mouth. Pressure-test and interrogate everything because the stories you don't challenge today will determine how you approach and live your life tomorrow. Remember...the quality of your life is determined by the quality of your questions. So be courageous and consistent in asking questions to ensure that you live YOUR life, and not the life you were told or taught to live.

I know I covered a lot, but I felt compelled to share this framework with you. So, remember, as you pursue your purpose, you will encounter many P.E.S.T.S. Though invisible, the P.E.S.T.S. will be formidable and pervasive. And how you manage them will ultimately determine your ascension, expansion, income, and influence. But here's good news: you have everything you need to address and defeat all P.E.S.T.S. that prevent you from doing what God has called you to do.

Believe that! Remember that! Soar!

ELDER WISDOM: LESSONS FOR THE JOURNEY

Our elders have the wisdom to help us win.

Declare Today: I will listen and learn from those who have come before me.

59

SOMETIMES PAIN IS THE TUITION YOU PAY WHEN YOU DON'T LISTEN TO WISDOM

Our elders tried to warn us. They told us that a hard head makes a soft behind. But of course, we would not listen. We had to do it our way. We had to have our turn. We had to have our say. And, boy, did we pay a high price for some of our decisions! Even today, some of us are still paying for some of the foolish choices we made in our teens, twenties, and thirties. Consequences are real, and some consequences last a lifetime.

Honestly, I could have saved myself a lot of heartaches and headaches if I had listened to my elders. But for some reason,

I would not heed their advice because I thought my elders just wanted to control me. I also thought their advice was outdated, juvenile, and too simple for high-tech times. But after two divorces, single-handedly raising my son, almost losing a million dollars, and suffering too many fools, I now understand that my elders were trying to teach me, or "learn" me, some fundamental truths about being a Black woman. They had years of experience, deep insight, and the spiritual discernment that I didn't have, but sorely needed. Regrettably, I had to learn the hard way that they could detect evil motives, sense danger, and identify opportunists faster than I could; only life will teach you that.

Unfortunately, I would not listen. But thanks to my constant and long attendance at the University of Adversity, I finally learned some hard but valuable lessons about love, life, and living that they tried to warn me about. I didn't listen thirty years ago, but thankfully, I am wiser and less arrogant now. I have accumulated many battle scars on my journey, and, fortunately, none of my ill-advised decisions and shady dealings were fatal. By the grace of God, I am still here.

In my reflection time, I often wonder why I was so reluctant to heed and honor my elders' time-tested wisdom. Not listening to them just seems absolutely ridiculous to me; ignoring their advice defies common sense. My elders had experience; they had history, and they had mother wit. They had endured and witnessed segregation, Jim Crow, police brutality, church bombings, and other atrocities. They knew stuff, stuff that nobody wrote about or really could write about. Back then, you could get lynched for telling the truth about some of the cruel things that some white people did to black people. Yet, like a petulant child, I discounted, protested, and resisted the very counsel I needed to prosper and grow. I even jeopardized my safety and the safety of my son.

I now realize that my elders were incredibly astute; they had to be. They had lived and survived over 80 years in a chaotic, unjust world; you can't last that long being stupid or naive. They did not have a formal education, but they had the type of knowledge that only comes from lived experience. They had lessons about life that had to be "caught," not taught. I have since learned that caught lessons are the ones that can help you the most when you are in a crunch or a crisis.

Now that I am getting older, I have learned to value and revere my elders, especially now, and I have incorporated many of their time-tested lessons in my life. Lessons like...the most difficult and painful experiences in life can only be overcome by prayer. I learned that lesson after I was laid off after working in one industry for thirty years. After I lost my job, I felt anxious and distraught, and it was my long talks with God that sustained me. During those tearful talks with God, I learned how to listen to my spirit, how to be patient, and how to be grateful. And I finally realized that the answers to life's most pressing questions are never found in books, but are only revealed in prayer.

I also learned that some people are street people, some are porch people, others are house people, and only a few are room people. That's how my elders taught me about relationships. They taught me that access to me must be based on a person's attitude, actions, and their reverence for God. If people lacked those three ingredients, they were relegated to the street and not the room. Why it took me two divorces and five heartbreaks to learn that lesson, I will never know. I painfully had to learn that access to me was a privilege that had to be earned and not a right to be had.

Today it seems funny that I once believed that my grandparents and parents were unlearned, uncouth, and unrefined. My arrogance and ignorance would be comical if the pain that I suffered from my insolence weren't so excruciating. But the older I get, the smarter my elders become. That's why I am more grateful and thankful for their wisdom today. I now understand that they provided good "learning" even when I failed to grasp the good lessons. I know... wisdom is sometimes wasted on fools.

So, if I am older than you are, and even if I am not, please heed my advice. Listen to your elders. Learn their lessons. Leverage their wisdom. Gain and glean from them because they already know some of what you need to know. Don't jeopardize your safety, your success, and your sanity by being a know-it-all.

My friend, you are going somewhere. Where you are going, you will need your elder's wisdom, and most of all, you will need Godly insight because God has given you a purpose. God has also given you a divine plan that you can only execute with wisdom, time-tested wisdom. So, heed so you can lead. Pray so you plan. Meditate so you can maneuver. And be patient so you can prosper.

Are you ready to take flight? Are you prepared to pursue your purpose? Are you prepared to flow in the ease and power of God? If so, let's soar because the best is yet to come.

Let's Dare to Soar Higher!

60

SOMETIMES YOU SEE BETTER WITH YOUR EYES CLOSED

My elders were so smart. They knew that sometimes you see better with your eyes closed. Of course, I didn't believe them, especially when they ordered me to turn off the lights and go to bed. I was afraid of the dark. Also, I was a bit nosy and I didn't want to miss out on anything.

But life has a way of showing you that closing your eyes sometimes perfects your vision. I know it sounds crazy, but there is something about darkness that removes all distractions that helps you focus and dream. That's why I eventually learned to appreciate the darkness because it allows me to fully experience the splendor of life with awe, wonder, and hope. It also gives my imagination room to tumble, twirl, and twist in ways that tickle my soul.

To my elders, seeing with your eyes closed was not just a nice thing to do; it was their survival. Let's face it. Being called "nigga," "boy" and "gal" could not have made them feel proud, dignified, or respected. So, closing their eyes and envisioning something new, better, and fairer gave them something to look forward to. It was the way they persevered and endured the assaults on their humanity. It was how they tasted and touched "real" freedom, something that they never really experienced, but something they hoped for their grandchildren.

When I was a child, I would often sneak into the house to listen to the grown-ups talk. Back then, kids and adults didn't participate in the same conversations, so I had to tiptoe quietly in the room to listen to their discussions. I rarely understood what they said, but I did hear names like Dr. King, Rosa Parks, and Mr. Evers. I didn't know who those people were, but they had to be important because the conversations would quickly turn into praise breaks or contested debates. I later discovered that the tenor and the intensity of the discussions were dependent upon who was in the room.

I would listen intently and see tears in my elders' eyes as they talked about their dreams for my friends and me. It seemed as if they closed their eyes tight as they could, almost squinting, to see a new reality. They closed their eyes to peer into a future where we could attend top-rated schools, own beautiful homes, attend colleges, and enjoy equal rights. I didn't know what colleges were, but I closed my eyes too because I wanted to see what they saw, or at least try to see what they saw.

Throughout my childhood, I constantly eavesdropped on my elders' conversations and watched as they closed their eyes. I tried to imagine what they saw because I knew they were imagining many advancements for Black people. Sometimes they even talked about God. I understood the God part because sometimes I saw God when I closed my eyes, too. However, the God I saw did not look like the pictures I saw in my church. The God at church was white. The God I saw with my eyes closed was Black and had a big white afro.

I personally learned about the power of closing my eyes when I was about six years old. During Sunday school, I told Mother Anne about the problems I was having at school. People were really struggling with integration, and many of the white kids and their parents didn't take too kindly to me being in their classrooms. I guess the government forgot that they could pass integration laws, but they could not legislate love. And, boy, my classmates and their parents didn't love me at all. My swollen eyes, bloody lips, and torn-up homework proved that.

Thankfully, the kids eventually got used to me. Or maybe they grew bored with hitting me. Either way, I was happy. I hate pain, and the daily humiliation chipped away at my delicate self-esteem.

Even though school got better, only slightly better, every time I talked about my dream of having fun at school, Mother Anne would say, "Baby, close your eyes so you can really see your future. You can't see it right if you just look at the world." Mother Anne was the consummate optimist.

Almost fifty years later, I am still heeding Mother Anne's advice. When life gets challenging or if I need spiritual guidance, I close my eyes. I shut them really tight and unleash my imagination. I let my imagination swirl and leap until I see new visions and life-altering miracles. I let my imagination run freely until it gets tired or until it settles down. Once it settles, I open my eyes and write down everything I saw, even if what I saw makes no sense to me. I have learned that my imagination, which I now know is the Spirit, always knows more than I know. So, I am always confident that what I wrote down will eventually make sense to me when I need it most.

If you are having a difficult time or if you feel stuck, why not do what my elders told me to do? Why not close your eyes? Why not remove all distractions and let your imagination run wild? Why not close your eyes and picture what Black life could be if the world was free of oppression, free of white supremacy, and free of institutionalized hate? Why not close your eyes and imagine how wonderful it would be if Black people, white people, brown people, tan people, red people, yellow people, and all hues of people loved each other and celebrated each other's differences? Why not think about how differently-abled people could thrive if the world thought about what they needed before buildings were built? Why not think about how the world can be if people could love who they really loved without judgment? Why not imagine how everyone could have what they needed if the super-rich didn't control everything and shared their resources with the poor? Why not sit still in the darkness and let the Spirit speak to your heart and to your weary soul so you can see new opportunities? Why not let your mind wander and wonder until it uncovers your truth? Why not let yourself see what needs to be seen so you can do what you were called to do?

Yes, my friend, close your eyes. See what you need to see to pursue your purpose. See your potential and new possibilities. See your patterns of self-imposed limitations, self-sabotage, and self-denial. See your inner barriers to love, joy, success, and freedom. See! And then patiently wait, trusting that God will show you more, and show you something bigger and bolder than you have ever seen before.

Are you ready? Close your eyes. Let your spirit roam freely. It's time to Soar!

Your purpose awaits.

61

EVEN THOUGH THEY WERE RAISED WITH YOU DOES NOT MEAN THEY WILL RISE WITH YOU

It's funny how you can be raised by the same parents, in the same home, with the same rules and be totally different than your siblings. Even though you learned the same lessons, were taught the same values, attended the same churches, something about the way you think, act and navigate in the world bears no resemblance to those who share your DNA. You don't really understand how it happened or when it happened, but you are different from your loved ones, as different as night and day. Even when you talk to your siblings, you realize that something is out of sync, off-kilter, or just plain weird. How did your family become so different and divided from you? What happened? Did your parents just pick up a few spare kids at the mall and give them the title of "brother" or "sister" and raise all of you under the same roof? Is that why your siblings are so different?

For years I thought that I was the only person who felt like a stranger in their own family. When I looked at the faces of the people I shared a home and genes with, I saw similarities. We had similar noses, the same shaped heads, and similar eyes. It was obvious that we were physically related, that we shared a genetic pool, but that was it. Nothing else was consistent. There wasn't a theme, a pattern, or a thread of consciousness that wove us together. We were all sojourners trying to find our own way amid constant relocations, poverty, struggle, and young parents trying to parent us while parenting themselves. But I digress.

What I know now for sure is that being raised in the same house does not guarantee that you are of the same spirit. Even though you are genetically related, you may be wired, shaped, and gifted differently because you have a distinct call on your life. No, you are not better; you are not greater, and you are not superior. But you are unique, maybe even peculiar. You discern that something is different about you because you think and behave in ways that appear strange, unorthodox, eccentric, or just plain odd compared to your relatives.

Unfortunately, you may be accused of being an attention grabber or a drama queen or king. But you are not trying to grab attention or stand out; you are trying to figure yourself out. You can't put your finger on it, but you feel an indescribable urge and an unexplained yearning pulling you in a direction that feels familiar but unknown at the same time. You know that something inside your soul is calling you, claiming you and compelling you to do things you have never done before. Yet, you don't fully understand yourself or comprehend the magnitude of what you are feeling.

As a child, nobody really explains what a calling, what a purpose, or what dharma is, or what it means for your life.

Nobody clarifies or affirms the impulses that are guiding you to new opportunities or awakening you to new realities. So, you are just left alone to deal with dreams you can't explain, visions you can't describe, knowledge you have never learned, and feelings you can't define. Have you been there?

Since your loved ones don't understand your oddness or your inclination for going against the grain, they judge it, even though nobody really knows what "it" is. That's why people with world-changing, life-defining, and society-shifting missions become outcasts, pariahs, and "black sheep" in their families. Sometimes people who don't play by family rules or comply with the culturally accepted norms even get socially ousted and rejected by the ones they need the most, their families.

It's so unfortunate because what family members don't understand is that their "deviant" kin is not bad at all. Different, but not deviant. What the family is actually seeing or sensing is greatness. Yes, the family is witnessing greatness that is budding, blooming, and maturing right before their very eyes. Granted, it looks different, but it is not deviant; it's actually divine.

When I think about how siblings sometimes feel about their gifted, attention-getting sibling, I am reminded of Joseph from the Bible. As a child, God gave him visions of greatness, grandeur, and power. Regrettably, Joseph was too young and too immature to know that some visions can't be shared with loved ones. So, he shared his vision, and his brothers were so threatened and jealous of his vision that they threw him into a dark, dangerous pit. Eventually, Joseph was sold into slavery and experienced more hardships. He spent time in prison and was wrongfully accused of flirting with his master's wife. At times, Joseph felt forgotten and tossed aside. But just in case you don't know how the story ends, what Joseph dreamt as a child ultimately comes true. He becomes a leader in a strange land, and through his leadership, a country survived a great famine.

So, purpose seekers, know that your vision, your calling, and your dreams will sometimes make you feel like a foreigner in your own family. And, your dreams may feel so threatening and baffling that your brothers and sisters may retaliate in hurtful ways. You may feel displaced, discounted, and attacked. You may feel lonely and misunderstood. But, be ready. When God plucks you out of obscurity, you may have a "Joseph" experience and feel alienated from the ones you love most.

My friend, you must accept this uncomfortable but irrefutable truth: even though you were raised in the same home with your siblings, does not mean they will experience the same height. You may experience greater success, more notoriety, and earn more money than the people you ate with, celebrated with, struggled with, and grew up with. Again, it does not mean that you are better. It just means that you are on a different path and that you made different choices. It means that you have surrendered to your true nature and that you have tapped into your gifts, which propelled you forward in the world.

As you are pursuing what you were created to do, be aware. Your family may call you selfish because you invest your time, money, and energy in developing your gifts and following your destiny. Your family may use guilt and societal pressure to influence you to stay in places that you have already outgrown. They may even use obligation to make you feel tethered to relationships that are no longer beneficial and healthy for what you feel divinely compelled to do. And as a last resort, they may call you foolish in attempts to discourage you because your dreams are beyond anything that they have ever seen or imagined in their own lives. But, don't get distracted and don't abandon your mission. Be courageous and stay committed. Know that the Inner Guidance, God, will lead you to your highest good.

Yes, you are different, not better or superior, but different. You are anointed to do great things in the world, and your loved ones are anointed, too, even if they don't realize it yet. But you can't wait for them to understand their greatness or recognize their calling before you pursue yours. You can't wait for them to encourage and embrace you and your purpose, either. You don't have time to waste. You don't know when your time on earth will end, so you must seize the moment and activate your gifts. You must do what God has consecrated you to do NOW with faith, focus, and fortitude.

I know it may feel like you are leaving people behind, but you are not. Remember, just because people are raised with you does not mean that they will rise with you. And you can't let their resistance or their failure to rise, clip your wings, or delay your destiny.

It's your time to SOAR so RISE! Take flight! SOAR High! And when you get to a certain altitude, don't forget to swoop back down and bring a few others up with you so they can experience a new dimension of God too.

Blessings!

62

YOUR NOW IS
NECESSARY

Sometimes it is difficult to be fully present in your NOW. You
know, your NOW, the place where you are in your life right
NOW. The emotional, spiritual, financial, intellectual, and
physical place where you currently reside. The NOW.

If the truth be told, sometimes people struggle with their
NOW. In fact, some people spend lots of time ruminating about
their past, wondering what could have been, should have been,
or what would have been if they made different choices in their
lives. Based on their understanding of their past or their
interpretations of their history, some rejoice, some rehearse, and
others lament. Some get so stuck in their memories or get so
paralyzed by their regrets that they lose momentum, abort their
own missions, and forfeit their dreams.

But others get too focused on their future. There's nothing
wrong with being proactive and optimistic, but they stay so
focused on what's imminent that they miss important clues that
they need to make progress TODAY. They keep looking so far

ahead that they fail to seize critical opportunities that are required to prepare, position, and "power" them for their next level. Or, they overlook crucial shifts, competitive trends, and technological advances that could alter the trajectory of their lives. Some are even so forward-thinking that they mismanage the fruitful relationships they NEED that offer peace, promise, and prosperity for the future.

Let's be honest. You can't change the past. You can't predict the future. All you can do is live in the NOW! The NOW!

My friend, your NOW is necessary. It is the time for you to extract the wisdom from your past so you can leverage that wisdom in the future. The NOW is a place to gain greater clarity about who you are, what you need, and what you truly desire so you can VOTE, make decisions, for yourself, and your vision. The NOW is a place to find your courage so you can follow your OWN conscience and not be seduced, coerced, and manipulated by the crowd. Your NOW is a place that you start making healthier connections based on your truth, authenticity, and purpose. Your NOW is when you remove the masks, the personas, the social costumes, the need to please, and your obsession with keeping up with the Joneses so you can be genuinely WHO YOU ARE! The NOW is the time to pull back the curtains, divest of your demons, close the gaps, and sanctify yourself.

My elders were right: Your NOW is a sacred place. It is a time of reflection, renewal, revival, re-invention, and restructuring of your life so you can serve the world in a way that brings fulfillment to you and illumination to others. Your NOW is the time to find harmony within your soul so you feel fully integrated and consecrated to fulfill your purpose.

NOW!!!

So, what are you doing with your NOW? What are you learning in your NOW? How are you growing in your NOW? Who are you forgiving in your NOW? How are you maximizing and optimizing your NOW?

Be present NOW! NOTICE Everything. Be OPEN to

everything. WONDER about everything! Welcome everything that your NOW offers. Do it NOW!

Your NOW is necessary. Why? Because eyes have not seen, and ears have not heard what God has in store for YOU!

It's time to Soar!

63

YOU CAN'T CHOOSE WHEN YOU ARE CHAINED

My elders warned me about chains. Being just three generations away from the most violent institution in history gave them a unique perspective about the indescribable horror of human captivity. They knew what it meant to be physically captured and emotionally controlled because their parents and grandparents shared stories, but really nightmares, about how Black people suffered during slavery. They said that white slaveholders were cruel and that Black people were dehumanized. For centuries, Black people were branded, beaten, maimed, raped, exploited, and sold for greed and gain. And even after slavery was legally abolished, very little changed. Many Blacks were still physically confined and socially restricted, and when they tried to assert their independence or demand equal rights, they were threatened. Blood-thirsty mobs, hooded night-riders, bombed homes, torched churches, and indiscriminate lynching kept black people "in their place." And what intimidation didn't do, Jim Crow laws legalized.

Yes, my elders knew a lot about slavery, and that's why they always warned me about chains. They said, "Baby, we fought hard to get the chains off your ankles. Don't let people put chains around your head." Honestly, I didn't know what they meant. I could not even imagine what chains around my head even looked like, nor could I imagine what it meant to be shackled. But just because I couldn't visualize the chains didn't mean that I didn't heed their advice. As a child, I learned to tuck my elders' wisdom and warnings away in my soul, knowing that God would help me recall the lessons when I needed them most. Trust me, those lessons kept me alive and sane for over fifty years.

Honestly, I didn't always agree with everything my elders said, but I did listen to their sage advice. Back then, we respected our elders more than our society honors and celebrates seasoned people today. We didn't dismiss their lived advice or experience; we listened because we didn't have books to teach us how to survive in racially hostile environments. Back in the day, you could not broadcast everything that happened without some retaliation. So, we had to rely on our elders to pass down the insight and strategies we needed to endure, albeit as second-class citizens, until we finally achieved equal rights. As a side note: equality still does not exist yet in America; old, institutionalized systems are resistant to change. But we are making strides toward fairness. But that's a different story.

I had to be around nine or ten years old when I finally understood the significance of the elders' advice about shackles. It was Career Day at my elementary school, and I was excited about sharing my future dreams with my classmates. I couldn't wait to tell them that I wanted to be a broadcaster like Carole Simpson and a writer like Mother Maya. When it was my turn to share, I stood up, marched to the front of the class, and proudly shared about my chosen careers. In my "white people" voice, the voice I learned from watching how Black women spoke to white people, I regaled them with stories about my dreams. Yes, I was going to be on the radio and in bookstores. I was going to be on TV and speak on stages. Me! Yes, I had a great future waiting for me. Boy, I was proud!

Unfortunately, I was the only person who was proud and excited. Nobody else seemed thrilled about my career aspirations, and I was quickly told that there were few *colored* newscasters and authors in the world. In other words, think again because those professions were above and beyond you. I was encouraged to pick something more realistic for a career.

I didn't have anything to refute or challenge my teacher's assertion. Heck, I was a kid. I knew Mother Maya wrote books, but I did not have the heart or confidence to challenge my teacher's estimation of me and my future. How could I? My teacher was an adult. She was an authority, right? She knew more than I did, right? Totally deflated and humiliated, I hung my head and shuffled back to my desk.

Since I received so much negative feedback from my teachers, I stopped sharing my goals and dreams. I could not understand their motives, but somehow my teachers made it their business to ensure that my expectations were low. For example, when it was Career Day, my teachers always highlighted prestigious jobs like doctors, lawyers, teachers, and veterinarians for the white kids. They had pictures, magazine covers, guest speakers, and everything. For the Black kids, even though it was just a handful of us, we were shown pictures of mail carriers, truck drivers, maids, and custodians. I was not interested in any of those jobs; I wanted to be on the radio and television and write books.

I wish I could say that my teachers' subtle and overt discouragement was short-lived, but it was not. Their comments about appropriate careers for people like me were so consistent that it felt as if they were trying to brainwash me into believing that my choices were limited or that I was disqualified from having bigger dreams. It was the craziest thing because I thought teachers were supposed to inspire students to think big and reach for the sky. But I soon realized that dreaming big was only for the white kids, not me. I was expected to stay on the ground, plead for scraps, and beg for handouts from the self-appointed elite.

Thankfully, I always remembered what my elders said about chains. I am not sure how I connected the dots, but I realized my teachers were attempting to put chains around my head. I recognized they were intentionally or unconsciously trying to chain me to a life of under-achievement, under-fulfillment, under-payment, and under-development. They were grooming me to be perpetually poor in spirit and in life. My so-called teachers somehow knew that they didn't have to put shackles on my legs or handcuffs around my arms if they put *their* limits in my head. Corrupting and shrinking my thinking would naturally encourage me to downsize and abandon my dreams. If I felt chained to inferiority and was successfully socialized to expect and accept crumbs, I would never raise my hand to eat at an abundant buffet replete with options and opportunities. And, of course, I would not raise my voice to demand better treatment for myself or my community.

What my teachers didn't understand was that my elders had warned me about putting chains around my head. My teachers didn't realize that I was taught to resist opinions and dismiss beliefs that didn't align with the mantras of the day. In the early 1970s, Jesse Jackson did his best to embed his "I am somebody" messages into the hearts and minds of Black children. And, I believed him; I was somebody.

My parents also made sure that I knew I had the right and the responsibility to have my own dreams and goals. At the time, my father worked for an organization called Project Equality, and I often overheard conversations about self-determination and self-actualization. Even though I didn't know what either word meant, I somehow knew that the words meant that I was not completely powerless. I instinctively knew that I had a modicum of agency and autonomy to create a life that felt good to my soul.

Eventually, my teachers could tell that I didn't heed their advice or accept their limited viewpoint on my ability. Since I wouldn't consent and comply with their sub-standard opinion of me, they labeled me a maverick, rebel, and a troublemaker. To them, I was "high-minded," which meant that I was an uppity negro who would not accept nor absorb their pejorative programming. I would not stay in the place prescribed for people like me.

But I could not internalize their negative judgments and low expectations for people who looked like me. Accepting that I was confined to a lifetime of menial jobs, poverty, and endless struggle was debilitating to my spirit and troubling to my soul. My spirit could not accept that my dreams had to die, especially before they even had a chance to live. I didn't want to be a maid, a garbage collector, or a mail carrier. There's nothing dishonorable about those professions, but I wanted to be what I wanted to be. I was a bold little Black girl with high hopes and big dreams. I didn't care what my teachers said; my future was not bleak, and their predictions were not true. I would have a career on the radio, speak on stage, and write books.

Thankfully, my father was a college student, proving that their assumptions about Black people were inaccurate. Black people could go to college and have "white" people jobs; unfortunately, that is what I called jobs that required a college education. Remember, my *teachers* taught me that, too.

I wish I could say that elementary school was my last experience with people trying to put chains around my head, but I can't. For the last four decades, people have continuously tried to enslave me or expected me to enslave myself. It's incognizable, but people actually expected me to relinquish or dilute my goals to accommodate their bigotry. Some have used manipulation, intimidation, ex-communication, blackmail, and abuse to "break my will," which was also the prevailing goal during the most horrific institution known to humanity – slavery.

It wasn't easy, but I have tried my best to escape being confined and pigeonholed. At times, I felt like I was running away like Harriet Tubman to secure my intellectual independence so I could have my own thoughts and live my own life. It was difficult then, and it is still difficult today. But I am committed to being free and radically thinking for myself, even if it means being by myself.

What I know for sure is that I am a revolutionary, a trailblazer, and a visionary. I refuse to concede to the tyranny of the crowd. I won't be dissuaded by the mandates of a mob. I am the boss of me. I have a brain, and I will create my own beliefs, think my own thoughts, and write my own narratives. No Chains for me!

My friend, you have a purpose, which means you cannot be chained to societal norms, historical beliefs, or cultural expectations. You cannot comply with any system that requires blind allegiance or demands that you hand over your dignity. You are a one-of-kind phenomenon with a unique perspective of the world, which means that you must maintain your intellectual agility and autonomy to do what God has called you to do.

Yes, my elders were right. Chains around your head will enslave you. You cannot become the highest version of yourself or contribute at your highest level if you are incarcerated by perspectives, policies, and principles that discount and degrade you. You cannot activate your gifts if you are suffocated and suppressed by the status quo, or numbed by conformity. You need to be free.

So, as you are pursuing your purpose, remember that you can't bloom in bondage, and you can't contribute in captivity. You need mental space to explore and examine the world in ways that expand your mind and feed your soul. To function at full capacity and with full creativity, you need room to stretch out and break free from societal boxes. You need liberation, mental liberation, to be who God created you to be.

My friend, question everything. Resist being mentally chained to any belief that weakens your insight, innovation, and integrity. Maintain a healthy disregard for established traditions and theories so you can shift your mind, sift through old paradigms and SOAR beyond limits. Stay free because you have a purpose, and your unique God-designed purpose can't be confined or defined by the dictates of the world.

Stay free because you have a job to do and a God to glorify!
Are you ready?
It's time to Soar!

64

INEXPERIENCE ALWAYS HAS SOMETHING TO SAY UNTIL REALITY SHUTS ITS MOUTH

As a child, my elders warned me and my friends about "talking out of turn." They said, "Until you have walked in somebody's shoes, shut your mouth. Don't put your mouth on somebody's life."

They were not playing with us either; their admonishments were stern, swift, and sharp. Life was different then. Talking "out of turn" or "running your mouth" was discouraged, and the entire community enforced the "no gossiping" policy too.

Even though I knew better, one day, I got caught gossiping. I thought I was secretly whispering about my neighbors' daughter. But of course, somebody overheard me "running her name through the mud." My neighbor's daughter was pregnant and unmarried, and since I knew three scriptures, I christened myself, judge, jury, and Jesus. I condemned the pregnant girl, talked about her hell-bound family, and even sent the pregnant girl to hell a few times before I got caught trashing her. And boy, did I get it. I got a whooping and a lecture. I still remember how Mother Mary gave me the evil eye when she said, "Child, don't put your mouth on her life until you have lived enough life of your own." Yikes!

As I said before, our elders were quick and direct with rebukes. They didn't sugarcoat anything; kids were not pacified or indulged. Our elders were committed to cultivating us to be wise warriors so we could contend with oppression, conquer obstacles, and create our own opportunities. But that's another story.

Since I have endured my own missteps and experienced a bit of personal ridicule myself, I now faithfully follow my elders' advice and keep my thoughts to myself. And when I am tempted to share my unsolicited opinions, I always remember Mother Mary's warning to, "Shut *your mouth because most people are usually doing the best they can, and what you can't.*"

As a coach, I have learned that there is always a back story to every situation; there is always more than meets the eye. You may not agree with the story, but there are always circumstances or reasons people do what they do. Also, there are always pieces of the story that you will never understand, even if you had all the facts. Life is tricky like that.

That's why it's important to understand this thing called **Inexperience**. I had to learn the hard way that Inexperience is always puffed up and prideful. It loves to weigh in on complicated issues, but it revels in folly and never researches the facts. As a result, it has lots of words, but little wisdom.

Inexperience also loves to talk, speculate, and advise about what could have been prevented or what should have been done, even though it lacks education, experience, or any willingness to make a difference. *Inexperience* offers little and adds little, yet shares much. *Inexperience* can be extremely irritating.

But when *Reality* shows up and exposes the contradictions and complexities of life, *Inexperience* usually shuts its mouth because it realizes that it knows nothing. *Inexperience* eventually understands that it does not appreciate the context or extenuating circumstances of a situation. It does not understand the history, the mitigating forces, or the systemic conditions that created the issue. It only has a shallow, cursory, and narrow understanding of the problem at hand. That's why *Inexperience* only recommends untested, unproven, and unscientific theories and therapies that can't be substantiated or implemented.

Now, just so that you know: *Inexperience* is stubborn. Though it provides information that is invalid, unethical, and irrelevant, it will not close its mouth. It will keep promoting its warped sense of truth, biased beliefs, and illogical solutions to anyone willing and desperate enough to listen. It will insist on judging, speculating, and hypothesizing until eventually, **Reality** steps in and says, "shut up and sit down until you get some sense."

My elders were right: shut your mouth, and don't "talk out of turn." Until you have walked a mile or even a few steps in someone's shoes, you don't know enough data to have an opinion or to determine what needs to happen in a particular situation. So, stay focused on your calling. Don't judge, and don't preach about someone else's life. You don't know what you will do until you have to wear the same shoes, in the same size, while walking the same path. As my elders used to say, "You never know what you will do until you have to do it." Wise advice, right?

Focus on you and what God has called you to do. And hopefully, when you need wisdom, you will have experienced enough *Reality* to shut *Inexperience's* mouth too.

Are you ready to focus on your own purpose? It's time to Soar Higher!

65

SOME SECRETS ONLY SURFACE IN SILENCE

When we were younger, our elders used to say, "Go sit your narrow behind down somewhere!" Do you remember that? I thought that my elders were being mean when they gave us that directive. But life has shown me that sitting down and stillness can have a sobering effect on your life. Life has taught me that it is in the quiet times when we turn down the volume in our minds and turn up the volume in our souls that we can really HEAR!

So, what do we hear? We HEAR what our souls are saying. We HEAR what our souls need. WE HEAR what our souls are yearning for. WE HEAR the cries of our souls pleading with us to be who we used to be before we were weighed down by expectations, reduced by socialization, and burdened by obligation. WE HEAR our abandoned destinies beckoning us to reclaim our divine callings so we can deliver our gifts to the world. We HEAR cries of our inner child begging to be unconditionally heard, seen, known, and loved without judgment. WE HEAR pleas of our authenticity urging us to take off our masks, abandon our public personas, and live freely. We hear our inner truth imploring us to accept who we are without defending, hiding, or pretending to be someone that we are not. We HEAR our minds requesting to be stretched and cultivated to heal the collective wounds of the world. We HEAR our spirits inviting us to shed old ways and outdated paradigms so we can embrace what's emerging in our lives. We HEAR God's urging us to step away from what we know so we can see what's new. When we are quiet, we hear!

Yes, when we are quiet and still, we hear secrets. We HEAR secrets from God that remind us that we are valuable and valued. We hear secrets from God that give us divine direction and data. We hear secrets from GOD that provide us with heavenly insight and inspiration. We hear secrets from God that bring us comfort and activate our courage. We hear secrets from God that confirm our calling, journey, and vision. We hear secrets from God that remind us we are not alone; God is always with us and in us. Secrets. Yes, if we are quiet, God shares secrets.

My friend, get still. Settle your mind and prepare to hear from God. Remove all distractions and filters. Turn off the TV. Turn off your phone. And then, wait and be open. Trust that the secrets will come when you least expect, and when they arrive, they will provide you with the plan you need and the peace you crave.

Never forget that God was speaking to us before we were born. Yes, God always spoke to us and continues to speak to us. God speaks to us in our dreams, through signs, through nature, and through our imagination. God will always speak to us.

My friend, my elders had it right. Go sit down somewhere. It's time to talk with God.

It's time To Soar Higher!

66

SOME DOLLARS AIN'T WORTH A DIME

"All money, ain't good money." My elders used to say that all of the time. But I didn't believe them until I became an entrepreneur. When I started my coaching business, I realized that some people were draining, disrespectful, and disruptive. In fact, there have been times when I wanted to pay some of my clients to leave, to take their butts and their business elsewhere. You know I am right!

So before you sign that contract, accept that agreement, ask for that raise, accept that promotion, take on that new client or get into a new relationship, ask yourself if it is worth it. Ask yourself if the money is worth the mess. Consider if the money you earn will be worth the misery you will endure. Determine if the blessing today will feel like a burden tomorrow. Stop to assess if the new event is the most effective use of your time, talent, and treasure. And most of all, determine if the new opportunity aligns with your divine assignment. Ask yourself critical questions before you accept anything—a job, a client, a lover, and even a perspective. And then use wisdom.

Often we create our own misery because we prematurely make agreements and decisions that cause us to live in defeat, deficit, and depression. Trust me. There is always more than meets the eye. That's why eyesight and insight are equally important; you need them both when you are determining how to move forward in your life and how to execute your purpose.

My friend, you have a purpose! And anything that jeopardizes your energy or integrity is not worth your time. So, heed the advice of my elders and remember that some dollars ain't worth a dime.

It's time to Soar!

67

YOU WILL PAY A
HIGH PRICE FOR
LOW LIVING

As a preacher's kid, the church was a constant influence in my life; my very existence revolved around it. For example, school, sports, and Girl Scouts meetings were scheduled around choir rehearsals, bible studies, and mid-week services. Bible quotes were often mixed with words of discipline, Bible stories were used to explain the news, and religious platitudes were used as personal greetings. Everything was based on church, because of church and involved church. The church was the focus of my life. It was my sanctuary, my playground, my classroom, my gathering place, my developmental center, my extended family, and my moral guide. Church was everything.

Although I learned many lessons from church, there is one adage that stays firmly etched in my mind. At least once a week, one of the elders, the church mothers, the deacons, or a seasoned somebody would say, "you will pay a high price for low living."

That statement was quoted so regularly that I could anticipate when the phrase was going to be used in a sermon, lesson, or prayer. Believe me, that saying was a staple in church gatherings. And, if I had a dollar for every time I heard it, I would be not rich but wealthy.

Even though I heard the phrase hundreds of times, I can admit that the statement was timeless advice. But there was one problem: everybody had a different interpretation of "low living." We all knew that the Ten Commandments was high living. And, we all accepted that over-indulging in drugs, alcohol, sex, and partying were examples of low living. We also all agreed that lying, greed, whoremongering, and any type of abuse was gutter-dwelling, also defined as "low living." But what about the activities, views, and issues that were not directly spelled out in the Top 10? What about the extenuating circumstances that didn't fit nicely into the "high living" category?

Trust me, I asked many questions because I wanted to live a good life, which to me, was a godly life. Most of all, I wanted to do something unique and meaningful in the world. I didn't want to jeopardize my future or miss out on opportunities to have what others considered "fun." I had witnessed too many people lose and destroy their lives by succumbing to reckless living and destructive addictions. I knew firsthand that yielding to "fun," or what was considered as "fun" was not fun at all. In fact, some of the secret, criminal activities I saw were dangerous and seductive, not fun. Families were disrupted, and futures were lost. What many people thought was harmless entertainment turned out to be harmful entrapment and chemical enslavement. I wanted a different fate; I had a purpose.

That's why I needed answers. I wanted clarification and spiritual direction. I wanted references, roadmaps, and rule books to keep me on a straight and narrow path. My future was too important to be governed by my feelings, promises of "fun" or random emotions. I wanted a definitive answer as to what made up "low living" to ensure that I didn't cheapen or ruin my life.

Suffice it to say; I never got a comprehensive answer as to what characterized "low living" and what constituted "high living." My other questions never got answered either. Questions like: what do you do when your own ideas, standards, and interpretations rub up against the socially accepted philosophies and touted beliefs? How do you still live "high" when you are required to live by a definition of "high" that contradicts your conscience? Who determines "low living" when there is variability based on culture and upbringing? Many of my questions could not be answered with certainty. That's why the Holy Spirit is so essential in our walk with God.

Since there was so much variability, I devised my own definition of "low living." For me, "low living" is about living without ethics, standards, and morals. It's when you are controlled by greed, immorality, injustice, sadistic beliefs, and serpentine practices that fail to honor God and God's people. And when you violate God and God's people, you will pay a high spiritual, political, and financial price for those abuses. You can even go to jail.

But, I have also learned that "low living" is when you downplay who you are, what you feel, and what you stand for to be accepted by the crowd. It is when you betray yourself and deny your exceptionalism and your God-given anointing to accommodate and appease others. "Low living" is when you trade little pieces of yourself for glory or gain. That's low living! Denying who you are or denigrating yourself is the worst; it's hard to get lower than that.

Granted, on the surface, not embracing who you are and celebrating your giftedness may not seem costly. Minimizing who you are may even be mistaken for modesty and humility. But when you fail to honor how God created you and ignore what God has called you to do, you suffer. You experience constant unhappiness, chronic underachievement, and chronic dis-ease. Don't believe me? Just look at the world. Many people are miserable now because they didn't cultivate their gifts or courageously pursue their goals. Or, because they have settled into places, positions, and with people who are beneath their desire, ability, and calling. Or, because they muted their voices, morphed their identities, and mangled their bodies to conform to societal norms and cultural standards. And now they are paying the high price of regret because they are stuck living lives that belie their potential and undermine God's promise for their lives. Now, that's "low living."

I am sure that my elders were referring to the Ten Commandments and other biblical texts when they warned us about the high price of "low living." But I had to learn the hard way that "low living" includes living in ANY way that robs you of your self-respect, self-love, self-confidence, and your God-given identity. I also had to learn the hard way that nothing creates spiritual bankruptcy and emotional poverty more than abandoning who you are and forsaking what God has ordained you to do — your purpose. So, I decided to live a "high life," a life in total alignment with God's desires for my life. Because, to me, living a "high life" is living a life of purpose.

My friend, living a purpose-filled life may not be the easiest life to live, but it is the path you were uniquely created to live. It's the path that will ignite your soul and inspire your heart. So, why not try to live it courageously, tenaciously, and unapologetically?

I don't know about you, but I plan to heed my elders. And as they lovingly warned me, I want to warn you that "you will pay a high price for low living." So, make sure you are living a "high life" full of your God-given purpose, a few good people, and inner peace. That way, you will pay the right price for something that genuinely fills your soul with endless value, joy, and meaning.

Are you ready?

It's time to Soar!

68

DON'T LET WHAT BIRTHED YOU YESTERDAY BECOME YOUR BONDAGE TOMORROW

"Baby, goodbye is a gift."

I didn't understand what Mother Bea meant when she told me that years ago. Goodbye and gift in the same sentence? That perspective was hard for me to grasp because all of my "goodbyes" had been tear-jerking, nose-sniffling, gut-wrenching experiences. They were not gifts, or at least that is what I thought.

But I learned that as we evolve, we will experience many goodbyes. We will experience many beginnings and endings. We will go through many births and deaths because life is a series of starts and stops. It is a process of learning, unlearning, and relearning. It is a journey of forming, norming, performing, and if you are intentional, transforming. Life is full of transitions.

But there comes a time in life when the people, places, and perspectives that birthed your new consciousness, your new sense of self, and your new clarity, will no longer be places of growth. Those initial birthing places that gave you life, love, and liberty will become places of oppression, suppression, and repression. If you stay too long, those places will become sources of bondage and will impede your ongoing evolution, elevation, and experimentation.

Those places are not bad; they are just no longer for you. They are no longer purposeful for your development, calling, and your path. And, if you stay in those outgrown, confining places, you will forfeit your dreams, desires, and destiny.

So, what can you do? You say, thank you. You thank those people who were instrumental in shaping who you are today. You thank those philosophies that helped you challenge convention, eradicate old paradigms, and question your old narratives. You thank those places that served as sanctuaries for your wounded soul. Lovingly, you say thank you with all the gratitude that your heart, mind, and soul can muster. Then, you MUST say goodbye. Maybe not goodbye forever, but goodbye for now because your journey continues and so should you.

Tell the old you, goodbye.

It's time to Soar!

69

DON'T WAIT UNTIL YOU'RE ALMOST GONE TO BE GRATEFUL

It is such a blessing and an honor to spend time with people who know that they are coming to the end of their physical lives. Knowing that they have limited time on Earth, they are not interested in empty platitudes; they don't care about being politically correct, and they are not trying to impress you with big words. When people are nearing the end of their physical lives, they drop all pretenses and posturing because they feel an urgency to share the truth, the unvarnished, unadulterated truth.

That's why if you are fortunate enough to spend time with people who are transitioning, you must cherish the experience. You must open your heart as wide as you can and listen. And as you listen with your heart, you will feel as if you are taking an intimate stroll down memory lane. You will learn of their great joys, painful regrets, passionate loves, empty relationships, celebrated successes, and heart-crushing failures. Since they are slowly transitioning and preparing to return to God, there is no embarrassment or little concern about egos. You will get to experience their true essence and despite the sadness and grief, it's beautiful.

As I was sitting with Mother Sadie, I learned so much about her world. I learned about the highs and the lows of seeing the world change from an industrial age to a technological age. I learned what it was like to participate in freedom marches, drink at "Black only" water fountains, and endure the degradation of entering restaurants from the back door. I had an opportunity to learn how risky it was to travel in the South and how racism was still present, but different, in the North. I heard a few painful stories about racism that made my blood boil because even in 2020, we are still fighting the same battles today.

I also learned some important life lessons. For example, I learned that it is important to hold grief in one hand while holding hope in the other hand because the road to progress will make you cry and cheer at the same time. I also learned that anger could be fuel, wounds could be wisdom, and forgiveness could build bridges between Black people, brown people, and white people. I learned much from those beside chats. Mother Sadie shared many lessons with me that created life-altering shifts and much-needed transformation in my own life.

But one day, she said something that hit me right in the middle of my heart. She said, "Baby, don't wait until you're almost gone to be grateful." That statement really touched my soul because it made me wonder if I consistently express gratitude to the people I love. Often, the people who share their precious time with us and love us the most, are the ones we overlook; we take their love and presence in our lives for granted.

When I reflected on my purpose journey, I realized that it was always the same seasoned saints who encouraged, advocated, and supported me. It was the same consistent few who generously shared words of kindness, greeted me with loving smiles, and always wrapped me in their loving arms. It was the same people who never sought the spotlight, kept my secrets, never missed a book signing, or a speaking engagement. It was the same ones who proofread my articles, served food at my programs, helped decorate meeting rooms, shared strategies for execution, gave me money for resources, and never thought any task was beneath them if it meant helping me. It was the same faithful folks, just a few, who provided the emotional and financial infrastructure I needed that helped me do what God had ordained and anointed me to do. It was just a handful of honest helpers who loved me into greatness and supported my every move.

Over the years, I have realized that the purpose journey is definitely a faith walk. To do what God has called us to do, we often walk up steep mountains and crawl through some desolate valleys. But thankfully, God sends people to walk with us, so we are not alone, especially when we are the most vulnerable or when we are tempted to throw in the towel.

Mother Sadie made me wonder if the people who loved me the most knew how much they enriched my life. So tonight, as you reflect on your purpose journey, think about the people who have always been there to support you when everybody else left you high and dry. Think about the people who made the calls, made the cakes, and made a difference. Then, call them, text them, or send them a letter to let them know that you are grateful for their presence in your life.

As Mother Sadie reminded me, I want to remind you, "don't wait until you're almost gone to be grateful." Don't wait until your breathing becomes shallow or your heart slows down before you say, "I love you." Tell everyone who has supported you that you love them, that you appreciate them, and that they meant something to your life. While you are growing, while you celebrating, and while you are being celebrated, don't forget to express your gratitude to the faithful folks who cared when others didn't. Yes, say thank you.

"Don't wait until you're almost gone to be grateful."

Thank you, Mother Sadie, for that important reminder, and I

look forward to seeing you again in the great bye and bye. But while I am here on Earth, I promise to do my best to honor your sacrifice and continue pursuing my purpose with power, grace, and love.

I Love you!

I will always Dare to Soar Higher!

70

FAITH NEEDS FEET

If you know anything about African American culture, you know that our elders used to tell tall tales. I call them "I used to walk" stories. All you had to do was complain about walking somewhere, and they would say, "When I was your age, I had to walk five miles to school." Not to be outdone, another elder would say, "That's nothing, I had to walk 10 miles in the rain without an umbrella to catch the bus." Somebody would top that, and they would say, "When I was 8, I had to walk 15 miles to school in the snow with no shoes and no coat." You see, it was a competition. Everybody had an "I used to walk" story, and I enjoyed listening to them share exaggerated tales about braving the elements.

One day I asked Momma Dee, "Why everybody always got to tell us how far they walked?" I put some sass on my question too. I had my hands on my imaginary hips like I was grown. I wanted an explanation. Child, you know Momma Dee corrected me before she answered me. Back then, our elders "kept a child in a child's place." Times were different then; we didn't talk back to our elders. We didn't get sassy attitudes; we didn't smack our lips or raise our voices. Age garnered respect.

After she chastised me for acting "grown," she said, "Baby, back then, faith had feet. We didn't have cars. We were poor, and it was hard to get cars on credit. Those car places would rip you off because some of us couldn't read. But that didn't stop us from going where we had to go. We just walked to school, we walked to church, and we walked to work. We walked because we wanted something out of life. We were going somewhere even if we had to use what the Good Lord gave us."

Wanted something out of life? I can't say I knew what that meant, but her message was clear. Faith required you to move. Faith had to have feet, or it really wasn't faith.

Momma Dee's message still resonates with me today, especially as I walk in my purpose. Truth be told... there have been many times when I didn't want to walk because the journey felt too hard or because the process required me to walk too long. Sometimes, I didn't let my faith walk because I didn't realize that faith would sometimes require me to walk by myself through some scary places and with some unscrupulous people. Sometimes I didn't let my faith walk because I could not see my way; I had no direction and no counsel.

Despite their challenging circumstances, my elders walked; they had faith. They knew that their own deliverance was in their feet. And so they courageously walked through some dangerous places and through some harsh conditions. Many times my elders were opposed, blocked, and sometimes restrained. They were hosed, mauled by vicious dogs, and dragged down streets. They were beaten, bloodied, and berated. They were spat on, insulted, and lynched. Yet, they walked. They walked full of hope that their latter days would be better than their former days. Their faith had feet.

My elders bravely walked, and since they walked, I now know that I can walk too. I now know that I can walk even if I am blinded by fear, doubt, and insecurity. I now know I can walk amid agony, abuse, and adversity. I now know that I can even walk alone because my faith has feet. And with each step, I can change my life, and contribute to the collective healing of the world.

As we end our time together, I hope your faith now has feet. And, I hope your faith gives you the courage to walk into places that are new, unpopular, innovative, and cutting-edge without you second-guessing yourself. I hope your faith walks you into situations that are beyond your experience, your culture, and your imagination armed with a fierce determination to add value and substance. I pray that your faith walks you into healing circumstances, wholesome communities, and loving partnerships so you can experience the true meaning of belonging. I pray that your faith walks you into nursing homes, prisons, halfway houses, drug clinics, foster homes, and homeless shelters so you can meet and understand the plight of those who have been pushed to the margins. I pray that your feet keep moving after every fall, get strengthened after every stumble, and run eagerly toward every fruitful opportunity. I pray that God fortifies your feet and orders your steps as you walk toward indescribable joy and fulfillment.

My friend, your purpose is calling you. You are being summoned to create what's needed, to fix what's broken, and to correct what's wrong. You are being positioned in places to meet people who are outside of your culture, your community, and your comfort zone so that your truest nature can be revealed and activated. Your mind is being expanded, and your energy is being renewed because you are stepping into a greater dimension of your destiny. You are going somewhere.

My friend, it is your time to be a vessel, conduit, and catalyst for change, connection, and creativity. It is time for your life to unfold into an unspeakable abundance that blesses humanity. It's your time for you to grab hold and launch into your purpose and let God take you where you need to go. It's your time. It's your time. It's your time. It's your time.

Your faith has feet.

You have everything you need.
Your purpose awaits.
Blessings to you as you Soar Higher!

EPILOGUE

Embracing your purpose means you have decided to SOAR! It means you have decided to cherish and activate the God-given blueprint that was designed for your unique assignment. It means you have made a courageous choice, knowing that the path of purpose will be filled with mountains and valleys, joy and pain, and, most importantly, clarity and complexity. It also means you have decided to be daring and risk rejection and ridicule for the ultimate reward – fulfillment.

Remember, you can't SOAR by yourself. You are indeed great, but you are more powerful and effective in a community. So, let your purpose pick your people because your purpose knows who is needed for every step of this journey. And, never forget that advanced technology alone is never enough; you need battle-tested wisdom that only comes through the lived experience of those who have gone before you.

As you create a life and a movement, hold tight to your integrity. There will be temptations on every side that will try to derail and seduce you. But be vigilant and prayerful because all entrapments start as enticements. Don't compromise your calling, and don't ruin your rewards.

Most of all, remember that you are a creator and an initiator. You were born to make a difference, and your greatest contributions will depend on your ability to stay true to who you are. So stay conscious and stay connected to your Creator. Listen and heed the Spirit. Trust that God will guide and protect you.

In everything, seek God first and seek God always because you are about to do something that has never been done before. And you can do it! It's the truth, your truth!

It's your time! Your purpose is calling.

Blessings to you as you launch, and continued blessings as you SOAR HIGHER in your God-given assignment.

Let's Dare To Soar Higher!

ACKNOWLEDGMENTS

To God, the Divine Protector and Orchestrator. Thank you for orchestrating my life in a way that prepared me for such a time as this. I am grateful and I love you.

My parents, Dorethia Jamison and Rev. Franklin Jamison, thank you for your love, support, and encouragement. I appreciate the sacrifices and struggles you endured for our family. I love you both.

My father, Rev. Franklin Jamison. Daddy, thank you for believing in me as an author. Your advice, support, and encouragement continue to elevate me and refine me as a writer. Writing with you is one of the highlights of my life.

My son, Tariq R. Abdul-Haqq. You are one of my greatest gifts. You taught me love, patience, and forgiveness. I love you, and I am excited to see what God has in store for you. You are an incredible writer and poet. I can't wait until the world meets you and experiences gifts.

Minister Carrole Moss, my Momma C. You have supported me, cheered for me, encouraged me, and loved me for decades. Your love warms my heart. I am so proud of you and your ministry. I love you.

Mother Lucille Grinnell. Thank you for unconditionally loving me and my son. Your love is healing and therapeutic. I love you.

My pastor and mentor, Dr. Kenneth Lee Samuel. Thank you for your leadership and development. You are one of the best orators and teachers in the world. I am grateful to serve with you and to be mentored by you.

Rev. Gwendolyn McCalep, thank you so much for your prayers

and support. Your attention to detail and your willingness to walk this journey amid your own personal challenges was God-ordained.

Janice D. Bonner, thank you for listening and helping me get clarity about the messages I wanted to share. Thank you. I appreciate you.

Natasha Gomes, thank you for crying with me and reminding me to breathe. I can't wait until the world gets to experience your incredible gift of love and creativity. Thank you!

Reche' Tariq Abdul-Haqq, thank you for always reading, editing, and offering constructive feedback. You have been one of my best friends for almost thirty years. Thank you!

Alex Okoroji, my sister-friend. You are brilliant. You are a creative genius. Your ability to see me and see my potential encourages me to try new things. Thank you, Sis! I love you.

Yvette D. Bennett, thank you for walking on another literary journey with me. I appreciate your insight, your eye for detail, and your willingness to cheer me on. I can't wait to cheer for you when you win an Oscar.

To my supporters who have cheered for me and loved me. Thank you for reading my books, inviting me to speak, reading my posts, liking my messages, and for sharing my work with your friends. I am grateful for your support and your role in my success.

Again, thank you for coming on this journey with me. I appreciate you and your time. I can't wait to see what God has in store for your life.

Blessings,
SharRon

ABOUT THE AUTHOR

SharRon Jamison is on a mission to help people become who they were born to be and not settle for what society has told, taught, or tricked them to be. She believes when people activate their innate talents, tap into their inner wisdom, and celebrate their uniqueness, they will pursue their God-given purpose with clarity, courage, and vigor.

SharRon received a BA from Hampton University in Hampton, Virginia, and earned her MBA from Nova Southeastern University in Fort Lauderdale, Florida.

SharRon is an international speaker, life coach, social justice advocate, business professional, licensed minister, proud mother, and author of three books: *I Can Depend on Me, I Have Learned A Few Things,* and *Deciding To Soar.* She is a co-author of *The Strength of My Soul: Stories of Sisterhood,* and *Triumph and Inspiration, Open Your Gifts, Faith For Fiery Trials,* and *I Bared My Chest.*

Learn more about SharRon at www.SharronJamison.com.

Made in the USA
Columbia, SC
26 December 2024

50612261R00187